Common Worship Today

Common Worship Today

An illustrated guide to *Common Worship*

by the Group for the Renewal of Worship

Edited by Mark Earey
and Gilly Myers

Consultant editors:
Colin Buchanan and Trevor Lloyd

HarperCollins*Publishers*

HarperCollins*Religious*
Part of HarperCollins*Publishers*
77–85 Fulham Palace Road, London W6 8JB
www.christian-publishing.com

First published in Great Britain in 2001 by HarperCollins*Religious*

1 3 5 7 9 10 8 6 4 2

The Scripture quotations contained herein are from the New Revised Standard Version
Bible, copyright © 1989, by the Division of Christian Education of the National Council of
the Churches of Christ in the USA, and are used by permission. All rights reserved.

Mark Earey and Gilly Myers assert the moral right to be identified
as the editors of this work

A catalogue record for this book is available from the British Library

ISBN 0 00 599381 4

Printed and bound in Great Britain by The Bath Press

Contents

Foreword

Twenty years ago my predecessor, Archbishop Runcie, provided an encouraging Foreword to this book's predecessor, *Anglican Worship Today*, and in the course of it said, 'When seeking lively and informed contemporary reflection on matters liturgical, I, like many others, have developed a habit of reaching for a Grove booklet.' I find I follow in his footsteps in sharing his high regard for the Grove booklets, in noting with admiration how the team which produced the delightful companion to the ASB has itself developed and grown, and in now commending that team's splendid provision to accompany *Common Worship*. You hold in your hands a rich and highly enjoyable contribution to the future of our worship.

May the worship of every parish bring glory to God and a deeper discipleship to his people – and may this book help in bringing the worshippers a fuller understanding of what they are doing.

George Cantuar:

Introduction

Liturgical change of any sort is inevitably a time of significant expectations, with some excitement, a touch of frustration and perhaps a little confusion. All of these have been in evidence as the Church of England has said goodbye to *The Alternative Service Book 1980* (ASB) and welcomed in its place not a new service book, but a new approach to worship – *Common Worship*.

Of course, there is a new book (or rather, several books), but *Common Worship* is much more. For a start it is available in many different ways. ASB services were available in the full book, in booklets and, for the adventurous, in service cards produced by the local church. Technology has changed all that, and now the majority of churches will be using these new services in locally produced editions, even if they use copies of the books as well. To facilitate that, the new services are available on disk, as modules for the *Visual Liturgy* service planning software and, of course, on the Internet.

But the most significant thing about *Common Worship* services is not how you get them but what you do with them. This has always been true of liturgy, but with *Common Worship* there is more scope than ever to make the services of the Church of England engage with the particular mission context in which a local worshipping community finds itself. It is this flexibility within a common framework, an emphasis on 'shape' and action rather than simply on words, which will produce the long term impact of *Common Worship*. The options and possibilities are too vast for us even to begin to explore them here (though we do try!), yet the basic principles are within reach of all of us, and it is with them that we begin.

This book is produced by the Group for the Renewal of Worship (GROW), better known as the people behind the Grove booklets on worship and liturgy. It has a noble predecessor in the earlier *Anglican Worship Today*, also produced by GROW, which was a guide to the ASB and was published in 1980. Those of us who have worked most closely on this present book wish to express our thanks to those who laboured twenty years ago on that volume. We are enormously grateful for their practical help and for the example of their general approach, but much more for their vision in producing *Anglican Worship Today* in the first place. That book has inspired all of us (and many others too). It had pictures. It had cartoons. It had diagrams. It was easy to read. It was full of practical advice as well as history and theory. And all this in a book on liturgy! It brought liturgy to life. And some of its contributors are to be found again here, duly acknowledged on page 8.

A prime mover among those responsible for *Anglican Worship Today* was Michael Vasey, who died in June 1998 while this new book was still in embryonic form. In the 1980 volume he was neither the editor nor the most prolific contributor, but his was the initial vision that set the project in motion, and so, to the extent that he was responsible for that book, he is also responsible for this. Not only so, but many of those who have contributed to this volume owe to Michael their love (or at least a lot of their understanding) of liturgy. On top of all that, he was one of the key thinkers and writers behind some of the *Common Worship* services. It is to him that we dedicate all that follows – with respect, with thanks and with love.

On behalf of GROW
Mark Earey and Gilly Myers – Editors
Colin Buchanan and Trevor Lloyd – Consultant editors

List of contributors

Anne Barton – Winchester Diocesan Officer for Development and Research for Liturgical Matters.

Colin Buchanan – Bishop of Woolwich and Chair of GROW.

Christopher Cocksworth – Director of the Southern Theological Education and Training Scheme (STETS) and member of the Liturgical Commission.

Anna de Lange – Reader and a lay member of General Synod and of the Liturgical Commission.

Mark Earey – *Praxis* National Education Officer, based at the Institute for Liturgy and Mission, Sarum College.

Jeremy Fletcher – Chaplain to the Bishop of Southwell, Associate Lecturer in Liturgy at St John's College, Nottingham, and a member of the Liturgical Commission.

David Gregg – Rector of Newton Longville, Buckinghamshire, previously minister in ten village communities in Carlisle, Ely and Oxford Dioceses and on the staff of the Board for Mission and Unity.

Carolyn Headley – Tutor in Liturgy and Spirituality at Wycliffe Hall, Oxford.

Anne Hollinghurst – Anglican Chaplain and accredited lecturer at the University of Derby, and Chaplain to Derby Cathedral.

James Jones – Bishop of Liverpool and member of the Liturgical Commission.

Chris Leach – Children's ministry consultant, and a freelance writer and speaker.

John Leach – Director of Anglican Renewal Ministries, and a writer and speaker on matters relating to worship and charismatic renewal.

Trevor Lloyd – Archdeacon of Barnstaple and a member of both the Liturgical Commission and the Liturgical Publishing Group.

Gilly Myers – Priest-in-Charge of All Saints' Church, Nottingham and secretary of both *Praxis* and GROW.

Robert M E Paterson – Team Rector of Cowbridge, a member of the Church in Wales Liturgical Commission and Chairman of the Welsh Partnership for World Mission.

Charles Read – Tutor in Christian worship, Cranmer Hall, Durham.

Jane Sinclair – Canon Precentor of Sheffield Cathedral and member of the Liturgical Commission.

James Steven – Lecturer in Christian Worship, Trinity College, Bristol.

Tim Stratford – Vicar of the Good Shepherd, West Derby, an outer urban estate parish in Liverpool.

Ian Tarrant – Senior Anglican Chaplain at the University of Nottingham and former CMS Mission Partner in Congo.

Phillip Tovey – Training Officer in the Diocese of Oxford and member of Oxford Diocesan Liturgical Committee.

John Waller – Team Rector of Watling Valley Ecumenical Partnership, Milton Keynes, with responsibility for the Church of the Servant King, Furzton.

Contributors listed by chapter

Most chapters involved several writers. Where this is
the case and one or more persons made the major
contribution to the chapter, this is indicated by the
use of **bold**. Otherwise contributors are listed
alphabetically within each chapter.

Chapter 1
Mark Earey
Gilly Myers
James Steven
Tim Stratford

Chapter 2
John Leach
Tim Stratford
Chris Cocksworth
Mark Earey
Jeremy Fletcher
Carolyn Headley
Phillip Tovey

Chapter 3
Mark Earey
Colin Buchanan
Carolyn Headley

Chapter 4
Tim Stratford

Chapter 5
Mark Earey
Jeremy Fletcher
David Gregg
Anne Hollinghurst
Chris Leach
Charles Read
James Steven
Tim Stratford
Phillip Tovey

Chapter 6
Colin Buchanan
Anne Hollinghurst
John Leach

Chapter 7
Mark Earey
Trevor Lloyd

Chapter 8
Colin Buchanan
Gilly Myers

Chapter 9
Colin Buchanan
Jeremy Fletcher
James Jones
Trevor Lloyd
Charles Read
Ian Tarrant
Phillip Tovey

Chapter 10
Trevor Lloyd
Chris Cocksworth
Anna de Lange
Charles Read

Chapter 11
Anne Barton
Chris Cocksworth
Jeremy Fletcher

Chapter 12
Trevor Lloyd
Charles Read
Chris Cocksworth
Carolyn Headley
John Leach
Gilly Myers

Chapter 13
Colin Buchanan

Chapter 14
Robert Paterson
Phillip Tovey
John Waller

Chapter 15
Charles Read

Chapter 16
Jeremy Fletcher
Jane Sinclair

Acknowledgements

Editorial team

The initial work of setting up the project and considering the shape of the book was done by an editorial team which comprised Mark Earey, Gilly Myers, Vernon Blackmore, Tim Stratford and James Steven.

We would like to acknowledge the work put into those early stages of the book by all members of the team and to record with thanks the work of Tim Stratford in the latter stages of the book's production, both in providing and taking photographs and in acting as an overall picture consultant.

Copyright texts

We are grateful for permission to use copyright material as follows:

Common Worship: Services and Prayers for the Church of England (Church House Publishing, 2000), is copyright © The Archbishops' Council, 2000. Extracts are reproduced by permission of the publishers.

The extract from *Rites on the Way: Work in Progress* (GS Misc 530 – July 1998) is copyright © The Central Board of Finance of the Church of England, 1998; The Archbishops' Council, 1999 and is reproduced by permission.

The extract from *On the Way: Towards an Integrated Approach to Christian Initiation* (Church House Publishing, 1995, 1998) is copyright © The Central Board of Finance of the Church of England, 1995; The Archbishops' Council, 1999 and is reproduced by permission.

Extracts from *The Book of Common Prayer*, the rights in which are vested in the Crown, are reproduced by permission of the Crown's Patentee, Cambridge University Press.

The ecumenical translation of the Lord's Prayer on page 71 is that prepared by the English Language Liturgical Consultation (ELLC), 1988.

The quotation on page 198 taken from *Threshold of Light*, edited by A.M. Allchin and Esther de Waal, published and copyright 1986 by Darton, Longman and Todd Ltd, is used by permission of the publishers.

Picture credits

Pictures are indicated below by the page on which they appear.

Where no other acknowledgement is given, the photographs in this book are © 'Images of Praise' and were taken by Mike Collins. We are extremely grateful for permission to use these photographs.

We are also very grateful to the following individuals for permission to use their photographs:

Tim Stratford: 17 (Aidan), 19, 23, 26, 30, 31, 33 (modern church), 41, 42, 45, 46, 48, 50, 51, 53, 55, 56–7, 58, 59, 64, 66, 73, 75, 79, 81, 89, 90, 91, 92, 97, 98, 99, 101, 102, 103, 105, 106, 107, 109, 114–5, 123, 124, 126, 133, 139, 146, 150, 152–3 (all), 154, 159, 161 (cross), 162, 171, 172 (all), 182, 184, 187 (book), 196, 197, 202, 208, 210, 213, 218, 235, 237, 241, 246 (choir)

Liz Simpson: 84, 87 (children with songbooks), 88, 108, 120, 132, 134, 147, 148, 156, 158, 164, 186, 187 (ringers), 193, 201, 215, 217, 221, 222, 223, 225, 226, 236, 239, 247 (sheep in field), 250, 251, 253

Duncan Myers: 87 (young people), 161 (clergyman), 165, 174, 185, 214, 216

Mark Earey: 18, 21

Betty Washbrook: 129

Ian Tarrant: 122

PWD: 35

Permission to reproduce other pictures is gratefully acknowledged as follows:
  Alexander, David: 36, 37
  Anglican World (Lynn Ross): 228
  Anglican World (J. Rosenthal): 65
  Bridgeman Art Library: 77
  Christian Aid/Still Pictures: 70
  Church Mission Society: 234
  Diocese of Southwell: 85, 110, 169
  Diocese of Southwark: 86, 111, 140–41,
  Hulton Getty Picture Collection: 149, 198
  Mary Evans Picture Library: 180
  National Portrait Gallery: 28, 94, 96, 151
  Salisbury Newspapers: 142-3
  The Worshipful Company of Pewterers: 27

Illustrations
The illustrations are by Roger Wade-Walker.

Cover
The photographs are all from 'Images of Praise', except as follows (numbering from left to right and top to bottom):
  Tim Stratford: 1, 5 and back flap
  Mark Earey: 6
  Diocese of Southwark: 7

St Agatha's

Welcome to St Agatha's!

People have been worshipping in this building for centuries, and on this site for longer still. Here are the people of St Agatha's on an ordinary Sunday at the end of 2000. Why are they worshipping in this way? Where do the forms of service come from? What have been the influences on the worship space, its layout and furniture, and on what it says about God and about the worshippers? Throughout this book we will be trying to answer these questions and exploring the thinking and the history that has brought St Agatha's, and the rest of the Church of England, to *Common Worship*.

How to use this book

Like *Common Worship* itself, this book is designed to be flexible. Many people will want to find out about worship, liturgy and *Common Worship* in a general way and will read the book right the way through. Others will come with a specific question, or a particular service that they wish to understand. We have designed the book so that, although it will work if you read it through from cover to cover, it will also be easy to dip into a particular section or to follow up a particular interest.

The first half of the book (chapters 1 to 6) deals with worship and liturgy in general, while the second half focuses on the particular services and resources of *Common Worship*. Each chapter is divided into a number of double-page sections. Throughout the book you will find some common 'threads'. Some of these cover fairly substantial themes, others are less significant and some are just fun.

The major threads running through the book are these:

 Mission – how does worship work in the context of mission? What are the connections to be made?

 The Bible – how is the Bible being used in worship? What is being revealed about attitudes to the Bible?

 Body, mind and spirit – how is this aspect of worship drawing on and using our senses, in drama, symbol, movement, and so on?

 Formation – how is worship forming us as Christians, in our assumptions, our understanding of God, our lifestyle choices?

 Pastoral – how is public worship linked to pastoral realities?

Chapter heading

Major themes
You will find major themes featured in this way. Each major theme has a distinctive icon.

94   COMMON WORSHIP TODAY

The Prayer Books begin

The origins of a Church of England worship book lie in the work of Thomas Cranmer, Archbishop of Canterbury, in the reign of Edward VI (1547–53).

There is a pre-history – and not solely a royal matrimonial one. When Henry VIII came to the throne in 1509, England was still, religiously, in the Middle Ages. When he died in January 1547, he released the English Reformation. Although he had detached the Church of England from Rome and had bound the clergy instead to the crown, he had actually delayed the dynamic effect of the Reformation, withstanding most of the reforming influences, whether from the continent or from within England. Now, however, his son ruled at only nine years of age and the actual power lay with a Council – one with a Protestant majority. The key persons on it were not simply resisting the power of Rome, but had also passed the litmus tests of that period of change, in their beliefs about the Eucharist, the supremacy of Scripture, justification through faith and the use of the common tongue in worship.

Thomas Cranmer
Much now hung on the person and the beliefs of Thomas Cranmer, the Archbishop of Canterbury and a member of the Council. His own theology had become reformed in Henry's latter years, and his doctrinal conviction and political opportunity were marvellously complemented by a unique skill – he was able to write brilliant English liturgical prose. His was to be the mind and hand behind the composition and compilation of a series of liturgical books in English, the strong influence of which would still be felt 450 years later. The usual method of authorizing these new Prayer Books was to be by Parliamentary Acts of

The Prayer Book as a wi
[The Church of England] ha
Christian truth in its historic formul
Articles of Religion, the Book of Ce
Ordering of Bishops, Priests and De
1975 Preface to

Thomas Cranmer, Archbishop

Ministry – how are the whole people of God (not just the people at the front) serving one another and using their gifts?

 Diversity of practice

 Practical tips

In addition, you will find items like these cropping up repeatedly:

 Did you know…?

 Extracts from *Common Worship*

You will also find that most sections finish with ideas about where to find related information if you want to follow something up.

 The law and…

Flexibility and resources

Uniformity, a succession of which enforced revised versions of the Prayer Book throughout the Tudor and Stuart eras. 'Uniformity' meant that each new Book superseded the previous one. It was asserted of each successive Book that it provided a good and godly doctrine, and that it was much needed for the current times.

Cranmer's initial stage-by-stage programme was launched in 1547.

1547–8

In the summer of 1547 Royal Injunctions simplified some of the externals of worship and the ornamentation of church buildings – and provided for the Epistle and Gospel at Mass to be read in English. A set of (reformed) sermons (or 'Homilies') in English was also authorized. Then, in autumn 1547, Parliament passed an Act to provide (among other things) for Communion to be distributed frequently and in both kinds – i.e. both bread and wine. In March 1548 this was implemented by the publication of *The Order of the Communion*, a brief devotional run-up to a distribution to the people, tacked onto the existent Latin Mass, but itself in English.

1549

In December 1548 Parliament approved the first Act of Uniformity. This imposed a complete, English-language Prayer Book to be used by all

> In 1551 the Puritan John Hooper was appointed Bishop of Gloucester, but he declined to wear the episcopal vestments and had to be put in prison for a short time as a means of persuasion – an event unique in history.

clergy from Pentecost 1549 onwards. The monastic offices were skilfully united into two daily services only, those for Morning and Evening Prayer. The Bible was to be read aloud, in substantial portions, in sequence and (like all else) in English. The Holy Communion service was a combination of old structure with subtly new wording, but was also – as must have been amazing to the worshippers – in English.

1550

The urgent flow continued. In 1550 there came the ordination services ('Ordinal'), published as a separate book from *The Book of Common Prayer* and totally reforming the concept and function of the ordained ministry. An Order in Council required the tearing down of stone altars.

1552

Cranmer's work matured with the 1552 Prayer Book, authorized by another Act of Uniformity and imposed from All Saints' Day. Now not only the wording but also the basic structure of central rites was changed. In the process all concepts of 'consecration' of the elements at Communion – or of the font at Baptism – were eliminated. The people of England were to be reformed by a single, uniform Prayer Book, enforcing Protestant biblical understandings and inculcated by the requirement of regular use.

1553

In this year the Forty-two Articles of Religion were produced in draft form. There was also, however, the death of Edward VI and the succession of the Roman Catholic Princess Mary. The Prayer Book was banned, the leaders burned and the Reformation apparently aborted. This was not to be the end of the story, though.

Changes in Henry VIII's reign
- A vernacular Bible, 1537
- A first English-language Litany, 1544

Changes in Edward VI's reign
- First Book of Homilies, 1547
- An Act for Receiving in Both Kinds, 1547
- The Order of the Communion, 1548
- First English Prayer Book, 1549
- Order in Council for the Breaking Down of Altars, 1550
- First English Ordinal, 1550
- Second English Prayer Book, 1552
- The Forty-two Articles of Religion, 1553

CONNECTIONS
Cranmer's Communion services – pp.150–51
Cranmer's Morning and Evening Prayer – pp.196–7

33–56

Common threads
Other common elements look like this.

Interesting features
Items of particular relevance or interest which are self-contained, rather than connected to similar items on other pages. These include explanations, quotations and Bible references.

Connections
This is where to look for ideas if you want to follow up the content of any page a little further.

St Agatha's – Celtic times

In the year 2000, Ann and her husband Ernest are ministers at St Agatha's. Ann is the vicar and Ernest is a non-stipendiary minister licensed to the parish. One Evensong, during a particularly long anthem by the choir, Ernest's eyes wander across to the plaque on the wall listing the parish priests over the centuries, going right back to the eleventh century. As he ponders on what it must have been like to worship here then, or even earlier, he feels himself drifting back through time…

A distinctive Christian culture

The parish of St Agatha's did not exist in Celtic times, nor was there a church building. When the lines of communication between Britain and Rome were cut in the early fifth century, the south and east of Britain were left with an organizational and military vacuum soon filled by pagan Germanic migrants. In the north and west a new, distinctive, Christian culture developed. Under continued influence from the Coptic tradition, an emphasis on communal monastic life was to develop. This distinctive Church is sometimes misleadingly called 'insular', but is more commonly called 'Celtic'.

Egyptian love of the desert is reflected in the Celtic Christians' appreciation of nature. Worship did not revolve around church buildings but was based outside in the glory of God's creation. However, there is evidence of religious architecture in Celtic carving on the stones of churches built where once there would

62 – Death of Boadicea

C1st

130 – Hadrian's Wall completed

C2nd

c.208 – Martyrdom of St Alban

C3rd

was in the Roman Church. Clearly Ernest has drifted back to a time well before the Synod of Whitby (663). Haircuts were not the only matter to be discussed at that meeting. Ernest has a vague memory that there was disagreement over the date on which Easter was celebrated. He cannot remember all the details, but sighs to himself at the thought that disagreement over the date of Easter still divides the Orthodox and Western Churches today. Maybe one day…

His attention is caught by some movement at the cross. The preaching seems to be over and the monk (if that is what he is) seems to be setting up a simple, portable wooden altar. Presumably they do not celebrate the Eucharist in this spot very regularly.

Statue of
Aidan on Holy Island

Celtic Rites

Rites used in worship were most likely to have been compiled independently in the Celtic Church by missionaries on their travels. The Stowe (C9th) and Bobbio (C7th) Missals clearly show forms of service drawn from a mixture of Christian traditions.

have been a Celtic place of worship. It is at such a place of worship that Ernest finds himself.

Worshipping at the crossroads

Ernest sees a small crowd of people gathered around a simple cross at a road junction. 'Journey' was a key motif for Celtic Christians, and those paperbacks on Celtic prayer that Ernest picks up in Christian bookshops always seem to include a lot of prayers to do with travelling.

A man standing by the cross seems to be preaching. He looks like some sort of monk, but his hair is cut in a very unusual way – there is a sort of shaved line, rather than a circle, in the hair. Then Ernest remembers that the shape of a monk's tonsure (the way his hair was cut) was different in the Celtic Church from the way it

The Lindisfarne Gospels

The Lindisfarne Gospels (dating from the end of the seventh century) suggest a very high regard for the Bible amongst the Celtic Christians. Bishop Eadfrith of Lindisfarne, successor but one to Cuthbert, is thought to have written the manuscript, which is also beautifully bound and ornamented. The Latin manuscript and decorative carpet pages are most beautifully executed – yet on each of the most elaborate ones a single, small, and probably deliberate, mistake is evident. The work of a man's hand was not to claim perfection that rightly belonged to the divine creator.

CONNECTIONS
The age of the spoken word –
p.72

St Agatha's – Anglo-Saxon times

As Ernest becomes conscious of time spinning on, the pattern of roads and tracks remains roughly the same, but close to where the Celtic monk preached at the crossroads there now stands a small stone building. He recognizes some unusually shaped stones and then realizes where he has seen them before. The short history of the church available for visitors to St Agatha's in 2000 highlights one or two

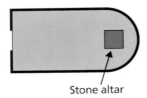

Stone altar

parts of the stonework thought to date from Saxon times – and here are those stones forming part of the first church building on this site. Some of the stones seem to have words on them –

Alcuin

At the end of the eighth century the English scholar Alcuin was living in France and had been entrusted with editing a copy of the new Gregorian Sacramentary sent there by Pope Hadrian I. His work shows a very elaborate provision drawn from contemporary Roman, Gallican (French) and Gelasian (fifth century) sources.

Church showing Anglo-Saxon features

perhaps Latin inscriptions. They are probably from a nearby Roman house or fort.

Light in the darkness

The church itself is a simple, one-room building. Ernest ventures closer and peers through the door, which is ajar. Inside it is dark, with just a few small windows and candles in alcoves. In the shallow apse sit three men, presumably the priests. The words sound like Latin – incomprehensible to most of the people living around the church.

As the service progresses, it looks colourful and elaborate. Ceremonial and vestments had undergone great development through the sixth and seventh centuries in Rome and Ernest notes that the changes had made their way into the Anglo-Saxon Church in Britain.

Anglo-Saxon font

Shining examples?

Violent warfare was an Anglo-Saxon way of life. Kings fought against neighbouring Anglo-Saxon kingdoms or against the Celts and, later, against Viking invaders. Revenge in the cause of justice was also a feature of the culture: taking 'a life for a life' was merely a man's duty to his family.

For this reason, some scholarly Christians were reluctant to translate parts of the Bible which might appear to condone such a lifestyle. One Anglo-Saxon cleric, translating into Old English from Latin, deliberately changed the end of Psalm 137. Thus 'happy is he who repays you … he who seizes your infants and dashes them against the rocks' became 'happy is he who takes his own son and establishes him upon the Rock'!

Ælfric, a late Anglo-Saxon, hesitated to translate Genesis in case the unsavoury aspects of the patriarchal narratives were understood as examples to be followed.

Getting involved

Lay involvement was inevitably limited, partly because of a complicated liturgy and partly because much worship revolved around the monastic community. However, the Anglo-Saxon Church opened up opportunities for women and under Roman rule it continued to tolerate double monastic houses, where male and female communities lived alongside each other. Most notably, Hilda of Whitby presided over just such a place.

Evangelists from Rome

These were the days when what today is Britain comprised several scattered kingdoms. In the north and the west, Celtic Christianity had flourished. Rome began its re-evangelization from the south and east. Pope Gregory the Great sent a band of 40 monks led by Augustine of Canterbury to preach the gospel to the heathen English. They arrived in 597. Conversion involved a deliberate acceptance of things Roman, including language and the primacy of the Bishop of Rome.

Augustine landed in heathen Kent, where Ethelbert was *Bretwalda* (senior to the other kings of Britain). He was already married to a Frankish Christian queen. Augustine had aimed to establish himself in London, but Ethelbert was keen that his see should be in Kent. Augustine began to use the pre-existing Roman church of St Martin's, Dorovernium (Canterbury). With the support of the *Bretwalda*, his mission was successful across the south and east of Britain, but the existing British (Celtic) bishops from the north and west were quickly offended by him. A conference he held with them, probably on the Welsh border, only exacerbated the situation.

By the time Augustine died in 604, Roman Christian influence only extended over Kent and part of Essex. It was not until after the Synod of Whitby in 663 that Roman ways began to dominate. It did not all go Rome's way even then, however. A more monastic structure was retained, whereas across most of the old Roman Empire dioceses were the most natural unit of administration. Worship revolved around the abbeys and monasteries. In many places the parishes were served by small communities of travelling priests from a minster community.

In addition, of course, Christianity was by no means the only faith – many still followed the old pagan ways and resented and opposed the 'new religion'.

St Agatha's – 1087

After the conquest of the Anglo-Saxons by William I in 1066, the new Norman kingdom bridged the English Channel. Christian traditions were brought more into line with the rest of the Western Church and so with Rome. The Church in Britain was given a structure which made it more fit to minister to the people of the land and more accountable to the state.

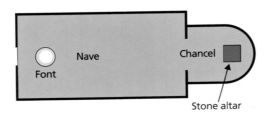

Nave — Font — Chancel — Stone altar

At St Agatha's

Ernest finds himself standing outside St Agatha's in 1087, the year after the Domesday Book survey was carried out. The tiny basilica has now been extended with a new rectangular room, a nave, in which the people could gather whilst the priests prayed. Looking around at the surrounding village, Ernest sees that the church still seems to be the only stone building there – a sign of security and safety.

Going inside, Ernest notices how draughty and cold it is. He will never complain about those overhead electric heaters again! The windows have no glass, just shutters. The walls are covered with pictures of saints, Bible stories and legends. Ernest goes to sit down, but finds there are no seats – just a long, stone bench along one wall in the nave. 'That must be where that saying comes from,' thinks Ernest, '"The weakest go to the wall."' In the apse-shaped chancel, standing free from the wall, is a low stone altar covered with a simple cloth.

As Ernest watches, a man appears, carrying lights which are placed on the altar and around the centre of the church. A congregation gathers and the priest, wearing colourful vestments, begins the service. It is all in Latin, as Ernest expected, but most of it is said out loud and some join in with the Creed. Parts of

Ordained ministers

By late Norman times most churches would have had a single priest working in them:

- a **rector** if the resident priest was in receipt of all the revenues (most often the case for the smaller churches);
- a **vicar** when some of the revenues were taken by absentee academic priests or for canonries, etc. (more often the case in larger churches).

Most of these clergy would have been in receipt of £3 to £4 per year, an average income. They were provided with a house and garden and perhaps 'half a hide' of land to farm. In 1247 the General Council of Lyons laid down that the parish priest must be not less than 25 years old, of suitable education and character, residing personally in the benefice. Should a patron fail to present an incumbent to a vacant benefice within six months, the presentation would pass to the bishop. All these rules still persist (in a changed form) in the Church of England today.

The ministry of the people

Liturgical roles were almost certainly all fulfilled by men in the Norman Church. The women's orders were very much separate from the mainstream of parish life. The liturgy was complex, the books needed to perform it were numerous, and literacy levels were low. Teaching (at least four times a year) would have been given in the vernacular. A choir would have been trained to contribute to the liturgy on the people's behalf.

Church with a Norman tower

the service are sung by a choir on a platform in the centre of the church. People stand or kneel on the bare earth floor, some saying their own prayers, some listening to the priest. Later in the service the centre of action moves from the choir's platform to the altar in the chancel. The priest can be seen facing the people through the smoky atmosphere caused by the candles and incense. Some of the congregation receive wafers and wine, going into the chancel for Communion.

The parish system

A much more organized structure for the Church had already been emerging in Anglo-Saxon times, but when the Norman lords arrived it was firmly established. This meant some degree of state control in Church matters. The parish system in embryo can be seen as early as the Domesday Book census of 1086. This marked a move away from the missionary communities, which had provided mutual support and strength in a pagan land. Religious communities which had built new churches and served them in limited ways could not meet the needs of a Christian country with its regular cycle of baptisms, weddings, funerals, Sunday and weekday services. The emphasis had moved from mission to maintenance. The clergy (though often married and with families at first) were no longer based in a religious community. They were under the authority of a bishop and a patron – and with measurable expectations.

St Agatha's – 1453

In the year that marked the end of the Hundred Years' War, and English withdrawal from France, we find the environment surrounding St Agatha's has developed, with the fields now larger and divided into long strips, marked out by pegs and stones. A few notable stone houses have recently been built in the village, along with a new moated manor house.

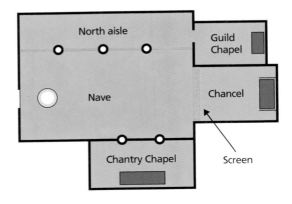

Building work

Ernest notices enormous changes to the church building. Two centuries earlier a lofty, square-ended Early English chancel had replaced the small, heavy Norman one. The arch between chancel and nave is now filled with a large wooden screen. Life-sized figures in painted wood stand out, set on a platform on top of the wooden screen: Jesus on the cross with Mary and John on either side.

Inside the building

The feel of the building is light and airy. The roof is higher, with light streaming in through a clerestory of Decorated windows. There is a new north aisle with a chapel at the end, parallel to the chancel and dedicated to St Mary. This chapel was paid for by a local guild, a sort of medieval trade union, and the guild priest says a daily Mass for the guild and its members, past and present. On the other side of the church another extension houses an enclosed chantry chapel. Here a chantry priest is saying Mass on his own for the repose of the soul of the late lord of the manor (who had left the money to build the chapel and to pay the priest).

The high altar, right up against the east wall of the chancel, with curtains on three sides of it, is richly decorated with a frontal bearing an embroidered picture. Above all this hangs the Blessed Sacrament in an ornately gilded pyx, shaped like a dove.

The service begins

At the high altar the service is just beginning. Candles are lit on the altar and a crucifix placed between them. The priest and his two assistants face east (with their backs to the people), wearing colourful vestments decorated more lavishly on their backs than on their fronts. As the villagers enter the church, they dip their fingers in the stoup of holy water, cross themselves and then stand in the nave. The only seats in the church are in the chancel for the officiating clergy, the lord of the manor and his family, and the parish clerk.

Familiar words

Ernest can hear little of the Latin words that the priest is using, though he recognizes the *Kyrie eleison* ('Lord have mercy'), the *Paternoster* (the Lord's Prayer) and the *Gloria in excelsis*. He notes that the choir are now situated in the rood loft, the platform over the screen between chancel and nave – where there is also a group of musicians. During the service, some are using rosaries to say their own prayers, and one or two wealthy people have little primers or prayer books of their own.

The Canon

After washing his hands and

Seeing is believing

In the Middle Ages the Bible was given great importance ceremonially, but was of little use practically. The Epistle was read from a large book carried from the altar. Another large book was used for the Gradual (or Grail), sung before the Gospel. Then the Gospel book was taken from the altar, attended by assistants and candles. There was no sermon or homily and the readings were in Latin. The villagers learned more from their eyes than their ears – through the wall paintings and stained-glass windows and the popular mystery plays that were performed in the church at major festivals.

Simeon with the child Jesus (Luke 2:28)

mumbling some prayers very quietly indeed, the priest begins the very long prayer of thanksgiving, intercession, commemoration and consecration (the Canon).

There is a deep reverence and bowing in the congregation when the priest lifts up the bread. A bell is rung, indicating that Christ has come down to be in the bread on the altar, for his sacrifice to be re-presented to God. At a later point Ernest notices something that looks like a mini-version of the sharing of the Peace that has caused so much trouble at the modern-day St Agatha's. In 1453 it is brief and formal and involves only the three ministers. There is a solemn blessing of the congregation, who do not receive Communion (they do so only rarely, and then only bread and not wine). When the priest and his assistants have received Communion and a final prayer has been said, one of the assistants stands and says to the congregation, '*Ite, missa est*' ('Go, the Mass is over').

CONNECTIONS
▣ Holy Communion from C2nd to C16th – pp.148–9

St Agatha's – 1561

This time the first thing Ernest notices is that the great west tower has been completed. Bells ring out to let people know the service is about to begin (there is a fine if they fail to attend). On the south side of the church there is a magnificent new porch, about 20 years old, with a chamber above it. Inside, though, there are even greater changes. The chancel screen is still there, but the rood loft and the figures of Christ, Mary and John are gone. The statues of the saints have been defaced and the wall paintings washed over. All the separate altars with their colourful frontals have disappeared, and even the great stone high altar in the chancel has gone.

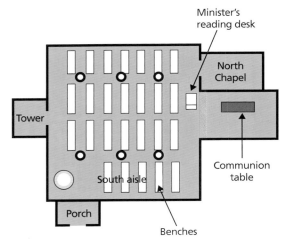

'Yes, it went years ago,' says a man standing next to Ernest. 'They ordered all the stone altars to be destroyed in 1550 because people thought that if you had a stone altar it was in order to make a sacrifice – and our Communion service is no longer a sacrifice of Jesus.'

A time of great change

'What has happened over there?' asks Ernest, pointing to where the chantry chapel used to be.

'That was all taken away when the chantries were abolished,' his neighbour replies. 'Someone made a lot of money out of that lot. You've no idea what we've been through. I remember the day – it was Whitsunday in 1549 – when we used the new Prayer Book, all in English, for the first time. That took some getting used to. And three years later we had another Prayer Book, even simpler this time. Then the next year the young King died and we all went back to Latin with Queen Mary. Those were terrible times, so many people burnt for not being willing to become Catholics again – we had them even in our own town here. But thank God for Good Queen Bess! It's three years now since she came to the throne and we've had another new Prayer Book for almost two years – almost the same as the one in 1552. Four radical changes in 10 years: I suppose you could say the Church is used to change now!'

Morning service

It is about 9.30 in the morning and people are coming in and sitting on the benches now filling the church. 'Are you going to take Communion?' Ernest's neighbour asks. 'Usually the service stops halfway through and we all go home, but today is a Communion Sunday: the minister announced it last week. We have to go and give him our names if we're coming. He reads us a long exhortation about how to receive Communion and really mean it.'

People are now singing a metrical psalm, led by the choir who are still over the chancel screen, but

> **Readers**
> The middle of the sixteenth century saw a brief revival of interest in the office of Reader. Readers were permitted to read the Scriptures and the services of Morning or Evening Prayer. The office of Reader was open to men only (this was not to change until 1969), and there was no question of them being allowed to preach.

now face west towards the people. The minister, wearing a long white surplice nearly down to his ankles, a black scarf and a hood, stands at his reading desk in the nave. He reads through Morning Prayer, and then an anthem and the Litany come before the beginning of the Communion service. When Ernest is just looking forward to hearing him preach, he begins to read a long homily from a book. The congregation look amazingly attentive. For Communion, the minister moves into the chancel, where a moveable table is set lengthwise, at right angles to the east wall.

Familiar words

Bread and wine are placed on the white cloth on the table, and people not taking Communion leave after the next prayer. Ernest hears the long exhortation on the meaning of Communion as if for the first time. He is impressed by the way the Prayer Book order makes sense in its right setting, and gladly joins the congregation as they fill the chancel when the minister says, 'Draw near...' Both bread (ordinary bread, too, not wafers) and wine are distributed to the communicants as they kneel around the holy table.

Other services

'Is this the only service?' Ernest asks his neighbour.

'No, there is Evening Prayer. Everyone will be back at 3 o'clock – even after two and a half hours this morning. There might be a Baptism after the second lesson. Then the minister tests the children on part of the catechism from the Prayer Book.'

CONNECTIONS
▶ **The age of print** – pp.74–5
▶ **The Prayer Books begin** – pp.94–5
▶ **Holy Communion from Cranmer to 1662** – pp.150–51
▶ **Readers revived** – p.32

1649 – Charles I executed
C17th

1742 – First performance of Handel's *Messiah*
C18th

1805 – Battle of Trafalgar
C19th

St Agatha's – 1662

Ernest suddenly finds himself inside St Agatha's another 100 years on, after the time of Cromwell and the Commonwealth, and just two years after the Restoration of the monarchy under Charles II. The church seems much lighter and Ernest realizes that all the stained glass has been smashed out and replaced by plain glass. There is now absolutely no trace of the old wall paintings, but up on the east wall at the end of the chancel is a brand-new panel with the words of the Creed, the Lord's Prayer and the Ten Commandments written on it. The table, now draped with a velvet cloth, is right up against the east wall again, surrounded by lovely wooden Communion rails.

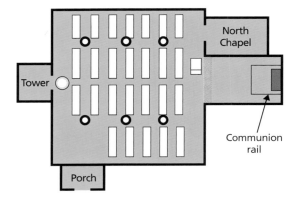

The penny drops

Looking up in the nave, Ernest sees the royal coat of arms above the chancel arch. The minister looks much the same as 100 years before, and the Communion service too is little changed. As the minister begins the consecration prayer, Ernest realizes why the Prayer Book rubric of 1662 instructs the minister to stand 'at the north side of the Table'. The rubric reflects the earlier situation when the holy table was set up lengthwise (that is, on an east–west axis) in the nave or chancel, making the north side one of the long sides. Since then the table has been put back in a permanent position against the east wall, but the rubric has not been changed.

Subtle changes

As he watches during what is now called 'the Prayer of Consecration' (the title was

Royal coats of arms became common in churches in the late sixteenth and seventeenth centuries

1373 – Mother Julian of Norwich has visions

C14th

1492 – Columbus lands in West Indies

C15th

1533 – Henry VIII marries Anne Boleyn

C16th

added in the 1662 Prayer Book), Ernest notices that the minister picks up both paten and chalice and lays his hand on them (as the rubric now requires) – something that he does not recall seeing in 1561.

When it comes to the distribution of the bread and wine, people go up to the Communion rail in an orderly fashion. Ernest

> **?** The Prayer Book Baptism service for those who 'are of riper years' was intended for those who missed out on infant baptism during the time of the Commonwealth.

notices another change: the remaining bread and wine is covered with a cloth. 'That'll all be finished up directly the service is over,' says an old man who notices Ernest staring. 'Time was when the parson would have taken that home for his breakfast – or so my old dad told me. But this new book we've had since St Bartholomew's Day has changed some of those things. I don't think it'll last.'

Some extras

Ernest glances through the lovely printed Prayer Book with which he is so familiar. His eye is caught, however, by some things he does not recognize. For instance, there is a Form of Prayer with Thanksgiving to Almighty God for having put an end to the Great Rebellion (29 May), a Form of Prayer and Fasting on the anniversary of the martyrdom of King Charles I (30 January) and a Service of Thanksgiving for the failure of the Gunpowder Plot (5 November). 'Now, there's nothing much like that in *Common Worship*!' thinks Ernest.

The Westminster *Directory*

In 1645 the use of the Prayer Book became illegal, and in its place came *A Directory for the Public Worship of God, Throughout the Three Kingdoms of England, Scotland and Ireland*. It was a deliberate attempt to create a unity in worship throughout the kingdoms which had not proved possible with *The Book of Common Prayer*.

The *Directory* was not really a service book at all, but a guide to ministers about how to conduct worship. It included:

- General instructions about the performance of the service and appropriate behaviour, such as: 'Let all enter the assembly, not irreverently, but in a grave and seemly manner, taking their seats or places without adoration, or bowing themselves towards one place or other.'
- Practical advice concerning the content of the service: 'We commend also the more frequent reading of such Scriptures, as he that readeth shall think best for edification of his Hearers.'
- Much advice about the sort of ground to be covered in extemporary prayer: 'Let the Prayer, Thanksgiving, or Blessing of the Bread and Wine, be to this effect; With humble and hearty acknowledgement of the greatness of our misery … To give thanks to God for all his benefits … All which he is to endeavour to perform with suitable affections answerable to such an holy Action, and to stir up the like in the people.'
- A few compulsory texts, for instance the words, 'I baptize thee in the Name of the Father, of the Son, and of the Holy Ghost.'
- Guidance about the administration of Baptism, the Lord's Supper, marriage, the burial of the dead, the keeping of the Lord's Day, the visitation of the sick, public solemn fasting, the singing of psalms and the observation of days of public thanksgiving.

Seventeenth-century pewter Communion vessels

CONNECTIONS
▶ **The seventeenth century** – pp.96–7

St Agatha's – 1780

Ernest notices that the whole church is now packed with high box pews, with doors and locks on them. He looks at the names painted on the doors and realizes that the pews are only available to those who have paid the rent for them.

The squire and his family have a particularly grand private pew, with comfortable chairs, a fireplace and curtains to keep out the draughts. Ernest feels sure he has seen parts of it before. A closer look reveals a clever bit of recycling, using wood from the old chantry chapel screen.

Some obviously poor people who cannot afford a pew are sitting on a couple of benches right at the back of the church. Ernest joins them. Visibility is bad because the pews are so high, and people cannot relate to each other except within their pews. At least the minister can be seen, in the high, triple-decker pulpit. The holy table now seems very small and isolated in the chancel, which is empty of other furniture apart from a bench for communicants.

The congregation takes a back seat
The service begins at 9.30 with Morning Prayer, read by the minister from the second stage of the triple-decker pulpit. Ernest notices that he is wearing a cassock under his full surplice, plus a hood and preaching bands at his neck. The parish clerk, on the bottom stage, wears a black gown. He makes the responses in the service on behalf of the people, apart from those responses now sung by the choir from their new gallery in the west end of the church. The orchestra up there with them seems to be the local town band.

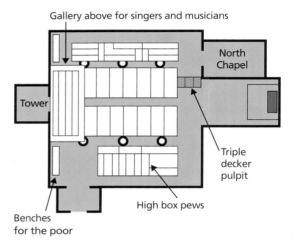

Gallery above for singers and musicians

North Chapel

Tower

Triple decker pulpit

High box pews

Benches for the poor

John Wesley

Metrical versions of the psalms are sung, and everyone turns to 'face the music'. 'Hm,' thinks Ernest, 'another saying I now understand.'

Now that their parts are taken by the clerk and choir, the people seem to have little to do but just be there, attending worship and listening to the sermon. The top deck of the pulpit is used for the sermon – an extremely long and tedious philosophical discourse. One advantage of the high box pews is that people can sleep unnoticed – but the church-wardens' staves are for poking them awake again.

At the end of the Litany people start to move around and Ernest starts to leave. Someone taps him on the shoulder. 'Sir, I believe there is to be Holy Communion today,' says a woman behind him. Clearly people were simply making the most of a break to stretch their legs. The Communion follows, apparently happening very infrequently, as the congregation do not seem

to know it very well. Large pewter flagons, cups and plates are used for Communion. The words of the service have not changed since 1662.

A new phenomenon

As he leaves, Ernest notices a group of people rushing off with Bibles under their arms. 'Methodists!' he hears someone mutter, and realizes that they must be members of the local Methodist class meeting, still coming regularly to the parish church for worship, but finding their spiritual nourishment elsewhere, in studying the Bible together and in listening to visiting teachers and open-air preachers. 'Clearly the Church, with its sermons on logic and right living like that one today, is nowhere near meeting the spiritual needs of ordinary folk,' thinks Ernest as he leaves. Walking up the road, he can just make out the sound of hymn-singing coming from one of the side streets...

Methodism

Although originally a renewal movement within the Church of England, the 'Methodists' were eventually made so uncomfortable within the established Church that it became inevitable that they would form a separate, non-conforming Church.

The chapels they built in the late eighteenth and early nineteenth centuries reveal the assumptions and priorities of their worship. The seats are all free pews. The front of the meeting space is often dominated by a large pipe organ and seats for a choir, reflecting the importance of hymn-singing. The Communion table is usually visible at the front, and sits below a high pulpit from which the service is led and the sermon is preached.

CONNECTIONS
▶ The evangelical revival – p.98

St Agatha's – 1867

Around St Agatha's almost all the old fields have gone, replaced by streets and factories. The smoke pouring from the factory chimneys makes the church walls look black. As Ernest approaches the church he is surprised to meet a group of protesters shouting, 'No Popery!' They represent evangelical opposition to the new ceremonial practices that the 'ritualists', or Anglo-Catholics as they became known, have introduced. After a number of years of disquiet, this year, 1867, marks the year that the Ritual Commission was formed to inquire into the legalities of the new ceremonial.

Free seats

In the church porch Ernest spots a notice advertising services. He has arrived in time for the main morning Communion. There is also a newly introduced 'early service' at 8.00 a.m. and the 6.30 p.m. Evensong in gaslight for the servants. Another notice proclaims that the seats in the church are now free. Gladdened by this, he makes for a seat in the new, low-backed pews.

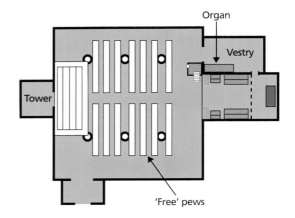

Pictures are back

From his seat Ernest is immediately struck not only by a better view of everything (the old high box pews have gone) but by all the new decorative features. Murals and stencilled Bible verses cover what in Georgian times were whitewashed walls. Colourful stained-glass windows likewise depict a variety of saints. There is a shiny new brass lectern shaped like an eagle.

A low stone screen separates nave from chancel, which is now raised two steps above the newly tiled nave floor. Ernest also notices lots of pipes and then, sensing the warmth, realizes that they must be for the newly installed hot-water heating system.

A new hymn book

A robed choir processes to the two rows of stalls on either side of the chancel. The opening hymn begins and the music comes from a new organ built into the old side chapel. Ernest follows the words in the new hymn book, *Hymns Ancient and Modern* – the first standard hymn book produced for the Church of England.

He notices the minister (or 'priest' as he prefers to be known) processing behind the choir with servers. The priest, dressed in the ancient Eucharistic vestments of chasuble, alb, stole, amice and maniple, proceeds to the altar, which is at the far end of the chancel, three steps above the chancel floor. The bare wooden altar table of Georgian times is now vested with coverings appropriate to the season in the Church's year and upon it a cross and six lit candles have been placed.

Same words, new actions

The words of the service follow the Prayer Book, with one or two additions. For example, after the familiar Collect for Purity, the *Kyrie* has reappeared and so has a gradual anthem before the reading of the Gospel.

The biggest change is in the amount of restored medieval ceremonial. The Gospel is processed to the entrance of the chancel where the reader crosses himself. At the offertory there

 The first official liturgical provision for a yearly Harvest Thanksgiving in the Church of England was in 1862.

seems to be an elaborate ritual with the plate and cup, at the end of which the priest washes his hands. Standing in front of the altar, he has his back to the people apart from when he turns to the congregation as he pronounces absolution, making the sign of the cross as he does so. He sings 'The Lord be with you' and the preface and *Sanctus*, adding in *Benedictus qui venit* ('Blessed is he who comes…'). As in other parts of the service, there is a strong sense of reverence and dignity.

When the congregation receive Communion, some of them wrinkle their noses at the new wafers, embossed with a crucifix, and some try to take the chalice into their hands as they used to do until the arrival of their new vicar. After Communion there is some elaborate washing up of Communion vessels.

CONNECTIONS
▶ The sacramental in worship – pp.42–3
▶ The evangelical revival – p.98

St Agatha's – 2000

Ernest recognizes the final notes of the anthem and his concentration jolts back into the year 2000. 'How things have changed,' he thinks to himself – meaning more than just the retail development covering the land once occupied by factories. 'It puts into perspective all those heated debates at the PCC about the new services.'

A re-ordered interior

Back in 1985 a platform was added at the front of the nave, raising the floor height to the height of the chancel. A new holy table (which everyone calls the 'nave altar') was placed in the middle of this platform so that the president could stand behind it, facing the congregation. During the 10 a.m. Sunday service, a group of instrumentalists and singers provide music with the aid of microphones and a sophisticated PA system. The entire floor of the building is carpeted, and some well-upholstered and comfortable chairs have

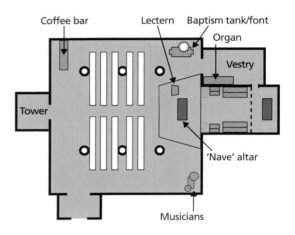

Coffee bar   Lectern   Baptism tank/font
Organ
Vestry
Tower
'Nave' altar
Musicians

Adult candidates

The twentieth century saw a decline in church attendance in England and a rise in the missionary role of the Church. Increasingly, candidates for Baptism and confirmation are in adulthood. Whole families are often baptized together, too.

Readers revived

The ministry of Readers was revived once more in 1866, initially to read services and say the Litany, although there was wide variation in their use in different dioceses. More comprehensive regulations in 1905 permitted limited preaching, under specific circumstances. Further changes in 1921 and 1941 extended this permission, although Readers were not allowed to preach at Holy Communion services until 1969, the year in which women were also admitted to the office. Nowadays Readers can perform nearly all the duties of an ordained deacon; their distinctiveness (reflected in their blue scarves) lies in being authorized lay ministers and they preach, teach and minister in ways appropriate to their situation.

been purchased. They are usually placed in a semicircle around the platform, but last Wednesday evening there was a Taizé-style service and the chairs were moved right out of the way, allowing the congregation plenty of space to sit in a group on the floor.

The Alternative Service Book

Ernest thinks back to the 1960s and '70s and all those experimental services, which culminated in *The Alternative Service Book 1980* – the first major changes to the words of the services since the turbulent days of the sixteenth and seventeenth centuries. What a shock it was to some in the congregation, who found themselves addressing God in contemporary language for

The simple layout of a modern church

The building's message
The way that a church building is laid out can make a difference to our understanding of God. Taking a lengthy walk to receive Communion – through the nave, under the chancel arch and right up to the east end – reinforces a sense of journey towards God and of God's transcendence. When the congregation is gathered 'in the round', about a 'nave altar', there is a greater sense of God's presence in the midst of the community, and of fellowship with one another.

the first time in their lives. As it turned out, the new words were the easy part – many found it even harder to get used to the physical contact (and the eye-contact) involved in sharing the Peace!

Lay ministry in worship blossoms

The ASB and the thinking behind it opened up many opportunities for laypeople in worship. They still have robed servers and choir at St Agatha's, but other laypeople are involved too – in leading the music, reading from the Bible,

leading the intercessions, distributing the elements at Communion, performing in dramatic presentations and, from time to time, dancing in praise. The outreach activities of the church result in many visitors and new families coming on a Sunday morning, so a large team of 'welcomers' helps people feel more at ease when they come into the imposing old building.

Flexibility and choice

'It's funny,' ponders Ernest, 'how some things become more like they were in the past.' He thinks of the number of different books he now needs in order to lead a single service. 'These old stones have seen it all before,' he muses. He thinks of St Agatha's monthly all-age service – based on the flexible structure of A Service of the Word. People really appreciate the words and pictures projected onto the large screen above the pulpit in those services, and Ernest recalls the ancient wall paintings. 'Liturgical change? There's nothing new about that!'

More Bible on Sunday
Both the ASB two-year lectionary and the *Common Worship* three-year lectionary increased the number of readings for a Communion service. From having just Epistle and Gospel in the Prayer Book, worshippers are now offered Old Testament, Psalm, New Testament and Gospel readings – though not every church uses all four.

CONNECTIONS
▶ **Holy Communion in the twentieth century** – pp.154–5
▶ **A Service of the Word** – pp.178–9, 182–3
▶ **The lectionary** – pp.236–9

CHAPTER 2

What is worship?

Some of the oldest archaeological evidence suggests that our ancestors, in every generation, in different places and in different ways, worshipped. Even in the post-industrial, post-Enlightenment, scientifically dominated West, many people still worship, and after a time of anti-religious assumptions there is once again a search for 'spirituality' among those who would not necessarily want to join the Church in its worship. The movement of peoples and their cultures around the globe and the growth of plural and multicultural societies in the West has highlighted just how important religious observance still is in the modern world. The number of regularly worshipping Christians may be on the decline in Britain, but the number of practising Muslims and Buddhists (to name but two) is on the increase.

Looking at worship 'from below'

One result of the Enlightenment spotlight falling on the Church is that anthropologists have looked at worship in the same way that they would look at other aspects of human life and work – that is, from a purely 'human' perspective. They are not interested in the theology of worship, or the rights and wrongs of different practices or texts. They simply observe

and record what they find in terms of external behaviours, which may or may not have religious meanings attached to them.

One way of doing this is to look at the ceremonies that are used. One model that has come from this inquiry is the 'rite of passage'. This theory was developed by Arnold van Gennep, who examined the initiation rituals of the tribes of Africa in the middle of the twentieth century. It has since been applied to Christian liturgy – with confirmation, for example, being seen by some as a rite of passage to adulthood in the Church. Others have looked at prayers and tried to classify the variety of beliefs and the types of deity that have been conceived.

Theories about how rituals work and the place of symbols in them have also been a major point of inquiry. Thus Victor Turner looked at the rituals of a Zambian tribe, derived some theories, and then applied them to his experience of a Catholic upbringing.

A Christian procession in Eritrea

Invitation to the numinous

On a more philosophical level, Rudolph Otto invited us to explore the idea of the numinous: the overpowering experience of the 'Other', an experience which he referred to as the *mysterium tremendum et fascinans*. This leads us to awareness of our creaturehood and so, perhaps, to awe and worship. He saw this experience as potentially open to all, even though not all have the experience.

To worship, or not to worship?

Historically, worship seems to have played a major part in most societies. In Christian terms, it is part of the way God made us. The strange thing, then, is not that human beings worship, but that so many people now choose not to – or, at least, choose not to do so in traditionally recognizable ways.

CONNECTIONS
🅜 **Culture and subculture** –
Chapter 5

Worship in the Old Testament

There are two basic aspects to an act of worship:

1. There is what *we* do. We pray, sing, read Scripture, reflect, meditate, use our bodies, join in with liturgy, and perhaps use our senses of smell and taste as well.

2. There is what *God* does. More and more today, it is expected that worshippers will in some way experience God during worship. It might be through a feeling of being close to God, a sense of having met with or been spoken to by him, or, even more dramatically, through a healing or the exercise of a spiritual gift.

Much academic ink has been spilt over how God's people in Old Testament times worshipped, but most of the discussion has been on the first aspect, and virtually none on the second. Of course, it is easier to gain objective information about the words and actions of Old Testament worship (collectively called the 'cultus') than about the subjective experience of the worshippers. What went on in the personal devotional life of the average Israelite is difficult to know, but we should not doubt its reality, nor confine discussion of Old Testament worship to the cultus alone.

Doing it God's way

We know that early worship as depicted in the Old Testament involved sacred places, shrines and altars, and some kind of sacrificial system. As the Israelites got to know their God better, one overarching principle became central: he was to be worshipped on his own terms. Large sections of the Old Testament contain highly detailed instructions for the conduct of worship, the equipment and furnishings required, the qualifications for leadership and the need to worship God in the place of his choosing. As the nomadic people settled in the Promised Land, the portable Tabernacle was eventually replaced with the Jerusalem Temple, and the worship became organized and institutionalized there.

When Israel went into exile in Babylon, worship in the Temple was no longer possible. It is generally accepted that the synagogue had its origins in this era, as people gathered on a smaller scale to pray and worship without the

A model of Solomon's Temple

A reconstruction of the tabernacle

framework of sacrifice. In addition, worship in the family home, regularly around the meal table and particularly at Passover, had long been a part of Israelite devotion.

Worship and the covenant

Worship reflected the two sides of the covenant relationship. God was their God: he had acted for them in saving power and gracious provision, and his character and his deeds were remembered and honoured in worship. Different festivals brought to mind and celebrated different acts of God and different aspects of his character.

The other side, however, was that the Israelites were his people, and so worship also drew attention to their successes and failures in living as God required. Paramount was the constant reminder of sin and failure through the sacrificial system and its provision for forgiveness. This, the New Testament author to the Hebrews tells us, could do nothing permanent about sin, but had the effect of teaching some important lessons about its nature and the necessity of a more radical solution.

What went on subjectively for the worshippers? We can only guess, but even the most cursory glance at the Psalms reveals a wide range of emotional responses to God and life. The use of the Psalms in worship would no doubt reflect the life experiences and emotions of the people, as they still do today.

We receive glimpses of both the 'epic' and the 'ecstatic' in worship in passages such as 2 Samuel 6 and 2 Chronicles 5, when, at times of great national celebration, the splendid and carefully organized liturgy and music is interspersed with wild abandon. At other times the people weep aloud as they are touched by a corporate conviction of sin.

A God who is present

The most important factor for the Israelites as they worshipped, and the thing which differentiated them from the surrounding nations, was that they worshipped a God who was present among them. His presence could not, of course, be contained in a building or a tent, but it could be known and possibly felt as they worshipped. For his presence to leave Israel was a national tragedy, which caused the nation to lose its distinctiveness (see Exodus 33). The return of God's glory, or presence, to the Temple, seen prophetically by Ezekiel, foreshadowed the coming of Jesus, the one to be named Emmanuel – 'God with us' – and the coming of the Holy Spirit on the Church, which meant that God would dwell in and among his people permanently.

Worship in the New Testament

We have no detailed information about how the earliest Christians worshipped. Jesus himself is both accepting and challenging in his attitude towards organized Jewish worship. He was brought up within the system, went to both the Temple and the synagogue, and taught that he had not come to do away with the law. Yet he was highly critical of the religious hierarchy for their deadness and legalism, their exploitation of the worshippers and their failure to recognize God's action when it was staring them in the face. His actions could indicate profound dissatisfaction with some aspects of Jewish worship at the time (see, for instance, Matthew 21:12–13). His first followers seem to have pursued a similar pattern.

For as long as they were allowed to, they continued to be a part of the Jewish worshipping community. Yet they were also aware that some of the key aspects of worship in the Temple (such as the priesthood, sacrifice and the Temple itself as the focus

of God's presence) had been fulfilled in the person of Jesus and in the community of his followers.

In his own teaching Jesus gave little explicit instruction about worship. We have some general guidelines about prayer and a form of words to use – the 'Lord's Prayer', which we have in two slightly different versions: Matthew 6:9–13 and Luke 11:2–4. He also urged the repetition of his actions (and possibly his words) at the Last Supper – 'Do this in remembrance of me' (Luke 22:19b and 1 Corinthians 11:24f.) – but we do not know that he anticipated the ritualizing of this into the public service of Holy Communion with which we are familiar. The nearest thing we have to teaching about worship from the lips of Jesus comes in the context of his conversation at a well with a woman from Samaria: 'God is spirit, and those who worship him must worship in spirit and truth' (John 4:24).

Continuity and fresh directions

The first Christians gathered at the Temple and in the synagogue, but they also built on the strong Jewish tradition of prayer, worship and learning in the home. They met regularly in each other's homes, where they prayed, praised God, learned about Jesus and shared food (Acts 2:42–7). As the numbers of Christians grew dramatically, homes were not always large enough, so the church in each city would find alternative places for gathering. The later persecution of Christians by the Roman authorities and by the Jewish religious leaders meant that secrecy and circumspection were required in some places.

The Jewish Sabbath was replaced in importance for the Church by the first day of the week, the day of Jesus' resurrection. This day above all became the main day on which Christians gathered to remember Christ, to build one another up in the faith and to praise the God who had saved them.

Form and freedom?

One model for the Church at worship is to be found in 1 Corinthians 14, where Paul explains that individual believers, inspired by the Holy Spirit, should contribute a song, a prophecy, a message in tongues, or something else which would build up the congregation. This chapter, with its final punchline that all should be done 'decently and in order', has been used to support many different styles of worship, some of them mutually contradictory!

One significant mistake, often based on this passage, is to believe that the early Church was not 'liturgical' in its worship. Naturally, they did not have some of the trappings of what we think of as 'liturgical' worship, such as service books, vestments and elaborate ceremonial. If we define 'liturgy' more accurately as the regular and repeated use of verbal formulae and physical actions, however, the New Testament is full of it. In an oral culture, and one used to the passing on of set prayers and teaching about God, it is extremely unlikely that there would not have been some set words and patterns used in worship. Somehow the Church managed to maintain the immediacy and freedom of the Spirit within a framework of recognized patterns and prayers.

Whatever forms were used, the New Testament makes it clear that early Christian worship was highly threatening to institutionalized religion, that it sometimes went wrong (for instance at Corinth – 1 Corinthians 11:17–22), but that it was vibrant, pervaded by the presence of the Spirit and profoundly attractive to the community at large.

CONNECTIONS
▣ **Liturgy and worship** – pp.40–41
▶ **The Lord's Prayer** – pp.70–71

Liturgy and worship

What is liturgy?

Our word 'liturgy' comes from the Greek word *leitourgia* and is usually said to mean something like 'the work of (or for) the people'. Originally it was used of public works of service done for the populace and, later, of religious rites performed on behalf of the community. It occurs in one form or another several times in the New Testament (for instance, Romans 13:6; 15:16; 2 Corinthians 9:12; Philippians 2:25), where it is translated as 'ministry', 'service', etc., but rarely as 'worship'. Acts 13:2, for example, reads: 'While they were worshipping [or 'ministering to' – literally 'liturgizing'] the Lord and fasting, the Holy Spirit said, "Set apart for me Barnabas and Saul for the work to which I have called them."'

Today, the word 'liturgy' is often used simply to mean the 'scripted' parts of a service (spoken or sung) which are not songs or hymns. However,

LIFE
WORSHIP IN THE WAY WE LIVE

LITURGY
PUBLIC SYMBOLIC WORSHIP

DEVOTION
PERSONAL SYMBOLIC WORSHIP

Liturgy is bigger than our personal, private worship, but smaller than the worship we offer with our whole lives.

Liturgy and mission

Liturgy and mission have often been seen as opposites. The received wisdom has been that if you want to make worship accessible, then the solution is to simplify as much as possible, remove difficult terminology and definitely avoid anything too churchy – such as liturgy.

There is, however, no intrinsic reason why liturgy (properly understood as structures and words, used repeatedly but flexibly in worship) should do more harm than good in the business of reaching out. Liturgical worship has many mission advantages:

• It connects with our whole being, body, mind and spirit.
• It gives us simple actions with symbolic meaning.
• It provides visual focus and stimulation.
• It gives us spoken words with which the outsider can join in (unlike songs and hymns, which need a familiarity with the music for full participation).
• It may give us a structure or an order of service, which can help the visitor to know what will happen next.

If some of the words in the liturgical texts are unfamiliar, then their meaning may be grasped if they are encountered in context, surrounded by more easily understandable phrases.

For most unchurched people, worship will be an alien experience no matter how simple or accessible it is made. Yet the atmosphere of worship and the sense that 'God is really among you' (1 Corinthians 14:25) are things that are apprehended rather than comprehended, and may be just as powerfully obvious in a liturgical service as in a more informal time of worship.

liturgical worship is better understood as a way of seeing worship. Such worship is:

Public – neither private devotion nor the gathering of a few like-minded individuals, it cannot become merely self-indulgent. In addition, it shows publicly what the Church believes and therefore it must not be misleading, unbalanced or idiosyncratic.

Corporate – it is more than a number of persons worshipping individually in the same place at the same time. It is a corporate act of the body of Christ, requiring give-and-take on everybody's part. In addition, the worship 'belongs' to everyone, and is not determined solely by the leader of the service.

Connected – it makes connections with the worship of the wider Church in every place and in every age, past, present and future.

Symbolic – it recognizes that public worship cannot be all that the worship of our lives must be, but it says things symbolically that we will live out in the rest of the week.

Embodied – it includes actions, symbols, movement, and not just words.

Formational – liturgical worship takes a long-term view. It deliberately considers worship not simply in terms of what it will do for us or for God today, but what effect, over time, it will have in forming us as Christians: our assumptions about God, our patterns of prayer, our lifestyles.

Liturgy in the New Testament?

Although there are no orders of service in the New Testament, there is some evidence of words that may have been quoted from existing hymns or spoken texts familiar to the writer and, perhaps, to the readers. Evidence for such 'liturgy' in the New Testament includes:

- Fixed exclamations, often in Aramaic even when used by Greek-speaking people, e.g. 'Amen', 'Abba', 'Hallelujah', 'Maranatha'.
- Doxologies, blessings and acts of praise, e.g. Romans 11:33–6; Ephesians 5:14; 1 Timothy 1:17; 3:16.
- Songs, e.g. the songs of Zechariah ('Benedictus'), Mary ('Magnificat') and Simeon ('Nunc Dimittis'), and the worship of heaven depicted in the book of Revelation.
- Credal statements, e.g. Romans 10:9; 1 Corinthians 8:6; 15:3–5.
- Gestures, e.g. 1 Timothy 2:8; 1 Corinthians 16:20; Acts 21:5.
- Annual festivals, e.g. 1 Corinthians 16:8.

CONNECTIONS
Worship in the New Testament – pp.38–9
Worship that connects – pp.60–61

The sacramental in worship

What is a 'sacrament'?

A sacrament is often described as 'an outward and visible sign of an inward and invisible grace'. The Church of England's twenty-fifth Article of Religion says the only two Gospel sacraments are Baptism and the Lord's Supper. It acknowledges

John the Baptist

JOANNES BAPTISTE ORA PRO

other sacramental activity in the world, but says that it falls short in one way or another from the sacraments ordained by Christ.

Making connections with God

Our Christian belief in the original goodness of creation, in the image of God in humankind and in the incarnation of the Son of God should make it obvious that God uses the physical and the spiritual together to make us what we are and to reveal himself to us.

Life as sacrament

In one sense the whole of life is 'sacramental', in that through the physical creation we can discover something of our creator and redeemer.

The Sacraments

THE LAW AND Sacraments ordained of Christ be not only badges or tokens of Christian men's profession, but rather they be certain sure witnesses, and effectual signs of grace, and God's good will towards us, by the which he doth work invisibly in us, and doth not only quicken, but also strengthen and confirm our Faith in him.

There are two Sacraments ordained of Christ our Lord in the Gospel, that is to say, Baptism, and the Supper of the Lord.

Those five commonly called Sacraments, that is to say, Confirmation, Penance, Orders, Matrimony, and extreme Unction, are not to be counted for Sacraments of the Gospel, being such as have grown partly of the corrupt following of the Apostles, partly are states of life allowed in the Scriptures; but yet have not like nature of Sacraments with Baptism, and the Lord's Supper, for that they have not any visible sign or ceremony ordained of God.

The Sacraments were not ordained of Christ to be gazed upon, or to be carried about, but that we should duly use them…

Article XXV of the Thirty-nine Articles of Religion

Whatever sacramental nature marriage might have may best be understood in these terms. *The Book of Common Prayer* describes it as 'signifying unto us the mystical union that is betwixt Christ and his Church'. Through all the shades of steadfast love and commitment which marriage can offer we can find out something about the bond between Christ and his people. This is 'sacramental', even though óur experience tells us that in an imperfect

world the connection between the symbol and the reality may sometimes be weakened.

Worship as sacrament

In a more focused way, Christian prayer and worship is sacramental as we draw ourselves consciously into God's presence. Similarly, such things as art, music, light, dance, action, prayer and word can be described as sacramental.

The Gospel sacrament of Baptism

In the first centuries the dramatic act of Baptism was undoubtedly itself a powerful inspiration to live a new life. The shape of at least some early (i.e. mid-third century) baptismal fonts seems to have been rectangular, resembling a stone coffin. The impact of such an image of putting to death the old self cannot be diminished. In Church history the dramatic element of Baptism has often been minimalized, as the size of fonts and the amount of water used has contracted, partly to do with the growth of infant rather than adult Baptism and the use of the sacrament in colder climates. Where human experience and the work of God are recognized as going hand in hand, however, there will be a tendency to reverse this. *Common Worship* offers a great deal of encouragement to bring back richness and drama in order to help our spirits resonate with God's work within us.

The Gospel sacrament of Holy Communion

Christian thinking has seen the sacramental nature of the Eucharist in three broad ways:

- Stressing the presence of Christ in substance, localized in the bread and wine, as Roman Catholic medieval theology did. Although the German Reformer Martin Luther moved away from the term 'transubstantiation', his thinking remained broadly in this category.

- Stressing the sacramental activity of God among the recipients through the *use* of the elements rather than *in* the elements, as many of the Reformers did.

- Stressing the mystery of God and acknowledging the difficulty of talking about heavenly things in terms other than metaphor, as many recent theologians have done, sometimes using the term 'transignification'.

> 'Twas God the word that spake it,
> He took the Bread and brake it;
> And what the Word did make it;
> That I believe, and take it.
>
> *Queen Elizabeth I*

CONNECTions
Initiation services – pp.116–17
Holy Communion – pp.144–5
Marriage – pp.210–17

The Word in worship

The Bible lies at the heart of the Church's worship. Some of it, such as the Book of Psalms, was written as a resource for prayer and worship before finding its way into the canon of Scripture. Much of it has inspired worship and forms the basis of liturgical texts. A fundamental aspect of the Church of England's worship is the Bible's formative nature in the development of faithful Christian people. The Word of God is proclaimed and dwelt upon in all sorts of ways whenever God's people gather, and the mooring of this to the Bible is strong in canticles, psalms, readings, sentences, songs and hymnody, Eucharistic prayers, litanies and responses.

The Word here and now

It is a strong part of the Church's understanding

that the Word of God is not just proclaimed as universal truth but is alive in every place in the here and now. It is part of the role of the Church to help the worshipping community connect their particular experience of life with the wider

---

The liturgical preaching context

The nature of liturgy seems to demand that worshippers are comfortable together on their journey in the presence of God. An ordered structure and common prayers enable and encourage people to open up their hearts and minds together. Anything that breaks a long-established pattern can be regarded as disruptive to worship.

Church of England tradition and architecture, which almost invariably includes a pulpit, seem to demand that a minister at some point during a service offers a sermon, an individual interpretation of the Bible. What the shape of the liturgy demands, however, is not necessarily this, but simply that when people gather for worship they read the Bible and reflect on God's Word as it applies to their place and their time. Drama, dance, conversation, group work, quiet, prayer and action are not inconsistent with this.

In a culture which is increasingly rejecting people who set themselves up as the 'authority', some less individualistic ways of reflecting on God's Word are an important development.

'Dialogue' preaching

Preachers need to be aware of the size of the congregation and logistics of the building, especially when using an 'interactive' approach. In a very large place it may be necessary for work to be done in small groups before somebody will dare speak from the front. In medium-sized congregations a roving microphone can prove invaluable. Small congregations can gather easily in a circle and talk most naturally. This is different from 'all-age' talks. Whatever questions are asked should be 'adult' (assuming that children do not form a large part of the congregation) and should allow people to speak to each other from their deepest experiences of life and/or faith.

New resources – new technology
Blackboards, flip-charts, overhead projectors and numerous cardboard inventions have been the stock-in-trade of family service preachers. Now computer display projectors and interactive whiteboards are accessible, and affordable new computer software is being generated rapidly. Educational material designed originally for schools can be particularly useful.

Models of preaching
Sermons often rely on preachers making a number of points about a biblical passage springing from their own experience of life in the local culture. This is demanding and not always appropriate, whether for a two-minute thought or a half-hour lecture. Other models exist:

- **Expository preaching** has strong post-Reformation roots and, amongst evangelicals in particular, has been an important way by which biblical passages are opened up verse by verse.
- **Family service preaching** has developed since the 1960s and often introduces imaginative visual aids or uses 'closed' questions (with right and wrong answers) to reinforce comprehension and maintain people's attention.
- **Meditative (or Ignatian) preaching** has evolved as a way of encouraging the imagination of the listener to interact with Bible stories. It employs much quietness and is, for instance, often part of a Good Friday service.
- **Dialogue (or interactive) preaching** has developed recently, especially in small congregations among the urban poor all over the world (including the UK). This involves the use of 'open' questions inviting adults to connect their experience to the Bible, encouraging theological creativity in cultures which have no share in current dominant academic thought-forms.

picture of salvation history. Frescoes, stained glass, art and sculpture (as well as reading, preaching, enacting and meditating) all represent ways through which God's Word has been translated and made accessible.

The Word in the world

Beyond corporate worship, the Church lives out God's Word in the actions of his people, in conversation, in discussion, in study groups and more. The liturgy and preaching present a wonderful opportunity for making these connections, but the 'sermon' label should not be allowed to limit the imagination. Such broadening is actively encouraged in A Service of the Word: 'The term "sermon" includes less formal exposition, the use of drama, interviews, discussion, audio-visuals and the insertion of hymns or other sections of the service between parts of the sermon...'

The nature of the God we worship

God's covenant people have always worshipped a named God, who is self-identifying. He reveals himself as 'the LORD, the LORD, a God merciful and gracious, slow to anger, and abounding in steadfast love and faithfulness' (Exodus 34:6).

A new name

The early Christians found their worship of this God, 'the Lord', taking place 'in the name of Christ'. The full meaning of the one name was becoming clear. Their experience of the 'steadfast love' of the Lord in Jesus' life, death and resurrection meant that they could no longer talk about God without also talking about Christ and the Spirit. Even less could they talk *to* God without talking in and through Christ and the Spirit.

Worship and the trinitarian God

Worship was seen not as a human activity directed towards a God 'out there', but a divine gift in which they were embraced by a God who welcomed them into his life of love. Christ was not only one to be worshipped, but the one in whom we worship. He is the paradigm

The Trinity, worship and life

Over recent years theologians have rediscovered the practical importance of the doctrine of the Trinity for Christian worship and human life. An ecumenical theological commission reported that

'a fresh awareness of the doctrine [of the Trinity] and its implications can lead to a renewal of worship and a deeper understanding of what it means to be a person, since the fulfilment of human beings is to be found in relationships in community and not in self-assertive individualism'.

'The Forgotten Trinity', British Council of Churches, 1989

CONNECTIONS
▶ **Corporate perspectives** – pp.48–9

A trinitarian mission

Our worship in the name of the trinitarian God leads us to participate more fully in the trinitarian mission of God. The prayers after Communion make clear that we who have been met by the Father, nourished by the Son and enlightened by the Spirit now offer ourselves as 'living sacrifices' (Romans 12:1) through Christ, 'sent out in the power of the Spirit' to live and work for God in our daily lives. Hence our sharing in God's mission in the world is also our true worship – in the world.

worshipper, offering his life and his obedience, and we, as those 'in Christ Jesus', are caught up in that worship.

God's name of love was later expanded to the full, trinitarian name of the Father, the Son and the Holy Spirit. This was the name into which people were immersed, or 'baptized'. This name would later be proclaimed in the Creeds and glorified in acclamations of praise.

Starting as we mean to go on

Often Christian worship begins with an acknowledgement that what follows takes place in the trinitarian name of God. This is a profound statement. Worshippers are admitting that they have no power of themselves to offer true worship. It does not take place in their name, nor does the worship leader have the ability to activate their worship. It is God who provides us with the power and ability to worship.

God gives us his Spirit to be the *energy* of our worship, to inspire – as the Prayer of Preparation says – all we do and say in worship. And we are

Trinitarian people

Christians have confessed the name of God in their worship for centuries, forming their understanding of God in the context of praise. We have also been commanded to form disciples in the name of the trinitarian God: 'Go therefore and make disciples of all nations, by baptizing them in the name of the Father and of the Son and of the Holy Spirit' (Matthew 28:19).

CW

Almighty God,
to whom all hearts are open,
all desires known,
and from whom no secrets are hidden:
cleanse the thoughts of our hearts
by the inspiration of your Holy Spirit,
that we may perfectly love you,
and worthily magnify your holy name;
through Christ our Lord. Amen.

Prayer of Preparation

In the name of the Father,
and of the Son,
and of the Holy Spirit.
Amen.

Optional opening sentence, Holy Communion Order One

Peace to you from God our heavenly Father.
Peace from his Son Jesus Christ who is our peace.
Peace from the Holy Spirit, the life-giver.
The peace of the triune God be always with you.

Introduction to the Peace for Trinity Sunday

And now we give you thanks
because you have revealed the glory
  of your eternal fellowship of love
  with your Son and with the Holy Spirit,
three persons equal in majesty, undivided in splendour,
yet one God,
ever to be worshipped and adored.

Short Eucharistic Preface for Trinity Sunday

May the Father from whom every family
in earth and heaven receives its name
strengthen you with his Spirit in your inner being,
so that Christ may dwell in your hearts by faith;
and the blessing…

One of the alternative Blessings

given Christ to be the *agent* of our worship, through whom – again as the Prayer of Preparation says – we 'worthily magnify' God's holy name. As we cry, '*Abba,*' the very sound of Jesus' worship is replicated in us by the work of the Spirit as we enter into Jesus' praise of God. God's life of love is not a life that we merely observe, but a life in which we share as we pray and praise in our time and place.

Corporate perspectives

The very idea of church (Greek *ekklesia*) is of a gathering. As Jesus modelled godly living, it was fundamentally lived out in fellowship with a group. His disciples, and the apostles, 'spent much time together in the temple, they broke bread at home and ate their food with glad and sincere hearts' (Acts 2:46). According to Acts 4, 'the whole group of those who believed were of one heart and soul, and no one claimed private ownership of any possessions, but everything they owned was held in common' (Acts 4:32). It was in this tradition (of *koinonia*, or communion) that the Christian Church was born. It is from an understanding of a trinitarian God as three persons that the Church draws its inspiration for a life of loving community.

Counter-culture

In the Western world today, which many would describe as individualistic, postmodern and consumerist, there can be no doubt that such

ways of being Church are counter-cultural. They were counter-cultural at the start of the first millennium too, but the New Testament reports a great attractiveness and magnetism about the early Church.

Worship in real community

In Britain, even down to the Reformation, religious communities were seen as reflecting a vital part of the very nature of the Church. Their history was of power, wealth and corruption as well as asceticism, love and service, but this was a movement which continually renewed and corrected itself. Much of the worship that the Church inherits today reflects its formation in these places.

Parish churches and other gathered worshipping communities need to reflect the Christian mandate to *koinonia*, or else their worship will not ring true. Public worship is offered in the first person plural ('we') and is deeply rooted in the traditions of community living. *Common Worship* encourages this in a number of ways.

Keeping hold of 'common prayer'

Variety and choice are watchwords of the age. Worship in today's world demands flexibility for local expression. Nevertheless, a great deal of the thinking behind the *Common Worship* material is intended to prevent local churches from casting loose their moorings to the wider Church. An ecumenically shared lectionary, a common shape to Holy Communion services and some definitive texts (the Gloria, Creeds, Lord's Prayer, etc.) all reflect this.

Offering an environment for relational expression

Relational matters are expressed Sunday by Sunday in many ways:

- In shared congregational responses.
- In encouragement of corporate activity during the Liturgy of the Word.
- In intercessions for Church, community, nation and world.
- In the offering of a sign of peace to fellow members of the congregation.
- In the sharing of bread and wine.

In the Baptism service the president is encouraged to present the candidates to the congregation and the congregation is asked whether it will support the baptismal candidates in their Christian journey. In the marriage service the whole congregation is asked to pledge its support to the couple in the years to come.

Reflecting the Trinity

The Calendar now names Sundays through the summer period up to All Saints' Day as Sundays after Trinity. Many of the Eucharistic prayers reflect on the nature of God as Father, Son and Holy Spirit in an ordered and conscious way. This helps focus the Church on the essentially relational nature of God.

Remembering 'the saints'

The Sanctorale (the list of saints' days) is an essential part of the Calendar which has been considerably revised. Churches are newly resourced to dig into the historical richness of human godly living with a wealth of supportive material. Services between All Saints' Day and Advent also help focus on the kingdom of heaven.

Sunday by Sunday and day by day

All this is not just for Sunday. The weekday lectionary, with its largely continuous cycle of readings, and daily prayer (in a variety of forms, but with common elements), are intended to encourage a regular commitment to pray with each other – or, at the very least, to pray on one's own with a consciousness of sharing in an activity with the whole Church of God, in every time and every place.

CONNECTIONS
The Trinity and worship – pp.46–7
Medium and message – Chapter 4
Baptism – pp.126–7
Marriage – pp.214–15
The Sanctorale – pp.234–5
The ecumenical lectionary – pp.236–7
Daily prayer – Chapter 11

A life-changing encounter with God

In both individual and corporate worship we exercise the privilege of meeting with God. We become aware of the eternal dimension of life and are reminded of the promise and hope we have in Christ. That in turn affects the rest of our life. Whatever age we are, and at whatever point we are in our Christian journey, this encounter is life-changing. Our worship forms and shapes us as we grow in our relationship with God, in our faith, understanding and spiritual maturity.

Worship and belief

Our understanding of God will be reflected in both verbal and non-verbal liturgical expression. Liturgy is a corporate mouthpiece, and a dramatic presentation of the great truths of Scripture and the received and current doctrine of the Church. Our theology forms our worship.

Our worship also forms our belief. As we worship God we are drawn into a deeper understanding of his nature. For example, the meaning of his love, mercy, forgiveness and faithfulness become real to us as we become aware of his holiness and our need of grace. As we declare the great truths of the Christian faith in the ancient Creeds, we are challenged afresh in our belief now. As we meet at his table in Communion, we grow in our understanding of Jesus' sacrifice and merciful provision for us, and we anticipate his return and our sharing in the heavenly banquet. So the words and actions that we use to express worship can also inform or strengthen our belief. We not only express what we already know, but are led into further knowledge.

Worship and discipleship

Liturgy teaches and guides us in our personal life. It enables us to respond to Christ's call to follow him and supports us in our calling as baptized disciples. From our first contact with the Church to the preparation we receive for our death, the worship and the liturgical provision of the Church accompanies, equips, encourages, admonishes and exhorts us. It exercises pastoral care, ministering to us at all major turning points and crises of life. It marks and ministers to us in each major commitment of vocation such as Baptism, marriage, parenthood, ordination, or offering for local ministry in the Church and community.

Worship expresses and forms our moral behaviour. The call to individual and corporate holiness is encapsulated in the liturgy in the reading of the commandments. It deals with the failure to live a holy life in confession, the Litany, exhortations, petitionary prayers, intercessory prayers and prayers of recommitment. Services of reconciliation enable an individual or a community to deal with sin, mistakes and the breakdown of relationships. Services of healing minister in situations that result from living in a broken world. Whole liturgical acts are founded upon an understanding of what is morally right before God. For example, the Marriage Service and Service of Prayer and Dedication after Civil Marriage provide for a particular approach to love and commitment.

In short, our discipleship is both expressed and formed through our worship.

Worship and the nature of the Church

Through our liturgy we express the life of the Church, as the corporate body of Christ as well as individuals who are in relationship with him. We not only tell the story, we are involved in it and are being informed and nurtured by it. We are formed by our participation in the teaching and preaching, the ritual, the sacraments, the Church's calendar, the cycle of the seasons and festivals which proclaim the gospel message, and through testimony, news and fellowship. We support one another and produce an environment of faith, which fosters the growth of faith.

In the way we meet together we also model our faith, which in turn forms us as we adopt the norms and practices of the community of which we are a part. Our worship models our understanding of ministry in the way priests, deacons, ministers and laypeople function. Our physical posture models our understanding of who we are before God and in relation to each other. We model our doctrine of God and humanity by how we treat each other and the strangers in our midst. Our worship both expresses and forms our understanding of the nature of the Church.

CONNECTIONS
▶ **Worship and doctrine in Anglican thinking** – p.63

Music and song in Christian worship

The story of the use of music in Christian worship reveals a profound ambivalence, with the pendulum swinging between splendid excess and puritanical fear of idolatry.

Psalms and spiritual songs

From Old Testament descriptions of worship we know that singing and the use of instruments

were part of worship in the Temple. We also know that synagogue worship included singing, and that the early Christians used hymns and psalms in their worship, as well as 'spiritual songs', perhaps under the spontaneous inspiration of the Spirit. Yet in the first few centuries of the Church there were those opposed to instrumental music, which was a prominent feature of pagan worship.

Complexity and emotion

The invention in the tenth century of musical notation meant that music could become more complex, as it no longer had to be learned by heart. Composers began to explore polyphony and harmony, which replaced the unison singing of plainchant. The more complex music became, however, the more inaccessible it was to the congregation. Music was increasingly 'performed' by experts, a trend decried by John Wycliffe in the fourteenth century.

The Renaissance period saw a flowering in all the arts, and composers began quite deliberately to pour emotion into their music. This period gave birth to oratorio, the sacred counterpart of opera, and the Roman Church embraced it gladly. The Reformers were not so sure. In two key figures, Luther and Calvin, the familiar ambivalence was played out again. Luther, himself a musician of some skill, was glad to see the best in art used to enhance worship, whilst Calvin feared the power of music to draw attention to itself rather than to point to God. He would only allow the singing of psalms, and only to simple tunes. This dualism continued in the English Church: Merbecke's simple settings of the new liturgy in 1550 contrasted dramatically with the florid and esoteric *Eton Choir Book* of 1500.

Music and emotion

The power of music to lift worship has long been recognized. Augustine said that 'he who sings prays twice', and the 1992 report *In Tune with Heaven* notes that 'worship without music does not easily soar'. Music has tremendous emotional power and the great composers knew how to use it. The branch of psychology which deals with the appreciation of the arts is called aesthetics, and work has been done in trying to understand more fully how music affects us.

The most common effect concerns memory. An emotionally charged event which involved music can be recalled when we hear the music again, and the same emotions are triggered. Sometimes music can affect us because of the way it is constructed. A fast, lively piece will speed up our pulse rate, helping us to feel exhilarated, while a slow, sedate piece will calm us down. Within Western culture a tune in a minor key feels sad, while a major key feels happy.

Sometimes there is emotional pleasure in the 'architecture' of clever composition or arrangement, and sometimes the inbuilt tension and resolution in the music can move us from agitation to relaxation. Of course, the effect is maximized when the words and the music fit well together.

Throughout the history of the Church, a fear of emotionalism and manipulation has produced an ambivalent attitude towards this emotional power of music. Nonetheless, the best and most popular composers have used it to enhance worship, so that we bring our emotions as well as our intellect into God's presence.

Breaking down barriers

Most composers wrote for both secular and sacred use, and the barriers between the music of the Church and that of the world were broken down. Another important development was the rise of contrafacta, the setting of sacred words to popular secular music, a feature which has continued to this day and was most notably demonstrated by William Booth of the Salvation Army, who famously said, 'Why should the devil have all the best tunes?'

Hymns and songs

The rise of Romanticism led to the use of ever more splendid church music, but a new force emerged with the evangelical awakening of the eighteenth century. Hymns, simple, accessible and memorable, became the major teaching tool

of Methodism and held sway as the most popular worship music until they began to be challenged in the 1960s by the new songs of the charismatic renewal. With their ancestry in spirituals, jazz, rock and pop, worship songs have gained wide acceptance, even outside charismatic churches. The quest is now on for worship music for the new millennium, as 'modern' charismatic worship feels increasingly dated and new music technology allows the boundaries to be pushed even further out.

 Hymns are not mentioned at all in *The Book of Common Prayer*.

CONNECTIONS
▶ **The evangelical revival** – p.98
▶ **Daily prayer** – pp.198–9

Worship beyond words

The Church of England was born out of one of the greatest acts of artistic vandalism in the history of our nation. Perhaps it was a sign of our prevailing culture (we have always treasured our authors more than our artists), but Henry VIII's dissolution of the monasteries was accompanied by the destruction of much great art. The opening up of the language of prayer so that it could be 'understood of the people' happened against a background of the destruction of much visual richness.

Since then, the Church of England has had an equivocal relationship with the aesthetic aspects of worship. The early seventeenth century saw colour and ceremonial return, only to be whitewashed out during the Commonwealth, and then flower again at the Restoration. It seems that Anglicans are suspicious of the visual, believing that we can control the meaning of language but that what is beyond words is somehow dangerous. *Common Worship* offers the opportunity to look at this again, not least because its language points to the poetic use of imagery.

The very stones shall speak – the building

Enter a typical Church of England church. What does it say to you? How is it arranged? What do your eyes fix upon? The very (un)tidiness of the building will let you know if the place is cherished. Its shape and organization will draw you perhaps to the pulpit and lectern, or to the holy table. The position of the font will speak about the place of Baptism as a sign of rebirth and affirmation of belief. The arrangement of pews and chairs will define the 'feel' of the worship. People facing each other worship differently from those who see only each other's backs.

Works of art

There may be things to look at. Stained-glass windows will bring light and colour. In many churches these have to be explained to the uninitiated, an amazing turnaround from the time when they were placed in churches for the benefit of those who could not read. The holy table and other parts of the church may have frontals in the colours of the Christian year. There may be also be sculptures or paintings. The charismatic movement

Banners can turn words into images

religious art obscure its object (and just because someone is thought to have been 'inspired by God' does not make the piece of art good!).

Movement and gesture

There are other aspects of worship which go beyond words. Movement, posture and gesture all deserve experiment and exploration, from the simple lifting of hands to the set-piece procession (outside the church as well as within). A trip to the font as a reminder of Baptism, standing for intercession to indicate that we stand with those for whom we pray, kneeling to confess our sins and raising hands as an expression of adoration: these can all take our worship beyond the familiar. *Common Worship* has almost no instructions about posture – not to discourage change of posture but to release it. It is time for congregations to explore movement as a way of expressing worship.

Art, music and movement come together in dance. For this reason dance is one of the most expressive acts of worship, and it is also the artistic medium which causes most division among worshippers. Liturgical dance brings people as whole human beings before the God beyond words. Done well, like the finest art, dance draws us into adoration.

A richness in worship

In all this it is of course possible to see only the performance or the medium. On the other hand, our churches would be impoverished if we had words alone, and our art would be disparate if we had no faith. Drawn together as the expression of a worshipping community drawn to God through Jesus Christ, the visual and aesthetic provide the height and depth of worship.

of the 1960s introduced banners and, more recently, icons have made an appearance in many places. Much of this art is born out of deep prayer and encourages prayer in return.

There is a tension here. Ever since God's people were commanded not to worship idols, there has been a suspicion of anything which could become venerated in its own right. It is possible for something which is intended as a vehicle of worship to become an object of worship, but where a piece of art liberates the spirit and draws us towards the God who cannot be seen or described, surely it has a place in our worship? We should not let questions of personal taste masquerade as theology. Neither should

Diversity and commonality

Who makes the decisions?

Who makes the decisions about worship in your church? If you worshipped in a Roman Catholic church, many of the decisions would be taken centrally by your denomination. You might not be worshipping in Latin, but you would be using an official translation of the Latin text of the service authorized in Rome. Readings would be from an internationally uniform lectionary almost every day of the year. Some things, however, would be a matter for local decision: the hymns or songs, the form of the homily, the choice of Eucharistic prayer.

If, on the other hand, you belonged to a 'new church' (or 'house church' as they used to be called), there would be very few external constraints on your worship – or at least, few constraints beyond those imposed by moral, rather than legal, pressure. The form and style of worship would be entirely determined by the leader. With no fixed forms of words, the direction and content of the worship would be determined by the service leader and, perhaps, the leader of the musicians.

The only fixed words in the service would be those of the hymns or songs. Bible passages would be chosen to suit the preaching. Intercessory prayer might or might

not happen. Confession might or might not happen. The service might last one hour or three.

Fixity and freedom

On the one hand 'fixity'; on the other 'freedom'

– but which is really the most free, and who is that freedom for?

In the first case the leader is fairly constrained, but the people are empowered: they know what they can expect for themselves and from the leader, and they have the right to complain if they do not get it.

In the second case the leader is free to be flexible and to respond to the spontaneous prompting of God, but the congregation have little power – they are dependent on the leader.

Levels of authority

Most arguments about freedom and fixity in worship are arguments about the level at which decisions about worship are taken. Should they be taken:

- at the **congregational** level – by the leader of the particular service, or by the church council, or a church meeting?
- at the **regional** or **diocesan** level – perhaps by the bishop?
- at the **national** level – by national denominational authorities, or national ecumenical bodies?
- at the **international** level – by denominational authorities, or international ecumenical bodies?

A middle way

In the Church of England, inevitably, it is a bit of a compromise. Some things are determined centrally (e.g. the form of Eucharistic prayers), but some aspects are determined locally (e.g. which Eucharistic prayer to use, whether or not to sing parts of it, which setting to use if you do sing, whether to use congregational responses, and which ones, etc.). Bible readings are determined by lectionary, but the number of readings is determined locally, and the lectionary itself has 'open seasons' when a local church may determine its own pattern. When it comes to songs and hymns, of course, it is a local free-for-all!

Commonality and the Anglican Communion

Every local decision brings a loss of 'commonality' across the Church of England and every decision by a province to revise its liturgy brings a loss of 'commonality' across the Anglican Communion – and that has become a big issue in recent years.

The Church of England's General Synod in session

CONNECTIONS
⋈ **Holy Communion** – pp.166–77
⋈ **The Lectionary** – pp.236–41

The Prayer Book legacy

The Church of England's distinctive forms of worship date from 1549, when a Parliamentary Act of Uniformity abolished the use of Latin services and imposed a uniform 'Book of Common Prayer'. Further Acts of Uniformity followed, until the last one came in 1662. The important words are **Uniformity** and **Common Prayer**. Anglicans have got so used to the idea that worship should be fixed in books that they still find it hard to think of worship in any other way. Even *The Alternative Service Book 1980*, for all its options and choices and 'other suitable words', still felt safe because it was all in one book.

Power to the king – and to the people

The reason for this lies in the roots of the Church of England itself. Ours is a Church formed against the background of a political agenda. This agenda was for absolute power to be held *centrally*, but in *this* country and by the *monarch* rather than by a Pope in Rome. The Act of Uniformity was designed to put all the power for determining worship into the hands of the crown and government. In conjunction with the use of printing, this centralization and localization of authority enabled a literally 'overnight' change in the doctrine expressed in worship for the whole country – something impossible to achieve in the same way when books had to be copied laboriously by hand.

In the process it also gave unprecedented power to the laity, who were now able to check on the priest because the books, the same in every church, were in English.

Simple and memorable

Thomas Cranmer (Archbishop of Canterbury

and the copying of good (or not so good!) ideas. In the West Rome dominated, but it did not crush local variation. In England the dominant form of service was that used at Salisbury (the so-called 'Sarum Use'), but other versions existed and were also being used.

Agenda for a new century

The end of the nineteenth century and the whole of the twentieth century saw the Prayer Book uniformity in Church of England worship begin to unravel in terms of the actual worship offered in Anglican parish churches. Nonetheless, the assumption behind the texts, of common forms of words shared across time and space, continues to set a large part of the agenda for arguments over new Church of England liturgy, and it has played a large part in the thinking behind *Common Worship*. It is also lodged deep in the minds and hearts of many regular worshippers.

1533–56) had a liturgical agenda of simplification, and the result was a supremely memorable Prayer Book and an ethos of stability that was exported around the Anglican Communion in the centuries to come.

The truth is that, although the words of the liturgy in the book were fixed, the ways of using, interpreting, singing, elaborating and omitting those words were various. Yet the myth of commonality was maintained and, indeed, it was *felt* that there was commonality because at least something – the liturgical text – was fixed.

Liturgy by evolution

It is often forgotten that, before the Reformation (and Counter-Reformation), liturgy had evolved in a much more gradual way. There was commonality, but this came about initially through a general consensus about good practice

Uniformity dissolves

The uniformity in worship, through a centrally controlled liturgical text, was not actually how the worshippers experienced worship. Over each generation and from church to church there were always differences in the way the Prayer Book services were used:

- The Prayer Book makes no mention of hymns, but once they became popular they introduced an element of choice and variety from one church to the next and from one week to the next.
- As society developed, services were developed for which there was no provision in the Prayer Book, e.g. Christmas carol services and Harvest Festival celebrations.
- Different churches with differing theological stances and traditions interpreted and enacted the Prayer Book services in vastly differing ways – from High Mass with vestments to a low church preaching service without even a vase of flowers on the holy table.

Matters such as what ministers wore (and were called), where they stood in relation to the holy table and what hymn book a church used were all giveaway signs of very diverse worship experiences, even though every parish was using the same basic service book.

CONNECTIONS
St Agatha's – pp.24–33
The age of print – pp.74–5

Worship that connects

The controversy over ritual and ceremony in the latter part of the nineteenth century and an inescapable realization that the worship of the established Church was no longer able to reach all sections of English society put change on the agenda for the twentieth century.

Out of touch

Chaplains in the Great War, returning from the front line, reported that troops were neither familiar with the Prayer Book services, nor able to make connections between those services and their current situation. It is, perhaps, one of the missed opportunities of the twentieth century that, although this realization was one of the pressures for change, its implications were not worked out in the change that was suggested. The proposed '1928 Prayer Book' was influenced far more by the internal squabbles in the Church over ritual and words.

Variety and flexibility

Cranmer's agenda for the Prayer Book was one of simplification of seasonal and other 'extras' and a tight uniformity from parish to parish and from Sunday to Sunday.

Mission perspectives

A new perspective on mission overseas during the twentieth century brought a change in perspective at home. Imperialism in religion, as in many other areas, was out – inculturation (the adaptation of worship to take account of existing local culture) was in.

Church of England worshippers began to learn at home what missionaries were proclaiming overseas: our unchanging God is worshipped in a variety of cultural styles (some adapted to the surrounding world, some self-evidently not) and this should be seen as a strength, not an unfortunate accident.

This is especially true of music in worship, and we must not identify good or correct worship with a single favoured cultural mode. There is a people factor too – other people, including children, are not a distraction from liturgy, but a vital part of what makes a loving congregation.

Being 'local' in a new context

Inculturation brought with it a new sense of the 'local'. In many ways *The Book of Common Prayer* was a 'local' order of service, in that it was specifically designed to be a 'use' for England. It had connections with the wider Church, but was not ultimately conformed to a complete package imposed from elsewhere (Rome, for instance). Ironically, that 'local use' ironed out some of the variety then existing between, for example, the Sarum and Hereford Uses, both current in England at the time of the Reformation. Such an understanding of 'local' suited Henry VIII's political aims – not least his desire to impose a greater sense of nationhood on a disparate land.

Our understanding of 'local' has changed, however. Politically, the end of the twentieth century saw a move towards national devolution within Great Britain, even at the same time as European integration continued to grow and develop.

Liturgically, it became harder and harder to find any single form of worship that would command assent in the splintering cultures of post-war England. A growing pluralism affirmed not only the existence of differing cultures but also the benefits of such variety. If it is good to affirm and understand ethnic cultures, why should we not do the same for youth cultures, rural and urban differences, 'third age' culture, and so on?

Local responsibility

The situation was ripe for the local congregation to take greater responsibility for the ordering of worship so that it should be appropriate for the community being served. The growth of 'family' services (aimed at helping parents with young families) and of so-called 'alternative worship' (aimed at young adults) were key examples of this. Official reports urged the General Synod and Liturgical Commission to provide forms of worship particularly suitable for urban contexts and for times when children would be present (especially at the Eucharist).

The ASB, the seasonal material that followed it, and A Service of the Word and *Patterns for Worship* have brought two changes:

- Much more **variety**, by way of seasonal material.
- Much more **flexibility**, by allowing (limited but real) choice in both structure and content.

Common Worship continues that pattern, applying the principles to all services.

In many ways, this localizing of decision-making (balanced by a greater stress on the importance of a recognizable structure and shape for worship) is an outworking of the Reformation principle – that those who know best what the worship should be like are those who know the context: the locals.

CONNECTIONS
- Inculturation – pp.80–81
- All-age worship and the 'directory' approach – pp.182–3
- Times and seasons – pp.242–3

Why is common prayer important?

The 1662 *Book of Common Prayer* has lasted strongly to the present day, and has bred the notion that there is a single Anglican 'style' of worship.

An Anglican 'style' of worship?
This common style is difficult to define, though the kind of adjectives used are 'structured' and 'ordered', 'dignified' and 'reverent', 'restrained' and 'objective', 'reasoned' and 'biblical'. The 1662 Prayer Book drew on the language of the King James Version of the Bible (and Coverdale's Psalter), but also exhibited a calendar and readings, a rota of psalmody and canticles, and collects and set prayers. The shape of its offices and of Communion has been well known; its confessions and absolutions have been familiar. In addition, the vesture of ministers has been a standard feature; choirs have had a recognized range of music; often Anglicanism has meant stained glass for windows, Gothic and neo-gothic for architecture, benign clericalism for leadership. The mood has been formal and even stylized, the preaching understated, the singing disciplined, and the length of any service entirely predictable. On this particular liturgical landscape, therefore, all have known exactly

where they were, without always distinguishing between rubric and convention.

The reality
In reality, Anglican worship has been far more diverse than this account suggests and *Common Worship* builds in an allowance for such realistic

---

Spirituality – memory and internalization
Repeated words and forms of praise and prayer become embedded in the consciousness, available to us whenever and wherever we choose to use them. So the frequent repetition of Scripture, psalms, canticles and prayers in our regular worship gives us a working knowledge for daily faith – learned by heart, for use from the heart. They become an active part of the conversation we have with God, speaking to us as God's living Word at the same time as we are using them to speak to him.

Now from henceforth all the whole realm shall have but one use.
Preface to the 1549 Book of Common Prayer

Ecclesia reformata semper reformanda – 'A church once reformed is always up for further reform.'
Reformation tag

Let all things be done among you in a seemly and due order.
1 Corinthians 14:40, quoted with approval in 'Of Ceremonies' at the front of the 1662 Prayer Book

May God preserve the Church of England; it is all that stands between us and Christianity.
Attributed to a past Parliamentarian

The Athanasian Creed was not written by Athanasius (nor was the Apostles' Creed written by the apostles).

and necessary diversity. Nonetheless, with all the variety, *Common Worship* is genuinely meant to be 'common' – in structure, in lectionary, in central texts and in sheer continuity from week to week. Worship together is not that which suits the taste of one person or one dominant party, but is where people who differ from each other in their social status, culture, tastes and personalities unite with each other to worship in the faith of Jesus Christ.

Unity without uniformity

In the midst of growing congregational responsibility for worship, and of flexibility of liturgical practice, there has also been a strong sense of what could be lost in this process. A fresh desire to express Christian unity through shared forms of worship has surfaced, both within Anglicanism and across the denominations. For the Church of England, the part that common forms of worship have played in forming a Church identity has made that feel all

the more urgent. Voices have urged the Church to consider seriously the impact of diversity on doctrine, on spirituality and on pastoral care.

Family likeness

The *Common Worship* solution is to stress the importance of a clear shape to services, with an 'evolving core' of common texts. This core of texts is provided, for instance, by limiting the number of confessions and Eucharistic prayers, and by perpetuating the use of familiar texts such as the Collect for Purity (now called the Prayer of Preparation), the *Gloria in Excelsis* and the Prayer of Humble Access. The result is not a new uniformity, but a sense of family likeness.

Feeling at home when you move

Common Worship means greater variety of words and practice from one congregation to another. Like visiting another home at Christmas, the core celebration is the same, but some of the words and ways of doing things may be unfamiliar. Being able to feel at home will depend on our willingness to delight in the family likeness rather than needing everything to be done in the same way as we do it 'at home'. The strong *Common Worship* emphasis on a clear structure and shape in worship, along with some common texts, should help.

Worship and doctrine in Anglican thinking

Worship and doctrine have always been closely linked in the Church of England. Canon A5 declares that the doctrine of the Church of England is 'grounded in the Holy Scriptures ... in particular such doctrine is to be found in the Thirty-nine Articles of Religion, the Book of Common Prayer, and the Ordinal'. Often the older Latin phrase *lex orandi; lex credendi* ('rule of praying; rule of believing') is used to sum up this close connection. The connection is two-way, however: worship ought to reflect good doctrine and it can also be a source of doctrine. It is a chicken-and-egg situation. One thing is clear: liturgy (along with hymnody) plays a key role in forming the most basic beliefs and assumptions about God in the minds and hearts of worshippers. 'Authorized liturgical forms embody doctrine, and the stance of faith of each Province is in part discerned from its liturgical forms' (*The Truth Shall Make You Free, The Lambeth Conference*, 1988, p. 66).

CONNECTIONS
Worship and belief – p.50

The Anglican Communion

The Church of England in Tudor times defended its freedom to depart from the ways of worship followed on the continent – whether Roman Catholic or Reformed. Yet this principle of freedom was the charter for iron uniformity in 'this realm of England' (and Ireland and Wales had to conform to England as well).

Uniformity at home – diversity away

Anglicanism since then has similarly upheld provincial independence in which one province may well differ from another, however tightly parishes within each province are expected to conform to the local authorized use. Yet in, say, the nineteenth century, the variation from the liturgical texts and culture of the Church of England was not great and, where it did occur, it was usually traceable to 'churchmanship' rather than to inculturation or local creativity. The 1908 Lambeth Conference could still speak of *The Book of Common Prayer* as a great bond of the Anglican Communion, and even the 1948 Lambeth Conference used similar terms. The one great concession Anglicanism made to new converts everywhere in the world was to adopt the vernacular tongue. Anglicanism could almost be defined by its common liturgical patterns, as much as by its common organizational and episcopal features.

> It is not necessary that Traditions and Ceremonies be in all places one, and utterly like ... Every particular or national Church hath authority to ordain, change, and abolish, ceremonies or rites of the Church ordained only by man's authority...
>
> *Article XXXIV of the Thirty-nine Articles of Religion*

Provincial powers

Eventually, however, the provinces used their powers. By 1950 completely separate Prayer Books were to be found in Ireland, Scotland, the USA and Canada, and separate Eucharistic rites existed in many other places. In 1950 the Eucharistic rite of the newly formed, united Church of South India struck a pioneering note (it was the first to have a conscious reference to Gregory Dix's book, *The Shape of the Liturgy*) and presented a challenge to the Anglican Communion.

Principles for revision

The 1958 Lambeth Conference, for the first time, provided principles for revising the Prayer Book. The 1960s saw the creation of new provinces and the flexing of the synodical muscles of older ones, a fast improvement in worldwide communications, the birth of the idea of alternatives within one province and, where English language was in use, the beginnings of

Wales

In 1920 the four dioceses of Canterbury province which were in Wales were separated from the Church of England, were disestablished and became 'the Church in Wales'. It continued the sole use of the 1662 Prayer Book until 1966, when it began using experimental rites in both English and Welsh. This led in 1984 to a complete series of new, bilingual service books and these have been followed by some experimentation in modern English uses.

St David's Cathedral, Dyfed

Worship being led at the 1998 Lambeth Conference

province and its influence comes through the internal merit of its recommendations. The 1988 Lambeth Conference passed a resolution asking the primates to appoint an 'Advisory Body on Prayer Books of the Anglican Communion' to offer 'encouragement, support and advice to Churches of the Communion in their work of liturgical revision'. The primates, at their joint meeting with the ACC in 1993, asked the IALC to fulfil this role.

modern language texts. These were assisted by the formation of ecumenical bodies which produced agreed English language texts, arising partly through the first widespread use of the vernacular by the Roman Catholic Church after Vatican II. From 1968 onwards, hardly any texts were newly written in Tudor English, and a vast updating of traditional texts was undertaken.

Networking the Communion

Since the 1958 Lambeth Conference, there have been some modest attempts at networking the Communion to assist provinces to keep in step with each other. Thus in 1965 and 1969 there were two drafts of 'Pan-Anglican documents on the Structure of the Eucharist'. During the period of intensive revision between 1965 and 1985, provincial liturgical commissions all over the world had in front of them the work of others who had already begun to revise their services.

The International Anglican Liturgical Consultation

In 1985 came the first International Anglican Liturgical Consultation (IALC). This loose organization has been recognized by the Anglican Consultative Council (ACC) as an official network of the Communion, and it held five full consultations between 1985 and 2000. Its findings do not have official authority in any

Ireland

The Church of Ireland underwent the same Reformation as the Church of England in the sixteenth century, and was bound by the same Prayer Books as the Church of England in the following centuries. In 1801 the union of the nations led to a 'United Church of England and Ireland', but disestablishment in 1870 separated the Church of Ireland and gave it independence from the Church of England. Thus in 1878 it produced its own (very slightly revised) edition of *The Book of Common Prayer*. It has engaged in major liturgical revision since 1970, and in 1984 produced the hardback *Alternative Prayer Book* in modern English.

Scotland

In 1637 a completely separate Book of Common Prayer was provided for the Church of Scotland, with a Eucharistic rite harking back in part to 1549. It proved abortive but seminal. In the eighteenth century the bishops of the Episcopal Church in Scotland devised new Eucharistic rites deriving from 1637, which reached their final form in 1764. These, in due course, influenced the rite of the (post-independence) Episcopalians of the USA. In Scotland the rite was revised in 1892 and incorporated into a whole Prayer Book in 1912, which was itself revised in 1929. Since 1966 a series of booklets has been issued, more recently in modern English, with a ring binder to collect them together.

IALC – Full Consultations

1985 (Boston, USA)	Children and Communion
1987 (Brixen, N. Italy)	Ministry of the laity
1989 (York, England)	Inculturation of the liturgy
1991 (Toronto, Canada)	Christian initiation
1995 (Dublin, Eire)	The Eucharist

CONNECTIONS
▶ **Writing liturgy ecumenically** – pp.68–9
▶ **The shape of liturgy** – p.157
▶ **Early twentieth-century change** – pp.100–101

Ecumenical commonality and diversity

Christians who would not even have prayed together 50 years ago now regularly share in joint services and weeks of prayer for Christian unity. They may even find themselves as members of Local Ecumenical Partnerships (LEPs), sharing a building (and often sharing worship) with those whose roots are in different denominations.

Cross-fertilization

One of the key features of the Liturgical Movement is that it has developed in parallel with this Ecumenical Movement and, indeed, the two have cross-fertilized each other.

From the Edinburgh World Missionary Conference of 1910, Christians meeting ecumenically began to pray and to worship together. This was soon assumed to be the natural pattern for all ecumenical conferences and gatherings, and continues as a major part of the World Council of Churches (WCC)

gatherings today. Prior to that, pioneering experience of ecumenical worship was gained by the World Student Christian Federation (formed in 1895), which included members of the Eastern Orthodox Church as well as Anglicans and Protestants. At the other end of the scale, evangelicals from different denominations were also worshipping together in Christian Unions.

This very act of worshipping together, and experiencing the worship of other Christian traditions, did much to break down barriers of mistrust and to allow Christians to recognize and acknowledge the work of the Spirit in unfamiliar forms of worship. This in turn created an atmosphere in which liturgists from different traditions could more naturally work together. The resulting convergence in patterns of worship across the traditions then fuelled the calls for a search for greater unity at the structural and theological levels ... and so on. It is significant that one of the key documents to come out of the WCC Faith and Order discussions, the 1982 'Lima' document *Baptism, Eucharist and Ministry*, has such a strong liturgical as well as theological element (including an associated 'Lima' Eucharistic liturgy).

Convergence

For the non-liturgical traditions, a fresh appreciation of liturgy as a clear framework rather than a straitjacket began to dawn. The result has been a genuine coming together. The liturgical Churches have discovered a new flexibility and the non-liturgical Churches have begun to appreciate the value of a clear and stable shape in worship.

Light from the East

In the West, a key factor has been a new appreciation of the liturgy of the Eastern Churches, which have preserved some of the earlier patterns now being rediscovered.

- The Eastern Churches have long had a strong family likeness, which is able to encompass ethnic diversity.
- There is a strong sense of the connection of earthly worship with that of heaven.
- There is a tradition of regular celebration of the Eucharist, without it becoming a private priestly event.
- The emphasis on *epiclesis* in the Eucharistic prayer reflects a theological appreciation of the role of the Spirit.
- There is a focus on resurrection and glory, in contrast to the more common Western liturgical emphasis on Christ's suffering and death.

A new environment

The ecumenical context meant that liturgical scholarship was now taking place in a less polemical environment. Other factors also worked in favour of a new ecumenical consensus:

- The discovery (or rediscovery) of early Christian worship texts – predating the Reformation and the East–West schisms – offered the possibility of shared patterns and words drawn from a common heritage.
- An emphasis on fundamentals, rather than secondary accretions, influenced not only texts but worship spaces, which increasingly were designed around three points of focus: table, lectern and font.
- A fresh emphasis on the Bible grew across the traditions, resulting in a restored balance between the liturgies of Word and sacrament.
- In the Church of South India (formed in 1947) there was a new, ecumenical Church in which to try out all these new ideas.

New shape – new texts

The fact that liturgists have also been working on texts ecumenically and providing agreed translations for use across the English-speaking world means that the current Church of England search for a 'family likeness' through clear shape and a core of common texts now applies far beyond the Anglican Communion. The result is a greater ecumenical commonality (a sort of 'Christian family likeness' without uniformity) alongside a greater Anglican diversity. One only has to attend a *Common Worship* service of Holy Communion Order One, a modern Methodist service of the Lord's Supper and a post-Vatican II Catholic Mass to see this family likeness at its most obvious.

CONNECTIONS
▶ **Writing liturgy ecumenically** –
pp.68–9

Writing liturgy ecumenically

Liturgical thinking, since the beginnings of the Liturgical Movement, has increasingly been an ecumenical exercise, with no one tradition or Church having all the answers. Liturgists of all traditions and countries work together and try to make the fruits of their studies available as widely as possible. Meetings of Societas Liturgica (an ecumenical 'learned society' which had its first meeting in 1967) bring together liturgists from all over the world every two years. They are kept in touch in the meantime by the international

The Joint Liturgical Group (JLG)

This group of British liturgists from several denominations was established in 1963, originally at the invitation of the then Archbishop of Canterbury Michael Ramsey, prompted by Ronald Jasper, a member of the Church of England Liturgical Commission. It was intended to serve the Churches by offering forms of service, texts, theological reflection on contemporary liturgical practice and encouragement for those seeking liturgical expression for the developing ecumenism. It was most famously responsible for the two-year lectionary which was incorporated into the ASB and into the *Methodist Service Book* of 1975. Its later attempt at a four-year lectionary (known as JLG2) was not widely taken up, being overtaken by the three-year *Revised Common Lectionary* (RCL).

JLG's work has been wide ranging and much of it has influenced the revisions of particular Churches. Among its work over recent years have been the following:

- *The Word in Season* – a collection of essays on lectionaries and the use of the Bible in worship
- *Singing the Faith* – a collection of essays on hymnody
- *Confirmation and Reaffirmation of Baptismal Faith* (1992) – a proposed rite for Local Ecumenical Partnerships
- *An Order of Marriage for Christians from Different Churches* (1999) – a rite for inter-Church marriages

JLG also did key thinking on Holy Week services and on daily prayer which has influenced the revised services not only of the Church of England but of many of the Churches in these islands. JLG is represented on the English Language Liturgical Consultation (ELLC).

journal *Studia Liturgica*, which first appeared in 1962. The Church of England Liturgical Commission has a Roman Catholic observer at its meetings and sends an observer of its own to the Roman Catholic Pastoral Liturgy Committee.

International Commission on English in the Liturgy (ICEL)

ICEL is an international Roman Catholic body, set up in the mid-sixties in the wake of Vatican II and with responsibility for producing agreed English translations of Roman Catholic liturgy. ICEL has played a key part in the ecumenical body ICET and in its successor, ELLC (see box on right).

Connections between the different organizations

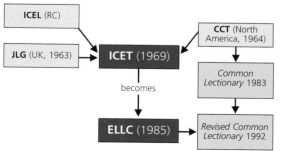

English Language Liturgical Consultation (ELLC)

ELLC is an international ecumenical forum for the formation of common texts for all those using English in their liturgy. It is the successor to the International Consultation on English Texts (ICET). ICET was formed in 1969, and soon began work on texts of such things as the Lord's Prayer, Apostles' Creed, and so on. This work culminated in the booklet *Prayers We Have in Common* in 1975. Once ICET's work was complete, it was allowed to lapse.

Discussion about a successor began in 1983, and in 1985 ELLC had its first meeting at Boston University. Its work was expected to cover many aspects of liturgy, including, but not limited to, the revision of the ICET texts.

ELLC has played a key role in commending the *Revised Common Lectionary*, produced by the North American Consultation on Common Texts (CCT).

In 1988 ELLC published *Praying Together*, a revision of ICET's earlier work. *Praying Together* contained agreed texts for the following:

- The Lord's Prayer
- *Kyrie Eleison* ('Lord, have mercy')
- *Gloria in Excelsis* ('Glory to God in the highest...')
- The Nicene Creed
- The Apostles' Creed
- *Sursum Corda* ('Lift up your hearts...' – the opening dialogue of the Eucharistic prayer)
- *Sanctus* ('Holy, holy, holy...') and *Benedictus Qui Venit* ('Blessed is he who comes...')
- *Agnus Dei* ('Lamb of God...')
- *Gloria Patri* ('Glory to the Father, and to the Son...')
- *Te Deum Laudamus* ('We praise you, O God...' – also known as the Song of the Church)
- *Benedictus* (The Song of Zechariah – Luke 1:68–79)
- *Magnificat* (The Song of Mary – Luke 1:46–55)
- *Nunc Dimittis* (The Song of Simeon – Luke 2:29–32)

Many of these texts have been incorporated (sometimes in amended forms) into *Common Worship* services. One of the key issues with which ELLC has wrestled is the vexed question of how to frame modern versions of traditional and well-known texts in inclusive language.

ELLC used the following guidelines in the revision of the ICET texts:

- In order to avoid pastoral disruption, only necessary changes should be made.
- Sensitivity should be shown to the need for inclusive language.
- The revision should allow for the fact that the texts are for use in worship. Ease of saying, hearing and singing is an essential factor.
- The revision should use language that is contemporary and suited to the original version of the ICET texts.

CONNECTIONS
▶ **The Lord's Prayer** – pp.70–71
▶ **Origins of the Lectionary** – p.237

The Lord's Prayer

Jesus said to his disciples, 'Pray then in this way: "Our Father..."' (Matthew 6:9), and so his disciples have prayed from that day to this. Of course, there are two different accounts in the New Testament, in Matthew and Luke, and Jesus himself draws different lessons for his disciples from the prayer in the two accounts.

Corporate use

The Christian Churches have generally agreed that the prayer was intended for corporate use, and have incorporated it into public worship. Cranmer included the Lord's Prayer twice in each of the main services in 1552, and thus made it absolutely central to all Anglican public worship. In particular he used it to begin a section of prayer, as with the collects in Morning and Evening Prayer and with the post-Communion prayers in the Communion service.

In the Communion service, the Lord's Prayer had been used in the West, from the time of Gregory the Great onwards, to 'top up' the Eucharistic prayer. With the reversion to a long Eucharistic prayer, which has occurred in almost all Anglican revision since the 1950s, the Lord's Prayer has generally been placed in that pre-Reformation position straight after the Eucharistic prayer, and that is how it is found in *Common Worship*'s Order One. In one or two overseas provinces, however, it has been lifted

The two versions of the Lord's Prayer in the New Testament	
Matthew 6:9–13	**Luke 11:2–4**
Within the Sermon on the Mount	**When the disciples asked to be taught to pray**
Our Father in heaven,	*Father,*
hallowed be your name.	*hallowed be your name.*
Your kingdom come.	*Your kingdom come.*
Your will be done,	
on earth as it is in heaven.	
Give us today our daily bread.	*Give us each day our daily bread.*
Forgive us our debts,	*Forgive us our sins,*
as we also have forgiven our debtors.	*for we also forgive everyone who is indebted to us.*
And lead us not into temptation,	*And lead us not into temptation.*
but deliver us from the evil one.	

> **?** In the East from very early times the Lord's Prayer grew a doxology ('for the kingdom, the power and the glory are yours...'), but this was not used in the Western Church until it passed into Anglican liturgy in 1662 (though not at every point of use). This was quite possibly from the defective Greek text of the New Testament then in use (see the Authorized Version rendering of Matthew 6:13).

from that context and placed instead at the end of the intercessions.

Modern versions

Since modern language English versions of liturgy began, there has been a series of 'international' ecumenical texts of the Lord's Prayer, produced by the International Consultation on English Texts (ICET) and its successor, the English Language Liturgical Consultation (ELLC). The Church of England text, after much debate about the best translation, varies from this in the ninth line. In general the *Common Worship* services print both the 'modified traditional' and the 'modified ecumenical' versions wherever they occur. The ELLC version is also printed in the main *Common Worship* book in the 'Prayers for Various Occasions' section, and the notes allow its use 'on suitable occasions'.

Is it 'eschatological'?

Suppose that the requests of the first half of the prayer, which clearly look to a heavenly outcome, are also the key to understanding the second half. Then...

- 'daily bread' becomes 'bread of God's coming day' (and possibly therefore Eucharistic bread)
- 'forgiveness of sins' is cast upon the canvas of the final judgement
- 'time of trial' becomes the ultimate testing of God's people
- 'evil' becomes 'the Evil One'

It all looks fairly plausible (check back with the biblical texts), but scholars are divided.

Versions of the Lord's Prayer permitted in the Church of England

Traditional – *Book of Common Prayer*	'Modified traditional' – *Common Worship traditional language version*	Ecumenical – ELLC, found in *Common Worship, 'Prayers for Various Occasions'*	'Modified ecumenical' – *Common Worship contemporary language version*
Our Father, which art in heaven,	Our Father, **who** art in heaven,	Our Father in heaven,	Our Father in heaven,
Hallowed be thy name.	hallowed be thy name;	hallowed be your name,	hallowed be your name,
Thy kingdom come,	thy kingdom come;	your kingdom come,	your kingdom come,
Thy will be done,	thy will be done;	your will be done,	your will be done,
in earth as it is in heaven.	**on** earth as it is in heaven.	on earth as in heaven.	on earth as in heaven.
Give us this day our daily bread.	Give us this day our daily bread.	Give us today our daily bread.	Give us today our daily bread.
And forgive us our trespasses,	And forgive us our trespasses,	Forgive us our sins	Forgive us our sins
As we forgive them that trespass against us.	as we forgive **those who** trespass against us.	as we forgive those who sin against us.	as we forgive those who sin against us.
And lead us not into temptation;	And lead us not into temptation;	Save us from the time of trial	**Lead us not into temptation**
But deliver us from evil;	but deliver us from evil.	and deliver us from evil.	**but** deliver us from evil.
For thine is the kingdom, The power and the glory, For ever and ever. Amen.	For thine is the kingdom, the power and the glory, for ever and ever. Amen.	For the kingdom, the power, and the glory are yours, now and forever. Amen.	For the kingdom, the power, and the glory are yours, now and forever. Amen.

The ***bold italics*** in columns 2 and 4 of the table above shows, in each case, a change from the previous column.

CONNECTIONS
ⓒ ICET and ELLC – pp.68–9

CHAPTER 4

Medium and message

The age of the spoken word

The flexibility of early oral worship traditions encouraged mission, but as worship developed in new cultures Church leaders struggled to retain control by putting things into writing. By the turn of the first millennium, the Church in the Western world looked to Rome. Even with the limitations of a manuscript medium and slow communications, this was the place to which innovation was referred. Only a few remote territories on the edge of the old Empire – such as Britain – were able to retain some local traditions.

Oral worship tradition

Before the advent of printing, Christians were not in the habit of carrying prayer books with them to church. Jesus taught his followers to pray without the need to resort to reading or writing. The Lord's Prayer was probably itself a memorable Aramaic rhyme, tightly framed and designed to be learned by heart. By around AD 75, however, it was already written down in Greek, as shown in the Gospel texts.

Scripture was certainly available to early Christians in written as well as oral traditions and was used liturgically (presumably systematically) in worship. Memorizing psalms and hymns and parts of Scripture was a primary way in which the early Church kept its traditions alive. Paul encourages worship in an oral tradition when he writes to the churches of Ephesus and Colossae (Ephesians 5:19 and Colossians 3:16).

Liturgical writing

The Didache (a second-century Church document) contains a simple outline for some parts of the Eucharist, mentioning the freedom for those who were 'prophets' to 'give thanks as much as they wish'. Justin Martyr in his First Apology (c.150) describes the Eucharist in outline, but again describes a certain amount of freedom: 'The president likewise offers prayers and thanksgiving to the best of his ability.'

By the time of Hippolytus of Rome (early third century), the liturgy was being written down and fixed by its leaders in ways that they could refer to over and over again. However, Hippolytus still states that the bishop may pray extemporarily, so long as the prayer remains orthodox.

Early worship books

Early worship books were probably primarily written by their first owners, and drawn substantially from other books of the time and from emerging practice. Recitation of the liturgy became very complex, requiring a substantial collection of books, each demanding considerable effort in manufacture. For instance:

- **Sacramentaries**, which contained the words needed by the priest for the Eucharist.
- **Lectionaries**, which contained the Scripture readings in full.
- **Antiphonaries**, which were the choirs' books, used for the parts of the Eucharist that were sung, including the antiphons used to introduce the psalm.

In the tenth and eleventh centuries compendia were developed such as missals (combining sacramentaries, lectionaries and antiphonaries) and breviaries (combining a calendar, psalms and everything needed for the various offices).

DID YOU KNOW? In the eighth century the French King Charlemagne appointed an Englishman, Alcuin of York, to supervise the writing of standard church services throughout his dominions.

Although the number of books reflected and encouraged a diversity of liturgical roles, the laity had no access to these books.

The travelling Dominican and Franciscan orders provoked the development of more portable breviaries, which soon found favour across Europe.

English patterns

Immediately prior to the printing revolution, the early oral roots of Christian worship had developed into complex and diverse traditions, perpetuated in each locality through writings which were both full of copyists' variations and adapted to local ideas and customs. In broad terms, however, the rather elaborate rites of Salisbury Cathedral (the 'Sarum Use') were at the heart of liturgy in the parishes of the northern province and most of the southern province, with only a few parishes and cathedrals using other variations such as those from Hereford, York or Bangor.

Alongside the formal liturgies of the Church, a shorter and simpler book of prayer, *Horae Beatae Mariae Virginis*, or, in English, *Prymer*, developed for popular use. It may have been around as early as the late tenth century. It surfaced in Rome at the end of the twelfth century and was translated into English early in the language's literary history in the fifteenth century. The use of 'prymers' developed particularly in England as a congregational aid to meditation and understanding in church services, whilst the priest negotiated the complications of the liturgy.

CONNECTIONS
Early development of the Eucharist – pp.148–9
St Agatha's 1453 – pp.22–3

The age of print

The importation from Germany of the printing press in the 1470s brought to the worship of the Church both new opportunities and threats. Its further development coincided with the Reformation and probably fuelled it, but the impact on worship went much further than that.

Printing and empowerment

Printing empowered both the centre and the edge of the Church in different ways. It gave those at the centre the opportunity to establish a much more uniform liturgy, whilst its economic impact led to the laity having better access to liturgical books. The Church always had the resources, but not the will, to put a Bible in every parish. Printing allowed others with fewer resources to realize this dream, whilst the powerful used it effectively to meet their own ends too. Printing limited variety and de-clericalized the liturgy at the same time.

Early books

When Johannes Gutenberg produced a printed Bible in 1455, it was hailed by Berthold, the Archbishop of Mainz, as a product of 'divine art'. It was quickly followed by a Psalter and by 1475 liturgical books were also rolling off the presses at Augsburg, Bamberg and Blaubeuren. By 1476 Ulrich Hahn had worked out how to print music with the text too, though this was rarely done – because of the variety of musical traditions, it was still often completed by hand. By the following year the first books were being printed in England, at William Caxton's works in Westminster.

Pictures were a significant aspect of early printed books and were often part of the accompanying sales pitch. By the end of the fifteenth century, Venetian printers were famed for their art. They invented beautifully engraved borders and the most famous amongst them, Aldus, introduced roman and italic typefaces that travelled the world.

The English scene

In England, Henry VIII's reign (1509–47) coincided with this period. The boundaries between what was done for the sake of the Church, what was done for the sake of Henry's political desires, and what was done for the self-interest of others involved, were not clear. What is clear is that printing and worship were together used for personal, political and faithful ends. Such was their power. Yet out of it all developed a resource for worship and spiritual formation which has served a significant cross-section of English speakers for centuries.

In 1541 and 1543 two editions of the Latin 'English Rite' were printed in London. They were unexceptional, except in the deletion of all references to the name, position and existence of any Pope. The patent which gave the owners of Eyre & Spottiswoode the right to print these books also suggests that they were valuable (in terms of balance of payments and employment) in the King's eyes.

The publication of the first English language Prayer Book followed in 1549. This book was accompanied by this promulgation: 'That no manner of person do sell the present booke unbounde above the price of ii shyllinge and ii pence the piece. And the same booke in paste or in boardes not above the price of iii shillings and viii pence the piece.'

Previously a Manuale and Processionale together would have cost seven shillings and the old Missale more than double that. It was essential for the new books to be affordable to parishes. Of course, the old books had to be destroyed – a matter of some heartache and pain.

A people of the book

This use of this new technology was to create a close association between worshippers and books. The books in turn enabled worshippers to take part in worship in ways which hitherto had not been

> **DID YOU KNOW?** When printing was first employed, scribes were not put out of work. At first they wrote musical notation into liturgical books. When the problem of how to print this was solved, they continued to execute the decorative initial letters.

> **Visual rubrics**
> The Sarum Processionale, containing music for special services, was printed in some 24 editions between 1502 and 1558. The 1523 Antwerp edition contains a complicated choreography showing by diagrams and symbols (tonsure, candle, book, etc.) where the different officiating ministers should be and what they should be doing.

open to them – initially by repeating phrases after the minister, but, in later years, by following in their own copies. Beginning with congregational singing of psalms shortly after 1552, by 1662 there were responses specifically written for the people (rather than the choir) and hymns were in common use by the time of the Wesleys in the eighteenth century.

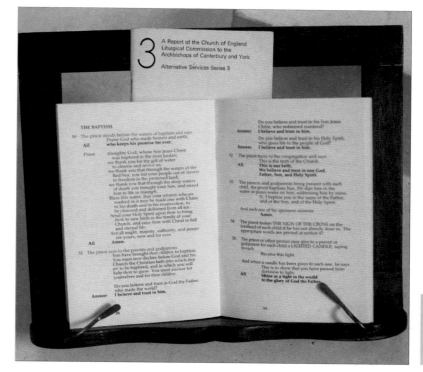

CONNECTIONS
▣ **St Agatha's, 1561** – pp.24–5
▣ **The Prayer Books begin** – pp.94–5

Language

After the Norman Conquest in Britain, the Anglo-Saxon language was regarded as the peasants' language by the new rulers and their lords, who spoke French. The universal language of the Western Church was Latin. By the thirteenth century, however, written English began to appear again and by the fourteenth century Chaucer was writing in English, and legal business could also be conducted in English. Books which emerged from Caxton's press in the late fifteenth century lent the language prestige and helped to stabilize its spelling.

Church and state

By the reign of Henry VIII, the time was ripe for a consolidation of the English state and he undoubtedly used language as a tool to this end. At the same time, this enabled the Church to make the faith plain through Bible, prayer and teaching.

The Bible had been translated into French in around 1250 and some French devotional books had been available since the twelfth century, so the upper classes had felt no need of material in English. However, Henry V had made English the language of the courts, provided that written reports were made in Latin. By the time of Henry VIII the new bourgeoisie of the City of London were also speaking English. He wanted to appeal to them and influence the masses as well, and this impulse also enabled the Church to connect properly with the population.

English prayers

In 1549 the first English Prayer Book was completed by Thomas Cranmer and printed. His own words about it to the King (then Edward VI) were, 'I have translated into the English tongue so

Scripture in English
Martin Luther published the Mass in German in 1525, Calvin's French Rite was published in 1541. The first English pieces to be used in liturgy since the days of the Celtic saints were chapters from the Old and New Testaments at Matins and Vespers each Sunday in every parish church. This followed the Injunctions of 1536 and 1538 placing a Bible in English in every church.

well as I could in a short time.' With the abbeys and monasteries gone, the bishops had a chance as never before to establish a national practice. What printing had made possible, the newly independent Church of England used with great effect.

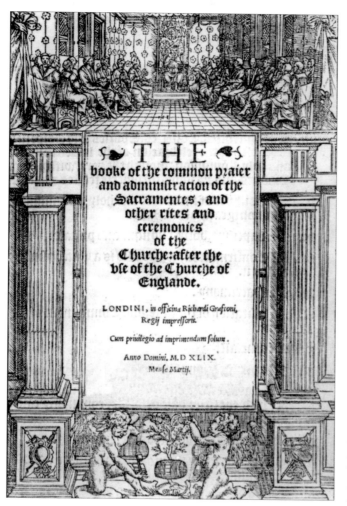

Cornwall, places where English was not spoken. The Act of Uniformity accompanying the 1552 Prayer Book was amended in 1559 by the Irish Act, which allowed services to continue in Latin in Ireland, along the lines of the Sarum books. The 1552 book was translated into French for the Channel Islands, but *The Book of Common Prayer* was not translated into Irish until 1608, as it was felt that few in Ireland could read the Irish letters (and they were difficult to print).

The age of common prayer

The 1549 and 1552 Prayer Books were originally intended neither as personal devotional manuals nor as books for the congregation. For congregational texts, the priest was to say each line first, inviting the congregation to repeat it after him ('…saying after me…'). Alongside the Prayer Books there was a series of editions of 'prymers' which continued to be published, including all that was felt necessary for the individual to read alongside the Bible during worship. These did not fall out of use until later in the century, when cheaper editions of the Prayer Book were printed.

A bare translation of the Sarum Missal and Breviary, however, was not the end of the road for Cranmer, who was encouraged by the continental reformers into a thorough revision. After some leaks of the texts by the printers, John Knox made a fierce attack against kneeling to receive Communion. The book was eventually published in 1552 and included the hastily drawn up 'Black Rubric', stating with reference to kneeling: '…we do declare that it is not meant thereby, that any adoration is done…'

By 1551, the 1549 English Prayer Book had also been imposed on Ireland, Wales and

A new age of common prayer and religious literacy was dawning. The printed Prayer Book became an increasingly important battleground over which the doctrinal issues of the Church were settled and was to become an ultimate reference point for that doctrine.

> **?** **DID YOU KNOW?** The first printed version of the whole Bible in English was made in France. Although licensed by the French king, the French Inquisitor General impounded the whole printing. Coverdale and Grafton eventually tracked down many of their precious leaves to a haberdasher who had been sold them as wrapping paper.

CONNECTIONS
⊠ St Agatha's, 1561 – pp.24–5
⊠ Inclusive language – p.83
⊠ The Prayer Books begin – pp.94–5

The information age

Time, increased literacy and reducing costs slowly diminished the power of those who controlled the printing presses. Global communications and a spiralling culture of choice and variety in a relatively secure political environment have made uniformity seem inappropriate. The Church of England was formed with 'common prayer' at its core, yet in more recent times it has been adapting to the new climate.

The need for diversity
The Royal Commission on Ecclesiastical Discipline reported in 1906 that 'the law of public worship in the Church of England is too narrow for the religious life of the present generation'. This came after 60 turbulent years in which nearly every jot and tittle of the Prayer Book had been tested in the law courts by

evangelical and high church parties. Each group had wanted to define Church practice according to its own understanding. It finally became obvious that precise definitions for appropriate worship were not possible. Eyes were also opened to sectors of society, especially among the urban poor, who had barely connected with the established Church's worship.

Limitations and fears
The stage was set for much more diverse practice, but the technology of books presented limitations – both to conception and to delivery. There was also a ghost lurking in the memory in the form of the *Directory for the Public Worship of God*, which had supplanted the Prayer Book during the Commonwealth period.

Practice leading the way
Clergy and congregations began responding flexibly to local needs, for instance by creating family services. *The Alternative Service Book 1980* officially opened up a new world of choice. Further resources such as *Lent – Holy Week – Easter* (1986) and *The Promise of His Glory* (1991) extended the seasonal scope, but broadly conformed to ASB rubrics. The material was still conceived within the limitations of books. It included complete services printed out for congregational use as well as additional material for the minister alone. Optional material was found in appendices which were difficult to access and use in the course of a service. Although cheaper

softback 'pew editions' of these books were published, few churches could afford to buy copies for the whole congregation. The only practical and economical way to use these services and resources was to produce local copies of the relevant services, or key parts thereof, for the congregation. The photocopier made that possible.

Computers and *Common Worship*

A new approach was signalled with the publication of *A Service of the Word* (1993) and *Patterns for Worship* (1995). Here was the 'directory' approach (clear frameworks and lots of choice over content) offered to the Church in a fresh way. Such material does not really belong in book form, though this is convenient for the authorization process. These resources belong to a new age of information technology. They are most at home published on computer disk, from which they can be tailored for printing on a local service sheet or processed through display software on a data projector. *Patterns for Worship* became the first Church of England liturgical material to be made available on disk as well as in

book form. It was followed by the enormously successful *Visual Liturgy* service planning software. The inevitable next step was liturgy on the Internet, and all the *Common Worship* services are available there.

Whilst the Church of England continues to publish normative rites, such as the *Common Worship* Communion services, its adaptation to a new culture and its embracing of new media suggest an increasing confidence. This does not insist on tramlines down which every local church must go, but instead encourages diversity. It accepts that differences between local cultures can be so great that permission to innovate and find new expressions of worship is required.

Pros and cons

The age of print and of belief in a common language brought advantages as well as disadvantages. Something which once helped empower laypeople to understand and take part in what had previously been the priest's liturgy may now be lost. Rubrics, which in national worship books helped everybody see the parameters of word and ritual, have changed in the new age to become instructions helping the congregation to understand what is happening and to know what to do next. Microphones, projection systems, computers and liturgical software all give power to those who control and use them.

There are dangers, too, of increased clericalism and increased disconnectedness from the wider Church. Along with the new technology there will be new lessons to be learned about the things that enable the people of God to worship together in spirit and in truth.

CONNECTIONS
◈ **St Agatha's, 1662** – pp.26–7
◈ **St Agatha's, 2000** – pp.32–3
▣ **Arriving at *Common Worship*** – Chapter 6
▣ **All-age worship and the 'directory' approach** – pp.182–3
◈ **The Westminster *Directory*** – p.27

CHAPTER 5

Culture and subculture

Inculturation

Over the last century there has been a great deal of thinking about the interface between Christian worship and the culture or cultures within which that worship takes place. Such thinking, about what has become known as 'inculturation', has become central to liturgical renewal and revision. Inculturation looks at processes: how the gospel 'gets into' a culture (and vice versa) and how the gospel and the culture change one another. It may also examine questions of cultural alienation and how this can be overcome.

Inculturation and the Church of England

Inculturation has become an issue for the Church of England for a number of reasons:

- Anglicans have become more aware of culture through the developing Anglican Communion.
- Our sister Churches have been exploring the possibility of being more inculturated, particularly in the development of music.
- Liturgical renewal has raised the issue of relevance and made us question things that were once regarded as unquestionable, e.g. the place of *The Book of Common Prayer*.
- Large numbers of people from a multitude of nations have made their home in Britain, making us much more aware of multiculturalism on our doorstep.
- Western culture has drifted from its Christian roots and now England is a pluralist culture rather than a Christian one.
- The Church has become aware that in some sections of English society there is a cultural gap, e.g. youth culture and inner-city culture.
- Those involved in international mission have been aware for some time of the dangers of 'imposing' an alien culture as part of the Christian package. Now those insights are being applied to mission 'at home' as well as 'away'.
- Postmodernism embraces cultural diversity and challenges us to use resources from a variety of traditions and cultures.

Anglican provinces are free to alter their own liturgy – 'every Country should use such Ceremonies as they shall think best…' (from the section 'Of

Exporting liturgical assumptions

Two traditions of eucharistic liturgy prevailed in the Anglican Communion until recent times:

- the 1662 *Book of Common Prayer*
- the Scottish/American tradition

These were exported around the world with the modern missionary movement. In some places new liturgies were composed, but they mostly followed an agenda set by the controversies of the 'home' Church. However, for the reasons mentioned above Anglicans have more recently espoused inculturation, for example in the 1989 York Statement, 'Down to Earth Worship', of the International Anglican Liturgical Consultation (IALC) and in the 1993 Kanamai Statement, 'African Culture and Anglican Liturgy'.

Inculturation can be seen in the new Kenyan Liturgies and the New Zealand Prayer Book. In England, A Service of the Word allows and encourages appropriate local flexibility. Much modern worship devised for and by teenagers and young adults also consciously explores and expresses cultural issues.

Ceremonies' in *The Book of Common Prayer*) – yet Anglicans have been fairly conservative in grasping their freedom.

More than just texts

Inculturation affects more than the liturgical texts. There has also been much experimentation in the realm of music, where traditional tunes from around the world have been incorporated into Christian hymnody. In some places local instruments are now used.

There are also examples of architectural innovation in the building and furnishing of churches and cathedrals in local styles. Vesture and ceremonial provide further opportunities for bringing local culture into worship.

CONNECTIONS
A new sense of the local – p.61
Music – pp.52–3
The Anglican Communion – pp.64–5
Postmodernism – pp.90–91
Arriving at *Common Worship* – Chapter 6

Why change the ASB now?

The Alternative Service Book 1980 was heralded as the greatest publishing event in the Church of England for 300 years. Why is it being changed now, after only 20 years of use? Part of the reason lies in changes to the culture, within which worship takes place.

- The English language has been changing and the ASB looked rather dated in this respect almost as soon as it appeared.
- The ASB went for a wholehearted 'modern'

approach to liturgy and no Prayer Book material was included. It was argued that this material was still available in *The Book of Common Prayer* itself. Nowadays, the move towards what some have called a 'postmodern' culture means that many people are happier to mix 'traditional' and 'contemporary' in the same service.

- Some ASB services did not have as much time spent on them as others when the ASB

Language

Language changes, often in a surprisingly short time, and there are significant differences between the language of *Common Worship* and that of the ASB.

'Inclusive language'

The ASB is a child of the 1970s – when people's ears were not yet fully attuned to how half the human race could feel excluded simply by words. Phrases such as 'we have sinned against our fellow men' were not seen as a problem then. A decade on, however, and it was a glaring problem. Many people no longer hear 'man' and 'men' as generic terms for the human race, even in contexts where this is the intended meaning. Gender-neutral words such as 'persons', 'people' and 'humanity' have replaced them. The media now speak of 'firefighters' and 'police officers' and, by and large, 'man' is now taken to mean a male rather than a human being.

The report *Making Women Visible* (1988) was written to define the principles by which language could be seen and heard to include both men and women, and since then all new liturgical writing has borne this in mind. There are specific problems (the phrase 'Son of Man', for example) and some phrases that do not yet ring with the weight of their predecessors ('forebears' rather than 'forefathers'), but overall the language of *Common Worship* is inclusive rather than exclusive of people.

An exception

The major exception to this is the phrase 'and was made man' in the Nicene Creed. This was retained because, to some, it sounded better than the alternative 'and became fully human'. It also avoids any echoes of phrases such as 'well, he's only human'. Time will tell whether resonance will prevail over offence.

Richer language

The ASB was accused of having flat and unpoetic language. This was unfair overall, but *Common Worship* has aimed at further richness and beauty in two ways. First there is a greater use of biblical imagery and poetic phrases:

- 'with opened eyes and hearts on fire' (Eucharistic Prayer D)
- 'the garden of your delight' (Eucharistic Prayer F)
- 'the silent music of your praise' (Eucharistic Prayer G)
- 'give to troubled hearts the light of hope' (Funeral, opening prayer)

Similarly, the Initiation services are crammed with biblical allusions.

Secondly, the ASB seemed to throw out all the language of *The Book of Common Prayer*. *Common Worship* seeks Prayer Book resonances in its new prayers, prints Prayer Book services within its main book, and provides Prayer Book texts for use in other services. The Collects, for instance, are full of Prayer Book echoes, in a deliberate attempt to enable the language of worship to charge the imagination and resonate with our tradition.

was being produced and so there is a need to devote more attention to them. A good example might be Morning and Evening Prayer, where the ASB did little to revise the Prayer Book other than modernizing the language and adding extra canticles. *Common Worship* provides a different model for Morning and Evening Prayer on Sundays. A closer look at daily prayer within the Church and a growing interest generally in 'spirituality' in our culture make good provision for daily prayer more central now, and *Common Worship* forms for daily prayer will address this.

- Some ASB services proved inadequate in use and needed a more thorough revision. The funeral service is a good example: hardly any minister used the ASB service 'straight' (though a few would claim that they did!). In practice most added and omitted material or changed the service around to make it more user-friendly and pastorally appropriate.

- Even the ASB services that worked well needed some adjustment at points to make them even better. The Communion services are a good example of this.

- The ASB provided more seasonal material than the Prayer Book, but even this was not very extensive and further volumes followed. *Common Worship* tries to bring this seasonal material together and make it easier to use.

- New technology – the personal computer and the photocopier – has made it feasible to use variety within a liturgical tradition accustomed to printed texts. Such possibilities both serve and feed the demand for more local choice and seasonal variety.

Subcultures and worship

Part one

Worship with elderly people

From the recently retired to the dying centenarian, 'the elderly' constitute a major category, both as a resource for ministry and worship and as a focus for pastoral and liturgical care. The demographic preponderance of older *women* calls for particular adaptation – for instance, some sensitive restraint in the liturgical use of 'family'.

Where?

As well as the regular worship of the Church, there are significant liturgical needs centred on hospitals, hospices, residential care units and private homes. Worship in church buildings may require adaptation in respect of seating, lighting, heating, kitchen and toilet facilities, large print resources, 'loop' systems, access ramps (including 'getting up' to Communion), and help with transport to and from church.

When?

Traditional Sunday morning times are probably more attractive to the elderly than to others, and a reluctance to be out after dark may make

afternoon worship in winter (followed by tea?) more viable than an evening option. Midweek (daytime) worship, particularly for women's groups, is often well supported. Evening 'home' Communions during the week can enable the participation of working people so as to express the continuing fellowship of the local church.

How?

Many elderly people have been nurtured in their faith principally through *The Book of Common Prayer* and the Authorized Version of the Bible. This needs to be positively affirmed, and joyfully provided, in this present transitional period – although it should not be assumed that the elderly are necessarily the most 'conservative' element in the congregation.

Coming to terms with the 'marks of mortality' can be greatly assisted by appropriate liturgy for the sick, the bereaved and the dying.

> **Using gifts**
> The positive contribution of the active elderly needs to be recognized and encouraged (e.g. leadership in intercessions, testimony, Scripture readings, stewarding, welcoming, music-making, etc., as well as more formalized 'accredited' ministries in public worship, the 'wisdom of age' in membership of worship groups, assistance in hospital chapels and ministry to the housebound).

Ethnic minority insights for Church of England worship

England itself is today highly multi-ethnic and multicultural. In many a Church of England parish and congregation, the so-called ethnic minorities are an ethnic *majority* and 'Sunday best' is as likely to include the splendour of traditional African costume or the sight of brightly coloured saris, as anything else. Requests for the translation of Church of England liturgical texts into other languages, such as Urdu (a request met in recent changes to the Canons), reveals a desire among Christians to express their ethnicity within their Anglican worship. Where this is enabled to happen there are insights for us all – particularly in a wider culture which is increasingly diverse rather than monolithic. This can be useful for those working with any form of specific cultural or subcultural group, such as the young, the elderly, and those in particular social groups or situations. Such insights include the following:

- A thoroughgoing engagement between Church of England liturgical structure and text and the needs and normal modes of expression within a particular culture. This can result in a vision of new ways of being 'Church of England', which subvert and reveal the implicit assumptions behind much Anglican liturgical text and practice.
- A freedom from an unhelpful 'English reserve', so often seen as an essential part of Church of England worship.
- A willingness to engage all the senses in worship, rather than settling for the more usual cerebral approach of much Anglican worship.

Subcultures and worship

Part two

Children and worship

Within living memory, children coming to church would literally be expected to be seen and not heard. They were thought of (and spoken of) as 'the Church of tomorrow', and they had to survive on a diet of worship designed exclusively for adults. Sunday School often happened in the afternoon, as an extra to the morning worship.

Two new agendas

More recently, however, two agendas surfaced which have radically affected the involvement of children:

- The Church realized that it had to take mission to young people more seriously, as those from the emerging youth subculture voted with their feet.
- The growing awareness of the need for

'inculturation' (changing the Church in order to make it more relevant to the surrounding culture) meant that 'child-friendliness' began to be seen as more important.

> **Children actively involved**
> Children are being involved in worship in other ways too. Rather than having it 'done to them', they are being allowed to take an active part, whether as lesson readers or intercessors, as acolytes and servers, as musicians or as part of the prayer ministry team.

Children came increasingly to be seen as the Church of today and not just of tomorrow, and Church leaders began to listen to their needs and to shape worship accordingly.

The results of this relatively new thinking about children are now regarded as normal good practice in most churches. 'Children's ministry' is now more likely to happen during the morning services, with children leaving for age-appropriate groups. The growth of 'all-age' or 'family' services has been dramatic, and child-friendly Communion services abound, with unconfirmed children increasingly being welcomed to receive Communion. *Patterns for Worship* was driven by the needs of all-age congregations as well as churches in 'urban priority areas'.

Above all, there is a recognition of the reality and value of children's spirituality. The academic work on 'faith development' by writers such as Westerhoff and Fowler, along with the experiential involvement of children in charismatic renewal, has led the Church to value and understand children more fully as inheritors, with adults, of the kingdom of God.

Youth culture and worship

The growth in the number of youth-culture styled services and the phenomenon of the 'youth congregation' have raised sharp questions around the subjects of inculturation, worship and mission. The value in terms of youth outreach can be clearly recognized, but how do these missionary endeavours relate to the wider body of Christ and more mainstream worship? This question has generated differing responses.

It must be borne in mind that youth culture is itself very diverse! Trends in the music world and the dress, language and culture which go with these play a significant part in influencing styles of worship – and these trends are not universal.

Youth-culture worship is currently influenced by the dance and club scene, Indie music and culture, and the new Celtic movement, among others. Meanwhile, the 'rock Communion' of the 1980s and early 1990s has largely become a thing of the past. The missionary challenge of inculturation is not only the diversity of youth culture but also its transience.

Relating youth worship to the wider Church

There are at least three discernible approaches to youth worship and mission.

1. A serious attempt to inculturate the gospel within the youth subculture of the day. The Church has to recognize that what it sees as 'mainstream' worship is itself a product of a certain culture, which should not be imposed on those who find it alien.

2. A youth-culture version of the 'seeker service' idea. In this, the youth-orientated worship service is seen in missionary terms as a 'shop window' onto the Church, with the hope that it will act as a way into more mainstream worship.

3. An attempt to keep and disciple young people already within the Church, by making their experience of worship more dynamic. In many ways an alternative Christian youth culture is created. Whilst there may not be in-depth engagement with the culture of young people beyond the Church, the spin-off from such youth worship may be termed 'missionary' in as much as it becomes something to which young people are happy to bring their friends.

Subcultures and worship

Part three

Worship in suburbia

So much of modern Britain thinks of itself as suburban that 'suburbia' has become the unspoken norm and one thinks, therefore, of rural or urban worship as the exceptions for which special provision should be made. Worship in a suburban context includes its own particular needs and constraints, however.

- Worshippers are often divided into two groups. Some have little sense of connection with the locality (because they work away from the area, and are at work for many more hours of the week than they are at home); others feel very much part of the community (such as those based in the home, caring for children or other relatives). Making connections between worship and the rest of life therefore becomes complex: connections with whom and for what?
- People who live in suburbs are used to a culture of choice in many aspects of their lives, such as entertainment, children's education, shopping, and so on. They are also used to travelling distances – either by car or public transport – to exercise that choice. This pick-and-choose mentality spills over into churchgoing behaviour. If people do not like the flavour of their parish church, then they travel to one which feels more comfortable (whatever their tradition).

Blessings in disguise?

This distancing from the local community poses a problem, but it can also give a church the freedom to develop a particular worshipping style, knowing that there will be another, contrasting, service going on just half a mile up the road. The challenge then remains: how do you offer a strong ministry to the local community, whilst developing a distinct worshipping style which attracts people from beyond it?

A challenge

Perhaps the biggest problem for worship in the suburbs is that suburban problems (and suburban sins) tend to be hidden and unspoken, covered by a gloss of affluence and respectability. On the whole, suburban congregations are more likely than urban or rural ones to include the comfortably off and those with influence and power in the wider community. These are the very people who often feel most comfortable with the status quo, yet to whom Christ issued some of his most profound challenges. Worship which has integrity must tread a fine line between the challenge of the gospel and the comfort of the gospel. The biggest challenge in such a worshipping context is to stretch the vision beyond the comfortable present to acknowledge the prejudice, injustice and oppression on which our own Western lifestyles rest and which they create.

Worship in an urban context

Most of Britain is now urban, but not all of Britain consciously thinks of itself in this way. Whilst the poor and powerless are likely to feel themselves 'urban', the more wealthy and those who have more choices are likely to feel themselves 'suburban'. In an urban context the gospel as good news can come alive, but a church which learned to present it first in an agrarian society cannot simply carry on doing the same thing.

No formula

There is no special formula for worship in urban contexts. In Victorian cities the 'Ritualists' clearly made powerful connections with the urban poor, but not nearly so much now. It may have been because they risked themselves for the sake of the worship that their parishioners were led to see something authentic in what their churches were about. Similarly, in South America there are churches which have risked all for the sake of liberating the poor from oppression. Their worship has connected with this, resonated with authenticity and shown the gospel to be 'good news for the poor' (Luke 4:18).

Starting places

Common Worship texts and services can give local worship shape and form. They are not the last word and there is scope for flexibility and experiment, particularly under the provisions of A Service of the Word. There is other material which comes from urban places and which can be used alongside this – most notably in Britain, the material produced by the Iona Community.

Worship in a rural context

A key feature of village and country town communities is that they are not physically linked to any larger community, and so they can be particularly prone to the parallel myths of self-sufficiency or isolation.

Features of rural communities
- A community consciousness with clear physical parameters.
- A population mix of the rooted (both those with long-standing family roots and those who have 'come here to die') and the rootless (commuter 'birds of passage' as well as weekenders).
- An English 'ethnicity', with a significant proportion of God-fearing agnostics.
- A liturgical focus on a beautiful, expensively maintained medieval church building.
- An involvement in a multi-parish benefice.
- A sense of living closer to the 'natural order' than urbanites (and suburbanites!).
- Often only one (usually Anglican) place of worship, or sometimes a smaller Free Church chapel as well.

Related issues and possibilities
- The need to offer a comprehensive (rather than eclectic) worship pattern in terms of the types of service offered and the traditions reflected.
- An affirmation of both traditional and contemporary liturgy.
- The special significance of creation ordinances surrounding childbirth, marriage, bereavement ministry, etc.
- An attitude of maintenance for mission, with liturgy as a focus for church-based evangelism and school involvement.
- The need to maintain a community focus for local worship rather than the cross-community 'pan-Anglicanism' of 'benefice' services.
- The opportunities provided by the agricultural year – Plough Sunday, Rogationtide, Lammas, Harvest.
- Recognition of the imperatives of ecumenical generosity through shared ministry, dual membership, united worship at festivals, local ecumenical partnerships, sacramental hospitality, and so on.

CONNECTIONS
⊠ **Iona Community** – pp.108–9
⊠ **Ritualists** – pp.30–31

Postmodernity and worship

The term 'postmodernity' refers quite simply to the present period of cultural transition caused by the collapse of confidence in the ideology of 'modernity'. Nurtured by the ideals of the eighteenth-century Enlightenment, modernity has been a period of unprecedented scientific and industrial growth, unbridled confidence in the power of reason, the development politically of the nation-state and the private individual, and the sustained rejection of traditional sources of authority (such as religion and the Church).

Disenchantment with modernity

The disenchantment with modernity signalled by the term 'postmodern' is being expressed in the following ways.

- Rejection of the core doctrine of 'progress'.
- Rejection of all overarching stories (or 'meta-narratives') which have traditionally brought cultural coherence and meaning. The postmodern judgement on such stories is that they have proved to be oppressive, imperialist and self-serving. Modernity's story of progress, for example, has been a story that has served the interests of the Western world, where wealth creation has been at the expense of developing countries.
- Acceptance of relativism. Since there is no longer any privileged story by which all other stories may be judged, we each have the freedom to choose our own stories. What is more, we also have the freedom to change, experiment with and develop our stories as best suits our sense of identity.
- Suspicion of logic and rationality. This can be seen in a preference for more discursive means of communication such as image and story.

- Rejection of the modernist sacred/secular split and an openness to the spiritual and mystical elements of life, e.g. the rise of interest in Feng Shui.
- A shift from a production-based society to a consumer-led society which is changing people's sense of self. The 'hero' of post-modernity is not the diligent worker but the consumer. This has encouraged a consumerist pick-and-mix approach to spirituality, plundering (rather than understanding) religious traditions for what seems to fit an individual's need.

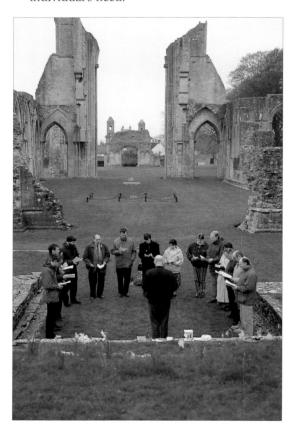

- Avoiding the temptation to be driven by concerns to make worship 'entertaining' for the spiritual consumers.
- Developing worship that encourages contemplation and reflection and a reordering of desires, pointing people beyond themselves to the desires of God revealed in his kingdom.
- Developing patterns of gathering for worship that are responsive to the increasing diversity of people's lifestyles and working patterns.

Worship and 'non-book' culture

Many church congregations expect to be given a book (or two) when they first arrive for worship, but outside the Church there are communities which are not so comfortable referring to books. It is no longer even true to say that this is a distinction between middle class and working class. It is shaped by age, local and family cultures, experience of school, library provision, expectations, and so on. Even where literacy levels are high, books have competitors such as the Internet, magazines and newspapers. Non-churched groups and newcomers in particular may have far more difficulty with being given a service book, or even a hymn book, than regular worshippers would.

Other options

It is important for the congregation to have something that helps them contribute to worship – and even more important for newcomers because they do not have any liturgical memory. There are many options and several issues involved here.

Simple service cards can meet the need, but they can make worship seem devalued or 'throwaway' for those used to a substantial book. Also, the simpler the card, the more likely it is that on some occasions you will want to do something different from what is printed. If you print a different order of service every week, the regulars will have to be glued to the card as well, in case something has changed.

Some churches are using overhead projectors or data projectors for spoken words as well as songs. This liberates people from books, but still relies on good literacy and has the disadvantage that, without a great deal of care, worshippers see only the text they are using and get no sense of the overall shape of the service.

Challenges for Christian worship

One attempt to respond to the concerns of postmodernity can be witnessed in the 'alternative worship' movement. The following are some of the challenges facing the worshipping life of the Church in the context of postmodernity.

- Ensuring that worship tells the big story of God's love for the world in Jesus Christ which brings freedom to all creation.
- Enlivening the symbolic dimensions of worship, such as those present in Baptism and Eucharist, so that they draw worshippers into God's story.
- Developing Christian communication that utilizes image and story.

CONNECTIONS
※ **Medium and message** –
pp.72–9
※ **Alternative worship** –
pp.110–11

CHAPTER 6

Arriving at *Common Worship*

How we got to *Common Worship*

Throughout the 450 years since Cranmer's first English Prayer Book, the Church of England (by its varying processes) has authorized the texts of its services, has stated that its texts reflect its doctrinal position, and has required its clergy (and others who lead worship) to use only those authorized rites. At times the penalties for getting out of line have been extreme. In Tudor and Stuart days the term '*common* prayer' betokened a law that was absolute – there was no flexibility for local circumstances, and no variety.

Revivals and diversity

The use of evangelical hymnody in Church of England services in the eighteenth century offered a first challenge to the iron concept that only the sheer text of *The Book of Common Prayer* could be used in public worship.

It was followed by the nineteenth-century Anglo-Catholic Movement, through which the Church learnt the hard way that there are virtually no enforceable sanctions against liturgical innovation.

When the proposed Prayer Book of 1927–8 failed it led to a new constitutional arrangement by which new 'alternative' services were authorized alongside the BCP for limited periods. Hence *The Alternative Service Book 1980* (ASB) was just that – *alternative*, not replacement.

Beyond the ASB

Into the 1980s and '90s services outside the range of the BCP were being 'commended' by the House of Bishops. Language was moving on. But all of this was taking place in a much wider context. Buildings were being re-ordered. Music styles were changing. Electronic reproduction and local editing were coming into vogue. A new Book for the year 2000 started to loom above the horizon.

The Age of Uniformity: 1534–1966

Monarchs	Book (and its year)	Characteristics
Henry VIII (1509–47)	[Split from Rome, 1534]	Roman Catholic rites in Latin kept unchanged
Edward VI (1547–53)	1549 Prayer Book	First full worship book in English, conservative, gently reforming
	1552 Prayer Book	Second full worship book in English, much more radically reforming
Mary (1553–8)	[Repealed 1552 Act of Uniformity]	Roman Catholic rites restored
Elizabeth I (1558–1603)	1559 Prayer Book	1552 Book with tiny changes
James I (1603–25)	1604 Prayer Book	1559 Book very slightly amended
Charles I (1625–49)	1645 *The Directory for the Public Worship of God* [Prayer Book forbidden by Parliament]	Advice and guidance for ministers in leading acts of worship. Hardly any fixed texts
Charles II (1649–85 – in exile until 1660)	1604 Book of Common Prayer used after Restoration in 1660	
	1662 Prayer Book	A very thorough revision of tiny details of the 1604 Book

Tracing the roots of *Common Worship*

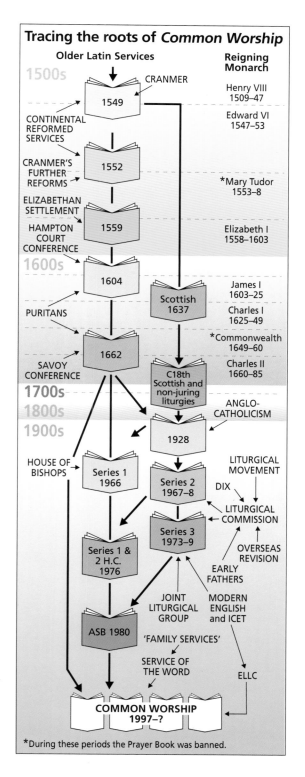

Older Latin Services

Reigning Monarch

1500s

CRANMER

1549

Henry VIII 1509–47

CONTINENTAL REFORMED SERVICES

Edward VI 1547–53

CRANMER'S FURTHER REFORMS

1552

ELIZABETHAN SETTLEMENT

*Mary Tudor 1553–8

HAMPTON COURT CONFERENCE

1559

Elizabeth I 1558–1603

1600s

1604

James I 1603–25

Scottish 1637

Charles I 1625–49

PURITANS

*Commonwealth 1649–60

1662

Charles II 1660–85

SAVOY CONFERENCE

C18th Scottish and non-juring liturgies

1700s

1800s

ANGLO-CATHOLICISM

1900s

1928

LITURGICAL MOVEMENT

HOUSE OF BISHOPS

Series 1 1966

Series 2 1967–8

DIX

LITURGICAL COMMISSION

Series 3 1973–9

OVERSEAS REVISION

Series 1 & 2 H.C. 1976

EARLY FATHERS

JOINT LITURGICAL GROUP

MODERN ENGLISH and ICET

ASB 1980

'FAMILY SERVICES'

SERVICE OF THE WORD

ELLC

COMMON WORSHIP 1997–?

*During these periods the Prayer Book was banned.

This chapter considers the 'books' (that is, the liturgical texts, published mainly, but not solely, in book form) that have both preceded and formed *Common Worship*.

After Charles II the 1662 Prayer Book ran on unchanged, unaffected by changes of monarch, until the nineteenth and twentieth centuries, when small alterations were made (or attempted) as follows:

- 1870 Prayer Book Lectionary Act. This changed the lectionary in the 1662 Prayer Book.
- 1872 Act of Uniformity Amendment Act (or 'The Shortened Services Act'). This permitted the shortening of some services in the 1662 Prayer Book.
- 1927–8 Prayer Book Measures. Two unsuccessful attempts were made to get Parliament to approve Prayer Books allowing alternative rites (1662 and rather more 'catholic' ones – including reservation of sacramental elements).

The Age of Alternatives: 1966 to *Common Worship*

Year/s	Services or features
1964	**Canon A5 entrenches *Book of Common Prayer* for doctrinal purposes**
1966	**Alternative Services Measure –** means uniformity much weakened by 'alternative services'
1966	Series 1 services (1928 type)
1967–8	Series 2 range of services
1968–71	**Modern language arrives**
1973–8	Series 3 range of services
1975	**Worship and Doctrine Measure allows longer-term planning**
1976	Synod decides to work for modern worship book
1980	*The Alternative Service Book 1980*
1983	*Ministry to the Sick*
1983–4	**Inclusive language arrives**
1986	**First use of 'commended' category for new services**
1986	*Lent – Holy Week – Easter* (commended)
1990	*The Promise of His Glory* (commended)
1993	*A Service of the Word* (with Affirmations of Faith)
1995	*Patterns for Worship* (includes A Service of the Word and much 'commended' resource material)
1997	***Common Worship* material begins –** the ASB replacement
1997	*Calendar, Lectionary and Collects*
1998	*Initiation Services*
1999	*A Service of the Word* (slightly revised)
2000	*Holy Communion, Wholeness and Healing, Marriage, Thanksgiving for the Gift of a Child, Funeral Services*
?	STILL TO COME: *Common Worship* material for Ordination, daily prayer…

The Prayer Books begin

The origins of a Church of England worship book lie in the work of Thomas Cranmer, Archbishop of Canterbury, in the reign of Edward VI (1547–53).

There is a pre-history – and not solely a royal matrimonial one. When Henry VIII came to the throne in 1509, England was still, religiously, in the Middle Ages. When he died in January 1547, he released the English Reformation. Although he had detached the Church of England from Rome and had bound the clergy instead to the crown, he had actually delayed the dynamic effect of the Reformation, withstanding most of the reforming influences, whether from the continent or from within England. Now, however, his son ruled at only nine years of age and the actual power lay with a Council – one with a Protestant majority. The key persons on it were not simply resisting the power of Rome, but had also passed the litmus tests of that period of change, in their beliefs about the Eucharist, the supremacy of Scripture, justification through faith and the use of the common tongue in worship.

Thomas Cranmer

Much now hung on the person and the beliefs of Thomas Cranmer, the Archbishop of Canterbury and a member of the Council. His own theology had become reformed in Henry's latter years, and his doctrinal conviction and political opportunity were marvellously complemented by a unique skill – he was able to write brilliant English liturgical prose. His was to be the mind and hand behind the composition and compilation of a series of liturgical books in English, the strong influence of which would still be felt 450 years later. The usual method of authorizing these new Prayer Books was to be by Parliamentary Acts of

> **The Prayer Book as a witness to the faith**
> [The Church of England] has borne witness to Christian truth in its historic formularies, the Thirty-nine Articles of Religion, the Book of Common Prayer, and the Ordering of Bishops, Priests and Deacons.
> *1975 Preface to the Declaration of Assent*

Thomas Cranmer, Archbishop of Canterbury 1533–56

Uniformity, a succession of which enforced revised versions of the Prayer Book throughout the Tudor and Stuart eras. 'Uniformity' meant that each new Book superseded the previous one. It was asserted of each successive Book that it provided a good and godly doctrine, and that it was much needed for the current times.

Cranmer's initial stage-by-stage programme was launched in 1547.

1547–8

In the summer of 1547 Royal Injunctions simplified some of the externals of worship and the ornamentation of church buildings – and provided for the Epistle and Gospel at Mass to be read in English. A set of (reformed) sermons (or 'Homilies') in English was also authorized. Then, in autumn 1547, Parliament passed an Act to provide (among other things) for Communion to be distributed frequently and in both kinds – i.e. both bread and wine. In March 1548 this was implemented by the publication of *The Order of the Communion*, a brief devotional run-up to a distribution to the people, tacked onto the existent Latin Mass, but itself in English.

1549

In December 1548 Parliament approved the first Act of Uniformity. This imposed a complete, English-language Prayer Book to be used by all

> **? DID YOU KNOW?** In 1551 the Puritan John Hooper was appointed Bishop of Gloucester, but he declined to wear the episcopal vestments and had to be put in prison for a short time as a means of persuasion – an event unique in history.

clergy from Pentecost 1549 onwards. The monastic offices were skilfully united into two daily services only, those for Morning and Evening Prayer. The Bible was to be read aloud, in substantial portions, in sequence and (like all else) in English. The Holy Communion service was a combination of old structure with subtly new wording, but was also – as must have been amazing to the worshippers – in English.

1550

The urgent flow continued. In 1550 there came the ordination services ('Ordinal'), published as a separate book from *The Book of Common Prayer* and totally reforming the concept and function of the ordained ministry. An Order in Council required the tearing down of stone altars.

1552

Cranmer's work matured with the 1552 Prayer Book, authorized by another Act of Uniformity and imposed from All Saints' Day. Now not only the wording but also the basic structure of central rites was changed. In the process all concepts of 'consecration' of the elements at Communion – or of the font at Baptism – were eliminated. The people of England were to be reformed by a single, uniform Prayer Book, enforcing Protestant biblical understandings and inculcated by the requirement of regular use.

1553

In this year the Forty-two Articles of Religion were produced in draft form. There was also, however, the death of Edward VI and the succession of the Roman Catholic Princess Mary. The Prayer Book was banned, the leaders burned and the Reformation apparently aborted. This was not to be the end of the story, though.

Changes in Henry VIII's reign
- A vernacular Bible, 1537
- A first English-language Litany, 1544

Changes in Edward VI's reign
- First Book of Homilies, 1547
- An Act for Receiving in Both Kinds, 1547
- The Order of the Communion, 1548
- First English Prayer Book, 1549
- Order in Council for the Breaking Down of Altars, 1550
- First English Ordinal, 1550
- Second English Prayer Book, 1552
- The Forty-two Articles of Religion, 1553

CONNECTIONS
⊞ **Cranmer's Communion services** – pp.150–51
⊞ **Cranmer's Morning and Evening Prayer** – pp.196–7

The seventeenth century – times of struggle

Mary was but shortlived as Queen (1553–8). After her death, Elizabeth I quickly made it clear that she was on the side of the Protestant Reformation. A new Act of Uniformity simply re-established Cranmer's Prayer Book of 1552, with three minor changes:

- The petition against the Bishop of Rome in the Litany was omitted.
- A new Table of Lessons was included.
- At Communion, the words of administration of 1549 ('The body of our Lord Jesus Christ…') were combined with those of 1552 ('Take and eat this…').

One section of the Act led to an unauthorized rubric appearing in the 1559 Prayer Book: 'the minister shall… use such ornaments in the church as were in use… in the second year of the reign of King Edward the Sixth [i.e. in the 1549 Book].' This rather unclear phrase was much fought over in the battles over the use of vestments in the nineteenth century.

Other moves (for instance, the Royal Order of 1561 directing that the lower part of the screen between chancel and nave should remain, or be replaced) gave a reassuring sense of a sovereign aiming for long-term stability, never contemplating a return to Rome, yet avoiding the most extreme Protestant views.

Pushing for further reform

Within the Reformers there were many who wished the Reformation to go much further. In particular they opposed:

- the wearing of even the surplice
- kneeling for Communion
- the sign of the cross in Baptism
- the use of a ring in marriage

Their basic principle was that nothing must be required in worship unless it could be shown to be commanded in Scripture. They tended to look to the continental Reformation and particularly to the Geneva of John Calvin. These Reformers became known as Puritans.

Against this thrust, the mainstream Church insisted that worship and structures must be *compatible* with Scripture, but not every necessary detail would be found explicitly in Scripture. Hence the Church had to make its

Oliver Cromwell, Lord Protector from 1653 to 1658

own sensible rules in each generation.

Hampton Court Conference

The Puritans hoped for more freedom from James VI of Scotland when he inherited the throne of England as James I in 1603. They met him on his way south with a petition signed by 1,000 people, asking for liberty in respect of worship. James for his part simply said he would convene a conference, and he did so at Hampton Court in 1604. There he heard the Puritans, assented to some tiny detailed changes in the Prayer Book, commissioned a new translation of the Bible (known today as the King James Version or Authorized Version), and rejected all other complaints out of hand. Indeed, he virtually turned the tables soon after by exporting episcopacy to Scotland and seeking to bring a fixed liturgy into force there.

Charles I and the Civil War

Matters became worse when Charles I came to the throne in 1625. Charles gave great scope to William Laud (Archbishop of Canterbury from 1633) to put further pressure on the Puritans to conform to the Prayer Book rubrics and canonical requirements. Laud went further, and insisted that the Communion table should be fixed against the east wall of the chancel, instead of being moveable. This was seen as highly provocative. Antipathy towards the King grew, much of it concentrated on the alleged wickedness of the bishops and the iniquities of Laud's archiepiscopate.

This led to the Civil War (1642), to the Westminster Assembly (1643) and to Parliament's prohibition of *The Book of Common Prayer* (1645). King Charles was beheaded on 30 January 1649, and the Commonwealth replaced the monarchy.

To replace *The Book of Common Prayer* there was not a new service book, but instead the *Directory for the Public Worship of God*. The *Directory* contained no full services, instead simply offering guidance for the minister about the conduct of worship. The Prayer Book's suspension proved to be only temporary. Apart from the brief reign of Mary Tudor, the use of the *Directory* was the only interruption to the use of *The Book of Common Prayer* – in one form or another – from 1549 to the present day.

Singing

We are used to singing hymns at all services, but there was virtually no provision for this in the sixteenth- and seventeenth-century Prayer Books – just a small foot in the door in Elizabeth's Injunctions of 1559, which stated that a hymn might be sung after Morning and Evening Prayer. Hymn books did not exist, though the psalms might be sung from Sternhold and Hopkins' metrical Psalter (1560) or, in due course, from Tate and Brady (1696). Hymns from that period, such as those of George Herbert (1596–1633), were written to be read as poetry rather than to be sung congregationally.

CONNECTIONS
The Westminster *Directory* – p.27
Music and song in worship – pp.52–3

The long reign of the 1662 Prayer Book

Restoration of the monarchy and of the Prayer Book

In 1658 Oliver Cromwell, the Lord Protector, died. Parliament lost confidence and in 1660 sent for Charles II. The Puritans expressed anxiety, as Charles significantly used *The Book of Common Prayer* in his own chapel, and the King promised them a conference, which took place with representatives of both Puritans and churchmen, from April to July 1661 at The Savoy. The result was the 1662 *Book of Common Prayer*, familiar to so many succeeding generations and basically the 1552 Prayer Book with only marginal changes.

The evangelical revival

The eighteenth-century evangelical revival stemmed from the persons of George Whitefield and John and Charles Wesley, all ordained presbyters of the Church of England. The background was the 'Holy Club' in Oxford in the 1720s, a group also known as 'Methodists'. This name stuck when the revival began in 1737–8, so that it became associated with 'enthusiasm' and its actual origins in the stiffness and formalism of the pre-revival Holy Club were forgotten. It is often said that Methodism was born in song, and hymn-singing passed into congregational life wherever Anglican parishes were touched by the revival.

Same texts, new context

Hymn-singing and preaching did not of themselves touch the text or order of the official liturgical texts. Evangelicals did not have doctrinal distinctions from their less enthusiastic neighbours. The difference was that they *really* believed what everybody else nominally believed. This difference did not affect the liturgical texts – instead it vastly altered the context and atmosphere in which worship was offered and brought great power into the preaching. The evangelicals, recognizing the liturgy as orthodox and pious, offered liturgical worship with a joy and enthusiasm which revolutionized participants and programme alike.

'…a whole new culture of Anglican worship developed'

Planting the Prayer Book around the world

The great worldwide missionary movement also had roots deep in this eighteenth-century evangelical revival, and it was as Anglican evangelicals took their mission into all the world that the 1662 *Book of Common Prayer* was planted in a vernacular language alongside the vernacular Bible in country after country.

The Catholic revival

A new movement in the life of the Church of England is usually dated from John Keble's

Assize Sermon of 14 July 1833. This was closely followed by the launching of the *Tracts for the Times* – hence the 'Tractarian' tag. The movement was also known as the 'Oxford Movement', because that was where it had its roots. The leaders – John H. Newman, Edward Pusey, John Keble, Hurrell Froude – seized upon the historic continuity of the ordinations of the Church of England with those of the pre-Reformation Church, and made much of it. In the Tracts and elsewhere they taught a strict adherence to *The Book of Common Prayer* in respect of daily offices, fasting, saints' days, vigils, and so on, but they also expounded doctrines of Baptism and Communion and established the use of a Roman-type confessional in such a way as to push the meaning of the Prayer Book rites towards the medieval outlooks which the Reformers had striven to exclude. Unlike the evangelicals, they were actively shifting the doctrinal weight of the Church of England.

Second generation

From roughly 1850 to 1900, as this movement's ideas on liturgy and worship worked through into practice, a whole new culture of Anglican worship developed. This included:

- Gothic Revival architecture
- translations of ancient hymns
- candles, credence tables, holy water stoups, crucifixes, statues, stone altars, riddel curtains
- cathedral-style choirs and robed servers
- medieval Mass vestments
- wafers instead of bread
- sacring bells
- stations of the cross
- a vast range of Roman Catholic ceremonial, including genuflection, crossings, eastward-facing position of the president at the Eucharist, and the mixing of water with the wine in the chalice.

There was a Public Worship Regulation Act in 1874, designed to bring back discipline, but in practice it was ignored. 'Catholic' clergy were not going to abate their practices, and bishops were reluctant to prosecute them and make martyrs of them.

From around the turn of the century onwards, these bold beginnings went on to include the use of Latin Masses, non-communicating Masses, reservation of the consecrated elements, devotions before those reserved elements, Corpus Christi processions, incense, invocation of the saints and exaggerated roles for the bishop with commensurate pomp, not least the adoption of the mitre. Between 1833 and, say, 1914 the worshipping face of the Church of England changed almost beyond recognition. Nonetheless, there was still (in theory at least) only one Prayer Book.

> ### A 'Christendom' model
> *The Book of Common Prayer* of 1662 assumes the whole country is Christian and Anglican and has no doctrine of 'going out' in mission. Its nearest approach is 'that we may … do all such good works as thou hast prepared for us to walk in'.

CONNECTIONS
◈ St Agatha's 1780 – pp.28–9
◈ St Agatha's 1867 – pp.30–31
◈ The Anglican Communion – pp.64–5
◈ Holy Communion in the nineteenth century – pp.152–3

The first half of the twentieth century

The Royal Commission

Near the end of the nineteenth century the 'Catholic' characteristics of so many clergy in the Church of England led to agitation in Parliament. Randall Davidson became Archbishop of Canterbury in 1903 and managed to steer the Parliamentary disquiet into a Royal Commission. Entitled 'The Royal Commission on Ecclesiastical Discipline', it sat from 1904 to 1906. It gathered vast quantities of evidence of Roman Catholic and kindred practices in the life of the Church of England. Its title '…on Ecclesiastical Discipline' reveals that the agenda was still not the development of the new, but how to adjust the old in order to make it enforceable.

The run-up to 1928

In 1908 Royal Letters of Business were issued to the Convocations of Canterbury and York to produce a new 'Ornaments Rubric' in conformity to the Commission's recommen-

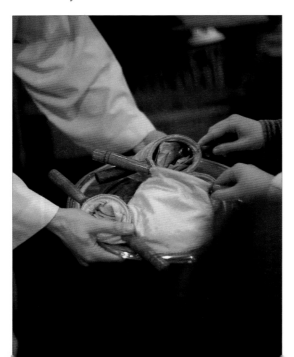

dations. Alongside this there was for a short time an 'Advisory Committee on Liturgical Questions' (1912–15), the only time between the Reformation and 1955 when there was any real attempt to involve those with expertise in the task of liturgical revision. During the First World War the attempt to find a new rubric about vestments phased itself into seeking a new text for the Communion service, and some informal progress towards that was made by the end of the war.

Devolved powers

In the years 1917–19 a great move developed to bring in a more representative Church government process. The 1919 Enabling Act endowed the National Assembly of the Church of England (later known as the Church Assembly) with the requisite powers of preparing legislation for a single reading only in the Lords and Commons. When the Convocations finally agreed some proposals in 1919 (including a new Communion service), the Home Secretary duly referred the whole business to the impending National Assembly. The Assembly set up a committee, which reported back in 1922 with a proposed whole new Prayer Book. After three years of debate, the matter (with a deadlock at a crucial point in the Eucharist) was remitted to the House of Bishops. They rewrote the proposed Prayer Book considerably and took it through the National Assembly in July 1927 (by votes of 517 for to 133 against), and thus on to Parliament.

The House of Lords approved the Prayer Book Measure on 14 December 1927, but in the Commons the next day the opposition made hay with a 'No Popery' cry and defeated the

Measure. The archbishops took advice, fiddled marginally with the Prayer Book, took it through the Assembly again (this time with reduced support), and lost it in the Commons again on 14 June 1928, in a less turbulent but no less decisive debate.

Aftermath of 1928

The bishops faced a serious crisis. They had insisted (under the very terms of the Enabling Act of 1919) that they needed the assent of Parliament and they had gone to Parliament twice to get it – and had failed. Should they lie down under it? Or could they return a third time? Both possibilities were wildly unattractive.

A new strategy

Ultimately, the bishops made a three-point plan and implemented it thus:

1. To publish the 1928 Prayer Book as it stood (as 'The Prayer Book as proposed in 1928'), without any authority.

2. To issue a statement saying that in the 'emergency', they would view its use as in accordance with the mind of the Church of England.

3. In the longer term, to devise ways of authorizing liturgy without going to Parliament.

The 'longer term' proved very long indeed – a Measure for delegating powers eventually went through Parliament in 1965, and thus there emerged a pattern of 'alternative services', authorized by the Church Assembly (or, after 1970, by the General Synod) without further recourse to Parliament. The position of the 1662 Prayer Book itself remained inviolable, but the 'alternative' services, requiring authorization by two-thirds majorities in each of the Houses voting on them, as well as the consent of the PCC in the parishes wishing to adopt them, were to come in alongside it. This new legal position came into force on 1 May 1966.

Controversial features of the 1928 Prayer Book

- Limited provision to reserve the consecrated elements from Holy Communion, ostensibly in order to communicate the sick and housebound (so the provision came as a rubric under 'The Communion of the Sick').
- The alternative order for Holy Communion reverted to a 1549-style Prayer of Consecration with an anamnesis paragraph after the narrative of our Lord's institution, and an epiclesis in the eastern position after that – the result being a prayer which neither Anglo-Catholic nor evangelical wished to use!
- Petitions for the departed in the intercessions in the Eucharist and also in the burial service.

The law of public worship in the Church of England is too narrow for the religious life of the present generation.
First conclusion of the Royal Commission on Ecclesiastical Discipline, 1906

The publication of this Book does not directly or indirectly imply that it can be regarded as authorized for use in churches.
Note added inside printings of the 1928 'Deposited Book'

Modern Roman Catholic liturgy

Early years – 1900–62

On the continent, pockets of liturgical renewal and reform appeared amongst Roman Catholics in the early twentieth century, though this 'Liturgical Movement' could trace its origins further back. Its characteristic thrust was to seek to make the liturgical participation of the laity active and authentic (including regular reception of Communion), and it called for the following:

- the use of vernacular language
- transparent ceremonial
- user-friendly music
- a developed lay spirituality

There were severe limitations upon such calls – Liturgical Movement advocates had to express total loyalty to the official (Council of Trent) liturgical texts, and affect conformity to the requirements of Canon Law and fidelity to the teachings and encyclicals of contemporary Popes.

First reforms

By the 1940s there was a cautious acceptance by the Vatican of some of the goals of the movement, and the first practical reforms came in the 1950s:

- The reform of Holy Week rites (e.g. enabling the Easter Vigil to be held on Holy Saturday evening instead of on Saturday *morning* as previously).
- The permission to hold Masses in the afternoon and evening, with a consequent relaxing of the previous rule that communicants must have been fasting from food from the previous midnight.

Opening the door

Then in 1959 John XXIII announced that he

> **Liturgy as the engine for mission**
> The liturgy is the summit towards which the activity of the Church is directed; at the same time it is the fountain from which all her power flows.
> *Vatican II, Constitution on the Sacred Liturgy, paragraph 10*

would call a Council. Few expected it to be far-reaching about liturgy, but, for those with eyes to see, there already existed enough points for reforming bishops to cite precedent on the one hand, and to urge that many other matters were, in principle, similarly in the sphere of discipline and not of revelation and could therefore be changed. Hans Küng, in his first book to be translated into English, *The Council and*

Christians converging on Liverpool's Roman Catholic cathedral

Reunion (1961), brought to the fore something which later proved pivotal at the Council: the existence of Eastern rites, with different liturgical texts and a wide use of the vernacular, all already, as Uniat Churches, under the aegis of the Bishop of Rome. Rome, on inspection, was not as monolithic as she appeared.

Vatican II

The Council opened in Rome in September 1962. It was clear from the start that there was a widespread desire for a renewal of the liturgy. In the event, the bishops succeeded in bringing the 'Constitution on the Sacred Liturgy' to its final text and adoption, as the first public statement from the Council in December 1963.

The Constitution was far reaching and has become the great charter for liturgical renewal within the life of the Roman Catholic Church. It advocated the following points:

- more systematic and substantial use of the Bible
- greater understanding of the structure and significance of liturgical rites
- greater use of accessible church music
- greater frequency of lay Communion (providing also for the cup to be given to the laity, particularly on special occasions)
- use of the language of the people of any place (instead of Latin), and agreement that this might be used in some parts of the Mass
- the practice of 'concelebration' in place of multiple private Masses

After Vatican II

Vatican II laid the groundwork, but the actual task of revision and renewal was still to come. Whole rites appeared in English. Latin, whilst still lawful, quickly passed out of common use. In 1966 four Eucharistic prayers were approved in Rome and passed into use in translation all over the world. The three-year Sunday lectionary (the ancestor of the Revised Common Lectionary and thus of the *Common Worship* Lectionary)

emerged. Great steps forward were taken in reading the Scriptures in English, in preaching, in congregational responses and acclamations, in lay-led (and often informal) intercessions, in congregational hymn-singing, in the use of the westward-facing position for the Eucharistic president and in the simplification of ceremonial. Almost overnight whole congregations were freely sharing the kiss of peace. Similar changes were occurring in the offices and other sacramental rites. By the time the Missa Normativa was published in 1970, not only the texts but also the ethos of traditional Roman Catholic worship had undergone a revolution.

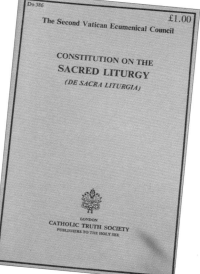

Ongoing renewal

The revolution did not stop then – far from it. Since 1970, year by year, further changes have come. There are Eucharistic prayers to be used with children, a pastorally sensitive Rite of Christian Initiation of Adults (RCIA), a sharing with other English-speaking Christians in the provision of common English forms of well-known traditional liturgical texts (such as the Lord's Prayer and the Creeds), and a host of other innovations. What is more, this welcome and wonderful gale of change, which has ripped through the doors and down the hallways of the largest Church on earth, has inevitably also whistled down the side passages and into neighbouring properties – not least our own Church of England.

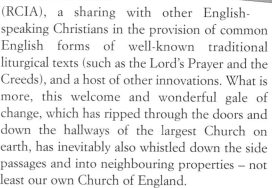

Not praying at the liturgy, but praying the liturgy.
Pius X, 1903

CONNECTIONS
Ecumenical liturgy – pp.66–9
Origins of the lectionary – pp.236–7

The first 'alternative services' – 1965–75

Changes in the law

The Prayer Book (Alternative and Other Services) Measure of 1965 redefined where 'lawful authority' lay:

- *The Book of Common Prayer* of 1662 remained normative and could only be altered or abolished by recourse to Parliament.
- A new concept was introduced, of 'alternative' services. These were services alternative to those in *The Book of Common Prayer* (i.e. for the same purpose, as, for instance, Communion or Marriage), and they could be authorized for periods of up to seven years, renewable once for another seven years, by two-thirds majority votes in the Houses of Bishops, Clergy and Laity of the old Church Assembly or, after 1970, of the General Synod. The service then had to have the consent of the PCC in any parish in which it was used.
- There was also provision for authorizing and making legal 'other' services outside the range of *The Book of Common Prayer* – such as family services, institution services and one-off events of many kinds. These would be at the discretion of the incumbent of the parish or of the officiating minister.

It will be noted that there was no space here for an individual bishop's arbitrary powers over liturgy.

The Measure (with the Canons dependent on it) was to come into force on 1 May 1966. Two sorts of material were then to be fed into the synodical mincing machine.

1928-type services

Under the new Measure all the services in the 1928 'Deposited Book', which had been used for nearly 40 years on the say-so of individual bishops, were to lose even that fig-leaf pretence of having 'lawful authority'. They would therefore have to be authorized as 'alternative services'. The Liturgical Commission would not assist this process (viewing 1928 as a distraction or even an obstacle), so the House of Bishops edited a set of rites from 1928 and published them in December 1965 as the 'First Series' (which later history has called 'Series 1'). These were then moved in the Convocations and House of Laity in May and June 1966. All went well until they came to the 1928 Confirmation service (which was in almost universal use by bishops). The House of Laity had strong opposition to it, and it failed to get two-thirds of the votes. There was also strong opposition to petitions for the dead in the Communion and Funeral rites, but these two just scraped through.

In time the Series 1 Communion was phased into Rite B in the ASB, the Marriage and Funeral services were regularly accorded another period of use up until 2000 – and have since been reauthorized alongside *Common Worship* – and the others had largely lapsed by 1980.

The Liturgical Commission's first work

In December 1965 the Commission also

The 'Interim Rite'

In the early years of the twentieth century a widespread, but unofficial, reshaping of the 1662 Communion service was undertaken, to follow a more 'traditional' shape, rather like the order in the 1549 Prayer Book, but with hardly any alteration of Cranmer's wording. It gained ground considerably after the 1928 debacle and was widely known as the 'Interim Rite'. It is the ancestor of *Common Worship*, Holy Communion Order One in traditional language.

published texts (the 'Second Series' – now called 'Series 2') in readiness for the new Measure to come into force. In a note of dissent, one member of the Commission, Colin Buchanan, opposed the Holy Communion text at two key places: the use of 'offer' in relation to bread and wine in the Eucharistic prayer, and the optional prayers for the dead. By various stages the Church Assembly came to an agreed result, and the House of Laity finally agreed in July 1967.

Other Series 2 services followed – Confirmation on its own in September 1967, full Baptism and Confirmation rites and Morning and Evening Prayer in 1968. A Series 2 Funeral service was also drafted, but when the House of Laity asked the Convocations to accept an agreed pattern of prayers relating to the departed, the Clergy refused to do so, and in 1969 the Laity declined to discuss the text. It went into limbo.

Into modern English

Between 1968 and 1970 there was a great shift in the English-speaking Christian world away from Tudor language and in favour of addressing God as 'you'. This gave birth to 'Series 3'. The International Consultation on English Texts (ICET) produced its first set of recommended common texts for English-speaking Christians, *Prayers We Have In Common*, and these were included in the new range of draft services. The new Eucharist was published in draft in September 1971. It was roundly attacked during its first appearance in the newly formed General Synod two months later, but was retouched and given final approval in November 1972. It was followed by a whole range of other Series 3 services and, although the Prayer Book remained the lawful norm of worship, a high proportion of Church of England worshippers were being prepared in the process for a whole book of alternative services, one in which God would be addressed as 'you' virtually all the way through.

> I will use the forms in the said Book prescribed and none other except so far as shall be ordered by lawful authority.
> *Final sentence of the Declaration of Assent made under the terms of the Clerical Subscription Act 1865, and used until 1975*

CONNECTIONS
◈ **Ecumenical texts** – pp.68–9
◈ **The 1928 Prayer Book** – pp.100–101
◈ **Revision of Holy Communion** – pp.154–5

The ASB and beyond

The law changes again

The introduction of 'alternative services' from 1966 onwards was subject to severe time limits, so the services were published solely in a cheap booklet format. The Church of England (Worship and Doctrine) Measure 1974 went much further, however, permitting General Synod to provide by Canon for unlimited use of 'alternative services'. In early 1976 a Synod working party recommended that the various Series 3 booklets should be brought together into a single substantial book of new services with a reasonable life expectancy. Synod

accepted the plan. There was still a strong (but probably erroneous) notion that 'Anglicans like to take their Prayer Book to church'.

Producing the ASB

This decision set an urgent timetable to get all new services authorized in Synod by the end of 1979, allowing a year for thorough, high-quality production of the resultant book for autumn 1980. Decisions were taken as follows:

- As individual services were authorized, they would remain in booklet form until incorporated into the ASB.
- Series 3 Communion alone had been in authorized use for sufficient time for a considered revision of its text to be worthwhile before 1980. Questionnaires on it were put out in 1977 and the revision was undertaken. This was to be the standard text in the ASB. All other texts – whether internationally agreed ecumenical ones or Anglican standard ones (like the confession and absolution in various services) – were to follow these forms.
- The book would include all the Sunday and Holy Day readings for the Eucharist (on a two-year cycle) set out in full for reading aloud. A thinner version of the book would simply contain biblical references (a decision which was later dropped by the group responsible for publishing decisions). A modern Psalter would also be added.
- One traditional-type service would be included alongside the modern ones. A hybrid Communion rite was going through Synod in the years 1975–6, and it was known at that time as 'Series 1 and Series 2 Revised' – later entitled 'Rite B'.

Synod approved the texts until the end of 1990 (later extended for a further 10 years) and *The Alternative Service Book 1980* was in the shops on 10 November 1980.

The ASB and after

The first task after 1980 was to bring into Synod texts which had missed the ASB – services for use with the sick, along with two smaller supplementary rites, The Blessing of Oils and The Reconciliation of a Penitent. Both these smaller rites were defeated in the House of Laity, but *Ministry to the Sick* was authorized from 1983. It included the first liturgical provision for anointing since 1549 and the first provision since the same date for taking bread and wine from the Communion in church to the sick.

New tasks after this were addressed with a distinct language shift. Drafting would now be in 'inclusive language'. The principle was spelled out in *Making Women Visible* (1988). This report recommended changes that could be made by taking advantage of the provision in Canon B5 that officiants could make alterations 'of no substantial importance' at their own discretion. Clearly, however, a more definitive set of basic texts was needed as soon as possible.

New services

Next came seasonal provision for Lent, Holy Week and Easter. These services were not 'alternative' to any in *The Book of Common Prayer* and did not need the full stages of synodical authorization. Instead they were discussed in the Synod and finally 'commended' by the House of Bishops and published in 1986 as *Lent – Holy Week – Easter*.

Another Liturgical Commission was appointed in the spring of 1986. In front of it was the plea of *Faith in the City*, which had been published

in December 1985, that liturgy should be more user-friendly for less literate worshippers and for the 'urban priority areas' (UPAs).

The major production to meet this challenge was *Patterns for Worship*, published in report form in 1989. It too was debated once in General Synod and then (after a delay whilst Eucharistic material was removed and A Service of the Word was separated from it) was 'commended' by the House of Bishops and published in colourful covers in 1995.

Via a similar route, *The Promise of His Glory*, a set of services for a 'winter season' from All Saints' (1 November) to the Presentation of Christ in the Temple (2 February) appeared in 1991.

The backlash

On the day in 1979 when General Synod authorized all the ASB services, a trio of great petitions was handed in, calling upon the bishops and leaders of the Church of England to honour their pledges in respect of the Prayer Book. Somewhat late in the day, the lovers of the traditional had come to realize that the modern-language texts had come to stay and were not just a passing cloud after which all would contentedly return to 1662. The Prayer Book Society has been a feature of the landscape ever since.

CONNECTION
Inclusive language – p.83

The influence of religious communities

A number of Christian communities have played a significant part in enriching, enlivening and influencing contemporary Church of England worship.

Liturgy finds new connections

Vibrancy of language and expression in worship has had a particularly creative and refreshing influence. *Celebrating Common Prayer* (1992) has modelled a plentiful and imaginative use of psalm, canticle and Scripture verses, giving a pattern of prayer steeped in rich and profound biblical imagery and phraseology.

The liturgy and songs of the Iona Community owe much of their appeal to a strong sense of poetry and wordcraft, combined with a radical commitment to justice, peace, inclusiveness and gender equality. The result is often arresting in its originality, liberating in its impact and sometimes not a little disturbing to comfortable complacency! It has re-emphasized for many the power of liturgy to confront, transform and spur into action.

Greater awareness of issues of inclusivity in liturgical language has been in itself an important factor in the widespread influence and use of the resources provided by other communities. Here the availability of prayers from groups such as the Saint Hilda Community (*Women Included*, for instance) has also been significant.

The welcome which the liturgy of the Northumbria Community has found, with its mixture of modern and ancient prayers and language, has been a reminder that in a postmodern setting there is no need to throw out the old in favour of the new – another major principle behind the *Common Worship* services. In particular, it has encouraged a greater sense of connection and continuity with the Celtic saints, to whom many have turned for fresh inspiration in recent times.

Finally, the desire for simplicity and yet a profound experience of prayer has found its echo in the enduring chants of Taizé. The simple beauty of much of the music and the simple, often intimate, words repeated many times are designed to penetrate deeply the mind and heart, so that the prayers of these chants become part of us, flowing over into daily work. The treasure many have discovered here is that of prayer shaping life. *Common Worship*, similarly, is intended to feed our spirits by providing familiar and memorable prayers (although the directness and simplicity of the Taizé chant is not always reflected in the new writing!).

morning, midday, evening and night prayer produced by, for example, the Society of St Francis and the Iona Community have been drawn upon frequently by local churches, as have the Northumbria Community's two volumes, *Celtic Daily Prayer* and *Celtic Night Prayer*.

Celebrating Common Prayer (a version of the Franciscan daily office) has also proved a particularly rich resource for the seasons, commemorations and holy days of the Christian year, and its influence has spilled over into the new *Common Worship* services.

What is it about the practice of prayer in some of these communities which has caused them to be so readily embraced? In general terms, there seems to have been a hunger to rediscover patterns of communal worship which offer structure alongside greater simplicity, and which often include the following emphases:

- reflection
- contemplation
- inclusiveness
- accessibility
- a sense of connection with life and the rhythms of life and season

The *Common Worship* services pick up and incorporate some of these lessons, making more provision for the use of silence and providing plenty of material for the celebration of the seasons of the Christian year.

A sense of rhythm

'Rhythm' in the life of prayer is perhaps one of the key aspects shared by many of the religious communities concerned. Resources for

Reflecting on Scripture

There has been a common emphasis on renewing the place of silence, reflection and contemplation in relation to the reading of Scripture. Specific direction on this is often included in the text and deliberate space allowed within the service. The Northumbrian Office sets out to promote this approach to Scripture further by deliberately using only very short passages. The *Common Worship* lectionary has a similar focus on the passages of Scripture themselves (as opposed to 'themes' imposed upon them) and encourages an engagement with the Bible on its own terms, trying to allow narrative passages to act as story and mixing that with other shorter passages.

Visual focus

There has been a rediscovery of the importance of a visual focus in worship. This may be in the form of a simple candle or many candles, a simple cross or the colourful image or icon which invites us to enter more deeply into contemplation of the mystery of God. Some of the communities have encouraged and highlighted the value of simple ritual or physical gesture, such as the symbolic lighting of a candle or passing on its light to another.

Such an emphasis on action, symbol and ritual has been reflected in *Common Worship*, especially in some of the pastoral material, for example in the funeral services.

CONNECTIONS
- **Inclusive language** – p.83
- **Daily prayer** – pp.198–9
- **Funerals** – pp.122–5
- **The Lectionary** – pp.236–41
- **Postmodernism** – pp.90–91
- **Inculturation** – pp.80–81

Charismatic, 'seeker' and 'alternative' influences

Charismatic renewal

When charismatic renewal began to influence the mainstream denominations in Britain in the early 1960s, many found that the new wine of their spiritual experience could not be contained within their established denominations. The result was the rise of the 'house church' movement, with small, independent fellowships meeting in homes, pubs and schools. This new movement had an immediate impact on the Church of England numerically, as many with a taste for things charismatic upped and left. Its effect on Church of England worship took longer to work through. In time Anglican churches began to use some of the new songs in their worship, but the greater challenge was yet to come.

Wimber and all that

The American teacher John Wimber first hit England with a large conference in Westminster in 1984. He came ostensibly bringing teaching on 'signs and wonders', but with him there also came a new musical style and a whole new philosophy of worship. Anglicans in particular resonated with his gentle, laid-back approach, and continue to be significantly influenced by the California soft-rock musical idiom. He developed a style in the Vineyard movement which was as little like 'church' as he could make it. Even where they do not fully embrace the Vineyard liturgy (45 minutes of non-stop singing, a space to listen for prophetic words, the

sermon, then prayer ministry), many Anglicans have adopted a Vineyard musical style, where worship equals singing, and the only goal of worship is intimacy with God. Where liturgical worship survives in such churches, it needs to be flexible enough to work with this self-consciously intimate musical style, which does not shy away from engaging the emotions. The evidence is that, used creatively, *Common Worship* can meet this situation.

Willow Creek

Another influence also came from America. The Willow Creek Community Church, near Chicago, has developed the idea of 'seeker services', where everything 'churchy' is stripped away to be replaced by a much more 'performance-orientated' service. High-quality music and drama is followed by biblical teaching, brought to bear on subjects like marriage, parenting or work. This has proved hugely

successful in the States, though less so in Britain, but again the drift away from the use of liturgy in worship is significant in churches which have embraced this model.

'Alternative' worship

Despite being disliked by some of those involved, 'alternative' worship has stuck as the generic label attached to a variety of highly creative services which have sprung up with a technological and multimedia emphasis and usually a consciously postmodern ethos. The 'alternative' label has also been misleadingly used at times to include services which have adopted a certain amount of the cultural clothing of 'alternative' worship, but have not necessarily engaged with the same cultural issues.

With a general revival of interest in 'spirituality', there has often been a parallel rejection of the Church and of organized Christian religion as institutional, hierarchical, dogmatic and lacking in true spirituality. The growing so-called 'New Age movement' is a testimony to this. In the Church, alternative worship groups have been a challenge from within, picking up on a similar critical agenda, namely:

- A critique of authority, power and leadership. Marks of alternative worship have been anonymity and group participation in the 'leading' of worship; rejection of a traditional church layout which distinguishes an 'up-front' role; adoption of a multi-stimulus approach to worship which avoids over-direction and gives space to the individual; rejection of a centralized uniformity in worship in favour of local creativity and authenticity in liturgy, music, and so on.
- An emphasis on issues of ecology and gender equality which is often reflected in the language of liturgy. Hence Eucharistic prayers will tend to stress the redemption of the whole creation, and God is almost as likely to be 'she' as 'he'.
- A reclaiming of the place of symbol, ritual, the senses, the visual, etc., in reaction to overly cerebral approaches. There is a plundering from traditions old and new in true 'pick-and-mix' style. Orthodox icons, computer graphics, incense and postmodern performance art often sit side by side.

Again, some of these emphases, in a less extreme form, are reflected in *Common Worship* and the principles behind it.

Implicit mission
Many alternative worship groups have not been explicitly missionary in emphasis, but the attempt to grapple consciously or unconsciously with the cultural questions raised by postmodernism have meant that issues of inculturation are taken seriously.

CONNECTIONS
⊠ **Inculturation** – pp.80–81
⊠ **Inclusive language** – p.83
⊠ **Postmodernism** – pp.90–91

Looking at *Common Worship*

The congregation of St Agatha's have the privilege (and responsibility) of worshipping in a building where Christians have worshipped, in different ways, for centuries. The very fabric of the building and its furnishings is a reminder to them every Sunday that they are just part of the long story of Christian worship in that place. As they grapple with the *Common Worship* liturgical material and the changes it entails, they are also reminded that they are not the first generation of worshippers in that place to have faced liturgical change – and they are unlikely to be the last.

In this part of the book we take a closer look at the *Common Worship* material – material which has been emerging since 1997 and which will form the Church's patterns of worship in the immediate future. We consider the various services and resources of *Common Worship*, dipping again into the historical processes that brought the services to their current form, but looking too at the practical realities of using this material to best effect in worship today.

Not a book, but a library

'Common Worship' is the name for the family of volumes replacing *The Alternative Service Book 1980*. In 1994 the Liturgical Commission suggested to General Synod that it would be better to produce a range of separate volumes rather than to squeeze all the texts for worship into one volume of 1,300 pages. The *Faith in the City* report of 1985 had said, 'To give people a 1,300 page Alternative Service Book is a symptom of the gulf between the Church and ordinary people in the Urban Priority Areas.' Ease of handling and access in a variety of forms was one of the aims in producing the new worship material. It is therefore available in printed volumes, in separate booklets of varying sizes, on congregational cards, as computer disks (both as text-only disks and as the Church's *Visual Liturgy* service-composing programme) and on the Internet.

The separate volumes are as follows.

Common Worship – Services and Prayers for the Church of England

The main volume contains all that is needed for Sunday worship. The Calendar, at the beginning, sets out the structure of the Church's year. This is followed by the outline structure, A Service of the Word, on which the services of Morning and Evening Prayer, which come next, are based. Then, moving towards the middle of the book, come the Holy Communion services, Thanksgiving for the Gift of a Child and Holy Baptism from the Initiation Services.

Collects and Post-Communions come towards the end, followed by the Lectionary references, with Canticles and Psalms at the back where they can be found easily.

Common Worship – Pastoral Services

Appearing at the same time, the second volume contains services for Wholeness and Healing, Marriage, Emergency Baptism, Thanksgiving for the Gift of a Child and Funerals.

Common Worship – Daily Prayer

The daily office book for the Church of England will appear some years after the main volume. The reason for this is that the Liturgical Commission is both contributing and listening to the debate about the nature of daily prayer which is going on in the Church. Should it be mainly for clergy, or for the whole people of God? Should there be a variety of forms, some simpler, some with richer material? Is the daily office basically about prayer and praise, or about reading the Scriptures? Members of the Liturgical Commission were heavily involved in revising the daily office book of the Society of St Francis, published in 1992 as *Celebrating Common Prayer*, so have been involved in the debate for many years already.

Common Worship – Initiation Services

The interim volume, published in 1998, contains a variety of services for baptism, confirmation, affirmation of baptismal faith and reception into the Church of England. The full volume, possibly including healing services, together with services and prayers for the ministry of reconciliation, will be published when the latter have completed their progress through Synod.

Common Worship – Times and Seasons

This volume will be a compendium of seasonal services and resources. Some of it has already appeared, in the years after 1980, in *Lent – Holy Week – Easter* (1986), *The Promise of His Glory* (1990), *Enriching the Christian Year* (1993) and *Patterns for Worship* (1995). Most of the new volume's content will also appear in a completely revised edition of *Patterns for Worship*.

Common Worship – The Ordinal

Revision of the services for ordaining bishops, priests and deacons is on the agenda of the House of Bishops and the Liturgical Commission, with a book of background essays due out in 2001. The ASB ordinal has been re-authorized for a further five years.

Something in common

All these volumes have the following things in common which distinguish *Common Worship* from the ASB:

- They contain a mixture of ancient and contemporary language material.
- They contain a mixture of authorized and commended material.
- They have no set date on which authorization expires.

CHAPTER 8

Initiation Services

'Baptism' to most of us means a memorable or dramatic start to something – as when a soldier has a 'baptism of fire'. Christian baptism has always been a 'new start', stemming from the baptisms carried out by John the Baptist.

John linked his baptism of repentance to the coming of the Messiah and to his promised gift of baptizing people 'with the Holy Spirit and with fire'. His baptism was then authenticated by Jesus when he submitted to it and began his public ministry. After that, baptism belonged with the Christian gospel. Jesus and his disciples are reported as baptizing during his earthly ministry (John 3:23; 4:2), and in his 'Great Commission' baptism was a basic means for his disciples to make new disciples (Matthew 28:19–20).

Water baptism was used in just this way from the Day of Pentecost onwards. On that day, when Peter has preached to the crowds, they are 'cut to the heart' and ask, 'What should we do?' He answers that the point of decision comes through being baptized: 'Repent, and be baptized every one of you in the name of Jesus Christ so that your sins may be forgiven; and you will receive the gift of the Holy Spirit' (Acts 2:37–8). In the Acts of the Apostles from then on, baptism is so regularly regarded as a basic ingredient that it can be taken for granted as having been received by all believers, as can be seen in all the churches to whom Paul writes his letters.

The meaning of baptism

What did baptism mean to the first disciples?

The New Testament is full of baptismal motifs: repentance, conversion, adoption, rebirth by the Spirit, being united with Christ in his death and resurrection, becoming a disciple, being put under the headship of Christ (or the name of the Holy Trinity), being transplanted into the body of Christ, walking in newness of life morally, and becoming an inheritor of eternal life and of the final resurrection – and thus it signifies all that is meant in being a believer at all.

As time went by, variety began to emerge – in the mode of baptism, the formula of baptism and the role of sponsors (which originated in the late second century in relation to infants). Much ink and energy has been spent agonizing over differences of practice from place to place and from one century to another. Should infants be baptized? What constitutes 'belief' and

> [God] has rescued us from the power of darkness and transferred us into the kingdom of his beloved Son.
>
> *Colossians 1:13*
>
> [God] saved us ... through the water of rebirth and renewal by the Holy Spirit.
>
> *Titus 3:5*
>
> So then you are no longer strangers and aliens, but you are citizens with the saints and also members of the household of God.
>
> *Ephesians 2:19*
>
> So if anyone is in Christ, there is a new creation.
>
> *2 Corinthians 5:17*
>
> Jesus is Lord.
>
> *The original baptismal confession, see Romans 10:9*

'repentance'? Are anointing and laying on of hands essential? What is the warrant for confirmation? It is a sad fact of the Church's history that an event of such life-changing importance should have caused so much division – yet maybe it is precisely because it is so important that the matter cannot rest.

Over the past 100 years there have been vast developments in scholarship and experience that have challenged the Church to reassess her initiatory practices. Differences have not all been resolved, but there has been convergence of thought between a number of denominations. *Common Worship* incorporates this thought in the Initiation Services, with renewed theology, enriched imagery and dramatic symbolism. The Initiation Services are, perhaps, the most radically changed and innovative of all the *Common Worship* services.

First-century developments

From an early date, probably near the end of the first century AD, the practice of immediate baptism slowly changed to one where some preparation and probation intervened between the application for baptism and the actual administration of it. During the second century AD the Church year began to acquire a more fixed shape, with the Easter celebration of Christ's death and resurrection as the high point within it (and with Easter kept on a Sunday – the day of resurrection). It was becoming usual for baptisms to take place on this festival. By the fourth century Easter had become the primary day for baptism, and Lent developed as a period of preparation for the baptismal candidates.

Baptism and infants

Was baptism given to infants? The earliest certain evidence we have of infant baptism comes from Tertullian in North Africa around AD 190–200 – urging that infants should *not* be

> They [Paul and Silas] spoke the word of the Lord to him [the jailer] and to all who were in his house … then he and his entire family were baptized without delay.
>
> *Acts 16:32–3*

> The Baptism of young Children is in any wise to be retained in the Church, as most agreeable with the institution of Christ.
>
> *Article XXVII of the Thirty-nine Articles of Religion*

baptized. So when did the practice begin? Or was it in fact there from the start, visible in Scripture itself? Consider the following points:

1. The Old Testament sign of the covenant of God, circumcision, was given to infants, yet its meaning, according to Paul, was that of a sign of the righteousness which comes through faith (Romans 4:12). If circumcision could properly belong to infants before they professed faith, is baptism, which is also a sign of the righteousness which comes through faith, not also appropriate for infants?

2. The Jewish baptism of proselytes (converts from other religions to Judaism) was known in the late first century AD, and families so baptized brought their children into baptism with them. If this practice began earlier – say, before AD 27 – it would suggest that converts to Christ took their children into Christian baptism with them. Indeed, there were proselytes there on the Day of Pentecost (Acts 2:11), to hear that the heart of Judaism is Jesus Christ, that the promise is to them and their children, and that they are to be baptized into the name of Christ (Acts 2:38–9). Did they not take their children into baptism with them?

By grace we have been saved through faith

A crucial feature of all the initiatory elements is that candidates come by faith – and without faith baptism is anomalous. Baptism formally unites candidates (adults and infants) to the visible Church and formally states that Jesus is Lord to them, yet the reality of believing in Jesus as Lord may still not enrich the lives of all who are baptized. In such cases, baptism is still baptism, given once for all for life. If, then, faith later dawns in people's lives, they are not baptized again, but simply rejoice that the inward is now in line with the outward. In many other cases, the 'belonging' aspects of baptism initially precede the 'believing' aspects. Faith and belief take time to develop. New members of the Church will need careful nurture as they continue to learn about, and to grow to know, the God in whose hands they have placed their lives.

3. In the New Testament there are several references to 'households' or families being baptized: Lydia's (Acts 16:15), the Philippian jailer's (Acts 16:33), Stephanas' (1 Corinthians 1:16), and possibly also Crispus' (Acts 18:8). These do not quite say that infants were baptized, but the very inclusive word for a whole household does not distinguish ages or suggest that all were above a certain age.

4. When adults were converted in New Testament times they were baptized on the spot. There was no delay, no probationary period. Baptism came at the very beginning, as a way of treating people as believers thereafter. Once this is grasped, do we have good clues as to when to baptize the children of believers? Surely they cannot be left out?

5. Not only are all to whom Paul writes baptized, but on occasion there are young children present to hear the word read out to them (cf. Ephesians 6:1; Colossians 3:20 and also – not by Paul – 1 John 1:13). The children are as much members of the baptized community as anyone else, and are being treated as believers.

6. The question also persists: 'How should believers bring up their children?' If the answer to that question is: 'As unbelievers to be converted later', then baptism is inappropriate. If the answer is that the children are being treated as believers from the start, however, then they should be baptized.

John the Baptist baptizing Jesus in the River Jordan

Baptism and confirmation before and after the Reformation

'Christendom' began from the time of the Decree of Constantine (AD 313), and it greatly affected the general use of baptism. Until then the standard candidates had been adults (accompanied by their children) and there had developed a lengthy catechumenate, culminating in intensive preparation during Lent for baptisms to come at Easter. The bishop presided over the Easter Eucharist; the candidates were baptized outside the assembly; they were then brought in to him and he would welcome them and lay his hands on them. Initially, the fourth century saw a rise in adults seeking baptism (as it became prudent for citizens to 'enrol' as Christians), but in the next generation there was bound to be a shift towards a preponderance of infants.

Augustine of Hippo

Very soon after, the teaching of Augustine (AD 354–430) also started to affect infant baptism. He taught that no child must die unbaptized, for fear of an unwelcoming next world. As many infants did die within hours of birth, the practice grew of giving baptism immediately following birth, and it was often done by midwives. This split baptism from all that had previously surrounded initiation. It became far less an ecclesial function and more an individualistic, postnatal inoculation against original sin.

A 'useful' service

The Baptism of such as are of Riper Years … may be always useful for the baptizing of Natives in our Plantations, and others converted to the Faith.

Preface to the 1662 Book of Common Prayer

The second Christian millennium

Such were the tendencies between AD 500 and 1000. The next 500 years saw further changes.

- Adult baptism ceased almost entirely, and infant baptism was universally used.
- Fonts, which in the eleventh century were often spacious enough for the total

submersion of infants, thereafter grew smaller (and were placed near the west door, to symbolize entry into the Church).

- Baptism within minutes of birth became usual, so that fonts were rarely in use for baptism.
- Godparents replaced natural parents as presenting 'next of kin'.
- The cup, which previously had been used to communicate infants with a drop of wine, was withdrawn, and only the wafer was given – which unweaned children could not receive, so their participation in Communion was delayed.
- This delay was seen as affording an opportunity to young children to learn some basic Christian truths – notably the Lord's Prayer and the *Ave Maria* – before admission to Communion. In time, first confession and first Communion came at the age of seven (a pattern found in the Roman Catholic Church to this day).
- Confirmation, already separated from baptism before AD 1000, was all the harder to get in England, where dioceses were often enormous and travel for bishops difficult. The practice was therefore widely neglected.

The Reformation

The Reformers remodelled the pattern they received.

- They retained universal infant baptism, but gave few good reasons for it.
- They treated baptism as one of only two sacraments of the gospel.
- They postponed admission to Communion until the 'years of discretion' (perhaps 13–15), at which point the children were to be confirmed and thus admitted. The catechism came within the confirmation service, and candidates had to 'make the grade' before being admitted.
- Baptism was to be conducted after the second lesson at Morning or Evening Prayer (but could be performed in homes in an emergency). The Reformers kept the mode of 'dipping' as the first option, and 'pouring' was

only a fall-back provision for children certified as too weak to stand dipping.

The 1552 services and the 1604 Canons both insisted that the clergy must search out unbaptized children and bring them to baptism. This was not so much through fear that children who died unbaptized would be lost (the Reformers were reticent on that point), but more through the need to make both Papists and Anabaptists conform to the Church of England.

The Restoration

In 1662 a service was added for 'The Baptism of those of Riper Years'. This was really to catch up on the children born between 1645 (when the use of the Prayer Book had been abolished) and 1662, because many children up to 17 years of age had not been baptized. In this service the candidates expressed their own faith (rather than by proxy via godparents), which raised a question as to whether they then needed to be confirmed. A closing rubric was added to require confirmation, almost certainly to ensure that they knelt in front of a bishop (and thus conformed to the rules of episcopacy and the Restoration Settlement), rather than because they would not have been properly initiated without confirmation.

Laying on of hands

A post-baptismal laying on of hands is often claimed as part of an 'original integrated rite' which has since 'disintegrated'. In fact, it is not found until the end of the second century in the West, and no practice seems to have derived earlier from the (abnormal) post-baptismal laying on of hands in Acts 8:14–17 and 19:1–6. Water baptism was full initiation. In the East a post-baptismal anointing arose by the fourth century and remains to this day, administered by the local presbyter. In the West the laying on of hands belonged to the bishop, but, after Augustine of Hippo's teaching on original sin, baptism was increasingly administered within moments of birth and confirmation had to await a visit by a bishop, so they were split from each other.

CONNECTIONS
▶ Is confirmation redundant? –
pp.124–5

Christian initiation from 1662 to 1980

The 1662 *Book of Common Prayer* provided the only legal rites until 1966, when alternative services began.

Baptism until 1966

Infant baptism remained the dominant use for hundreds of years. Until the 1950s, at least two-thirds of the infants born in England each year received baptism in the Church of England, and adult baptisms were correspondingly rare. There were, however, some divisions arising within the practice of infant baptism.

(a) The Gorham Judgement

The 1662 services state that the baptized are regenerate, but the Articles teach that baptism is only efficacious under the right conditions. What, then, would be the 'right conditions' for infants? In the early nineteenth century the view arose that for infants there are no conditions attached: such baptisms are unconditionally efficacious. It took the famous Gorham Judgement in 1850 to rule that a conditional view was still in accord with Anglican doctrine.

Baptism in Congo

(b) The rise of afternoon baptisms

The 1662 Prayer Book was provided for a rural society. The Industrial Revolution ushered in urban parishes with thousands of parishioners and a birth rate sufficient to provide dozens of infants for baptism each month. Baptisms therefore moved away from the main services and special 'baptism services' were held on Sunday afternoons. Although contrary to both Canons and rubrics, this has run on to the present day but is now declining.

(c) First glimpses of baptismal reform

The large numbers of baptisms also laid bare a great gap between parents bringing their children for baptism (without much other sign of Christian discipleship) on the one hand, and adult believers on the other. This used to be seen as normal where the population has generally viewed itself as Christian and 'C of E'. Augustine-based superstition about the fate of those dying unbaptized has also played its part in the 'folk religion' approach. Statistics suggest that these numbers are running down as the country secularizes.

In recent decades a conscience has developed about 'indiscriminate infant baptism', and the revision of the Canons and of the liturgical texts has, in a very gentle way, reflected the same concern.

Confirmation

From the Reformation onwards the theory of confirmation was difficult to implement, for bishops did not easily get round large dioceses and often catechizing by the vicar of 13–15-year-olds led to admission to Communion without the benefit of a bishop. After 1830 new dioceses were created, bishops were allowed to retire (previously many were immobilized by age or ill-health), suffragans were appointed, and the railways spread. Suddenly bishops were around, confirmations could occur, centres for annual confirmations were fixed, and preparation became more serious.

A sacrament?

The immediate doctrinal knock-on effect was that Anglo-Catholics taught that confirmation is the sacrament of the gift of the Holy Spirit, and water baptism is only the preliminary half of an initiation which is one sacrament (even if given in two parts). With confirmation available, this doctrine entered into the framework of the Church of England and not only made great claims for the rite itself but also made it indispensable for admission to Communion. The age fell to 10 or 11 in many parishes, and a higher wall than ever before arose between Anglicans and Free Church people.

The effect of this was worldwide. Provinces which revised their Prayer Books after 1900 regularly slipped Acts 8:14–17 into the confirmation rite and treated this highly exceptional Samaritan episode as a norm. The proposed but rejected Church of England 1928 Prayer Book used the same basis, but, when the 1928 rite was re-introduced as an 'alternative service' (Series 1) in 1966, it was defeated in the House of Laity, where many did not believe the passage gave warrant for confirmation, or

reckoned that the rite gave an inflated view of its significance.

The run-up to the ASB

The Liturgical Commission's 1959 report, *Baptism and Confirmation*, started from the idea that baptism and confirmation belong together in a single rite and strongly emphasized the role of the Spirit in confirmation. It also located baptism and confirmation within a Eucharistic context, a further innovation.

More recently there is a greater willingness to see baptism as complete sacramental initiation. Series 2 services were authorized in 1967 and 1968; then Series 3 services in 1978 enabled infants and adults to be baptized together. The services of Thanksgiving for the Birth of a Child and after Adoption were added, and all was ready for the ASB. Meanwhile, as confirmation lost its doctrinal pretensions, Communion tables were reopened to Free Church people from 1972, and from 1997 young children could be admitted to Communion prior to confirmation.

The Gorham Judgement

In 1847 the Bishop of Exeter declined to institute one George Cornelius Gorham to an incumbency to which he was lawfully nominated, on the grounds that he did not believe in the unconditional regeneration of all infants in baptism. Gorham applied for an injunction to the Court of Arches, who in 1849 upheld the Bishop's decision on the grounds of Gorham's heresy. Gorham then appealed to the Judicial Committee of the Privy Council, and in 1850 he won on appeal.

CONNECTIONS
⊞ **The first 'alternative services'** – pp.104–5
⊞ **Augustine's teaching on the necessity of baptism** – pp.120–21

Christian initiation from 1980 to 2000

The 20 years of currency of the ASB, at the end of the twentieth century, were a period when the Church of England – at least in urban contexts – was slowly losing touch with the general run of the population. Funerals declined slowly, marriages fell enormously, and infant baptisms also dropped steadily. There have been immigration effects too – millions now belong to other faith communities, far beyond the position in 1980. Yet a greater decline is due to the ongoing secularization of society, and with that has been a steady erosion of church youth activities. On the other hand, services more closely adapted for families with young children have grown during the same period. How, then, have these trends affected patterns of Christian initiation?

Fewer infant baptisms...

We are seeing the end of the traditional English expectation that (except in Baptist, Salvation Army or Quaker homes) all infants would be baptized. This has led to improved preparation for infant baptism (and a questioning about the conditions upon which it should be available), and also to provision of 'dry-run' alternatives to baptism: services of thanksgiving for the gift of children.

> **Baptism and Eucharist**
> Baptism is complete sacramental initiation and leads to participation in the eucharist. Confirmation and other rites of affirmation have a continuing pastoral role in the renewal of faith among the baptised but are in no way to be seen as a completion of Baptism or as necessary for admission to communion.
>
> *IALC IV, Toronto 1991, Recommendation (c)*

An unusual font cover

...and more adult baptisms

The trend has meant that an ever-growing proportion of those seeking confirmation at a mature age have not in fact been baptized as infants, and so baptisms of those of 'riper years' have become common – very often done within the context of a confirmation service with the bishop presiding.

Informed scholarship

Then there is the question of whether confirmation is truly an 'initiation' service. Since 1970 new biblical and patristic scholarship has led to an understanding of water baptism as the sole sacrament of initiation into the Christian life. This affects the confirmation of those baptized in infancy in two major respects:

1. Admission to Communion can be broken free from confirmation and given at a much earlier age on the basis of infant baptism.
2. Confirmation does not then have its age forced down in order that children of 10 or 11 may receive Communion, but instead its age may move up to come genuinely on the threshold of adulthood.

Is confirmation redundant for those baptized as adults?

This very question about confirmation also implies that, contrary to 1662, those baptized as adults do not need confirmation at all, and the laying on of the bishop's hands is redundant. They do not need to ratify their baptismal vows, for they made them only a few minutes earlier. Yet the original 1959 provision, of a service for adults which combines baptism and confirmation, runs on in the *Common Worship* services, and the querying of it has not yet reached the point of reforming it!

Patterns of preparation

As confirmation (with or without baptism immediately preceding it) has been moving away from pre-adolescents to adult believers

> ? The International Anglican Liturgical Consultation (IALC) in 1991 called for confirmation to be delegatable to presbyters.

(often adult converts), there has been a growing interest in patterns of preparation, stimulated by the Roman Catholic experience of the Rite of Christian Initiation of Adults (RCIA), which takes the preparation in stages and is as interested in assimilating candidates into the life of the people of God as it is in filling them with head-knowledge about the faith. This gave rise to the Church of England report *On the Way*, and has led to references to both sponsors and testimony in the *Common Worship* services.

The catechumenate

Particular strengths of the [catechumenal] approach include:

- Attempting to integrate personal formation, sacramental initiation, and incorporation into the life and mission of the Church.
- Recovering of the significance of baptism for the ongoing life, calling and mission of the Church.
- Emphasizing that the Church has a vital role in the welcome and formation of new Christians.
- Realizing that coming to faith is a journey in which the enquirer needs the prayer and support of Christians.
- Taking seriously the need to respect the starting point of an enquirer and to learn from those whom God is leading to faith.
- Making clear that initiation and formation involve experience and reflection as well as instruction.
- Identifying of four elements that should be part of Christian formation:
  - worship with the Church
  - growth in prayer
  - listening to the scriptures
  - service and witness in the community.
- Using progressive rites to help mark an individual's journey in faith and to enable the Church to support them in prayer.

On the Way: Towards an Integrated Approach to Christian Initiation, 1995, paragraph 6.1

CONNECTIONS
ⓒ **Confirmation, a sacrament?** – pp.122–3
Ⓜ **'Rites on the Way'** – pp.142–3

Initiation and the people of God

The rethinking of baptismal theology as described in the previous pages has influenced the *Common Worship* services, which express the following points about the role of the people of God in initiation:

- Initiation is the task of the whole Church. It is part of our mission; none of us can be a passive onlooker, for we all have a part to play.
- Baptism is indicative of our belonging and nature. It is not an event that we ascribe to the past and leave behind, but an indelible mark identifying believers with Christ and the whole baptized community.

The congregation

Gone are the days when the minister was the only point of contact with the baptismal candidates, and that is just as well. Recent research has demonstrated that the most significant influence in coming to faith is the friendship of ordinary Christian men and women. Moreover, most

The part of the congregation
The president addresses the whole congregation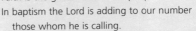
Faith is the gift of God to his people.
In baptism the Lord is adding to our number
those whom he is calling.
People of God, will you welcome these children/candidates
and uphold them in their new life in Christ?
With the help of God, we will.
From the Presentation

We welcome you into the fellowship of faith;
we are children of the same heavenly Father;
we welcome you.
From the Welcome

people who become believers do so over a period of time averaging four years. So we all have a role in befriending, story-sharing and living alongside others who are seeking the way to follow God.

Even those of us who are not involved directly with the candidates will nevertheless have words to say in the service that express the nature of the Church's role:

- We pledge our support at the Presentation.
- Everyone joins in with the Profession of Faith, the faith shared by the whole community into which the candidates are to be baptized.
- At the Commission we are reminded again of our responsibility to help bring up infants in the faith.
- We welcome the newly baptized (and their families) and we share the Peace.

It is our task to support in whatever way we can, to welcome and to pray. The congregation needs to be around for it all to make sense.

Parents, godparents and sponsors

When the candidate to be baptized is an infant, *Common Worship* has questions at the Decision addressed 'through [the candidate's] parents, godparents and sponsors'. Whether or not we believe that parental faith should be a

 Parents can be godparents to their own children.

prerequisite to infant baptism, there is no doubt from other parts of the *Common Worship* service that the onus is on the parents and godparents to bring the child up as a Christian. It is the role of the Church to support these key players, and to offer guidance in their responsibilities – often with the wisdom of experience. Adult candidates may also have sponsors – members of the Church with a specific role of giving personal support and encouragement to the new believers.

When baptismal candidates are teenagers or adults, they will not need to be 'brought up' in the faith by their families. However, the active support of more mature Christians who will pray, teach and encourage is invaluable. People who offer to commit themselves to the candidates in this way can be their sponsors. They might already have accompanied the candidates on their journey of exploration and worked with them through their preparation for baptism.

The candidates and *Common Worship*

A striking feature of the *Common Worship* Initiation Services is the 'journey' motif which runs through the services. There is a sense of pilgrimage, and we might be reminded of those pilgrims of old: travellers on a road with a common destination, young and old from many walks of life, gathering up others from towns and villages as they passed through, telling their stories along the route until they reached the 'holy place' to worship.

Naturally, for our baptismal candidates, the journey will begin before baptism and continue beyond it. Here are some of the expressions of pilgrimage that are found in the service:

- Journey
- Story
- Way

Journey

There is a great deal of biblical language suggesting the journey theme reflected in the services. We talk about the candidates 'walking'– walking in the way of Christ (Presentation), walking in the light (Giving a Lighted Candle) and walking in newness of life (Prayer over the Water). After the Baptism the president prays for the newly baptized as they join 'the company of Christ's pilgrim people'. They do not walk alone.

> In baptism God invites you on a life-long journey. Together with all God's people you must explore the way of Jesus…
>
> *From the Commission*

Story

It is so important that we tell our stories to one another. In our 'disposable' culture, living for the experience of the moment, people will often

How to give a testimony
There are various ways in which the Testimony might be approached:
- Those brave enough can stand up in front of the congregation and speak (though strict time limits may have to be adhered to).
- Being guided through a discourse by a friendly interviewer can help.
- Reading a prewritten account will avoid the fear of forgetting the important points.
- If it is more appropriate, candidates could be invited to write 50–100 words in advance, to be printed at the back of the service sheet or in a special booklet.

dismiss tales of yesterday, seeking instead the excitement of tomorrow. Yet if we are to grow in knowledge and love of one another and of God, we need to risk sharing our own stories and to

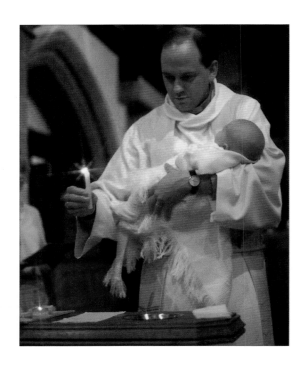

Do you reject the devil and all rebellion against God?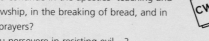
I reject them.
Do you renounce the deceit and corruption of evil?
I renounce them.
Do you repent of the sins that separate us from God and neighbour?
I repent of them.

Do you turn to Christ as Saviour?
I turn to Christ.
Do you submit to Christ as Lord?
I submit to Christ.
Do you come to Christ, the way, the truth and the life?
I come to Christ.

From the Decision

Will you continue in the apostles' teaching and
    fellowship, in the breaking of bread, and in
    the prayers?
Will you persevere in resisting evil…?
Will you proclaim … the good news of God, in Christ?
Will you seek and serve Christ in all people…?
Will you acknowledge Christ's authority
    over human society…?

From the Adult Commission

listen to others. The *Common Worship* services have an optional spot for a bit of story-telling at the Presentation – i.e. the Testimony.

Testimonies are not compulsory, but hearing how God has engaged and dealt with people of our own time will be a great encouragement to the Church. It is an option which is definitely worth thinking about.

Way

Jesus said, 'I am the Way…' Some of the first believers were described as followers of 'the Way' (Acts 24:14) and as such they patterned their lives as disciples of Jesus. The Adult Commission in the Baptism Service gives us a summary and reminder of the marks of this discipleship.

Logic and flow of the services

The structure of the Initiation Services has a certain logic and flow, leading the candidates from the recognition of what God has done,

Delay baptism for infants?
The requirement of the present Canons is that, where parents ask for baptism for their child, there should be no delay, 'save for the purpose of preparing or instructing the parents or guardians or godparents'. Parents and godparents are asked some searching questions in the service, so it is clear that, for families asking for baptism with little idea of its significance, there may need to be some very thorough preparation in the meaning of discipleship, including participation in the 'community of faith'. So 'delay' may be appropriate for this purpose.

through the big turning point of accepting Christ as Lord, passing through the waters of baptism and being incorporated into the new community, the body of Christ. *Common Worship* reverses the logic of the ASB questions at the Decision, reflecting this pattern.

The prayers of the people

According to Justin (c. AD 160) and Hippolytus (c. AD 215), the first thing that the newly baptized did was to join the other believers in the prayers. Up until that point they had not been allowed to do so. Why not involve the newly baptized (or confirmed) in leading the Intercessions?

 In any year the Church of England baptizes more adults than the churches of the Baptist Union.

CONNECTIONS
Baptism and infants –
pp.118–19
The part of the congregation –
pp.126–7
Questions to parents and godparents –
pp.126–7
Structure –
pp.134–7

Baptism and admission to Holy Communion

Communion of all the baptized

In the New Testament, baptism is the gateway into the life of the Church. Thus it would be unthinkable that anyone should be baptized and then not receive Communion, unless he or she had withdrawn from Communion or had been excommunicated. The members of the body of Christ could be measured equally by their baptism or by their participation in the Lord's Supper. At whatever age children were baptized (and we think infant baptism is apostolic), they joined the rest of the congregation at the Lord's table.

The pattern changes

We have seen, however, that after AD 500 baptism happened very soon after birth, while receiving Communion was not only delayed until long after baptism, but became rare even for adults and finally was forbidden for young children. The Reformers thought catechizing to ensure a mature understanding would protect young people from error, and they raised the age of admission to Communion from 7 to 13, catechized within confirmation and in principle made confirmation the key for the admission.

Admission of baptized persons to Holy Communion before confirmation

Guidelines agreed by the House of Bishops

a …every diocesan bishop will have the discretion to make a general policy whether or not to entertain new applications for 'communion before confirmation' to take place in his diocese … The bishop should satisfy himself that both the incumbent and the Parochial Church Council support any application, and that where appropriate ecumenical partners have been consulted…

b The incumbent must ensure that the policy adopted for his/her parish is clearly and widely understood … The bishop should be satisfied that the programme of continuing Christian nurture is in place leading to confirmation in due course.

c Before admitting a person to confirmation, the priest must seek evidence of baptism. Baptism always precedes admission to Holy Communion.

d There is a question regarding the age at which children may be admitted to Holy Communion. In general the times of the first receiving should be determined not so much by the child's chronological age as by his or her appreciation of the significance of the sacrament. Subject to the bishop's direction, it is appropriate for the decision to be made by the parish priest after consultation with the parents or those who are responsible for the child's formation, with the parents' goodwill. An appropriate and serious pattern of preparation should be followed. The priest and parents share in continuing to educate the child in the significance of Holy Communion so that (s)he gains in understanding with increasing maturity.

e [This further handles issues of preparation and nurture, requires the keeping of a register and the issuing of certificates about such admission to Communion, and insists that no one admitted to Communion in one place should be debarred from it in another.]

Is confirmation essential?

The Anglo-Catholic movement from the 1880s onwards wanted children to be communicant from 10 (or even younger), but to be confirmed first. Some even advocated a combined infant baptism-and-confirmation so as to admit the newly baptized directly to Communion.

Sacramental initiation complete in baptism: does baptism admit to Communion?

From 1970 theologians and official commissions have increasingly firmly concluded that water baptism is complete sacramental initiation. The two instances of a post-baptismal laying on of hands by an apostle in the Acts of the Apostles (in chapters 8 and 19) appear as exceptional rather than normative, and it looks as though the roots of confirmation do not lie there at all and the service we have can be adapted for different purposes. Understanding this has had far-reaching (though slow-arriving) implications both for admission to Communion and for confirmation. In the 1970s a few provinces of the Anglican Communion admitted unconfirmed children to Communion on this principle. In England, however, it took from the Ely Report in 1971, through three rejections by General Synod, to Spring 1997 for the go-ahead for such admission to Communion to be given.

The IALC Statements

Meanwhile, International Anglican Liturgical Consultations in Boston, USA, in 1985 and in Toronto, Canada, in 1991 affirmed almost unanimously (with strong English participation) that 'baptism is complete sacramental initiation and leads to participation in the Eucharist'. The Toronto Statement, *Walk in Newness of Life*, has deeply affected world Anglicanism, even in England.

The message gets through in England at last

Between 1991 and 1996 the House of Bishops slowly took aboard these principles, and it was helped by further reports – as well as by changes in its own membership. In March 1997 it issued guidelines for the admission of unconfirmed children to Communion (printed opposite). Dioceses generally have opened the doors.

A glimpse into the future?

There remains a gap, in respect of younger children, between the Boston and Toronto (and surely biblical) principle of Communion at and from baptism and the House of Bishops' guidelines, which discuss age and preparation prior to admission and view baptism as necessary in the background, but do not see it of itself admitting to Communion. The guidelines seem to anticipate an age of around seven. That gap shouts, as do so many children themselves, for baptism to lead immediately to Communion in the coming years.

 Within the Church of England people are currently admitted to Communion by a number of different routes:

A	B	C	D
Infant baptism (Growing years)	Infant baptism (Child years)	Infant baptism Into Communion	Adult baptism (Delay, or not)
Confirmation	Into Communion	Mature	Confirmation
Into Communion	Mature confirmation	confirmation	Into Communion

A is traditional, and in some dioceses leads to confirmation as young as 10.

B follows the House of Bishops' guidelines and leads to admission to Communion at 7 or 8 (and to confirmation as a personal ratification of baptismal undertakings at 13 or older).

C is baptism-admitting-to-Communion, including in infancy, and then confirmation as a personal ratification.

D is the present pattern for adults, with confirmation as an unexplained (and unnecessary?) addition following affirmation of baptismal faith for oneself at baptism.

A further pattern would be baptism-admitting-to-Communion for adults, with no need of confirmation. This would be true to Scripture, but is currently not permissible.

CONNECTIONS
◉ **International Anglican Liturgical Consultations** – pp.64–5
◉ **The history of confirmation** – pp.120–23
◉ **1st Century Baptism** – pp.118–19

Common Worship:
symbolic action in initiation

Every culture throughout history has had symbols to give sense and meaning to life. Using symbols is a natural part of being human. They can help to give identity to a community, and a good symbol will have many levels of meaning. Symbols can be words, actions or pictures that strike a chord within us, resonating with memories or experiences and triggering a vast range of responses.

Symbols can be a powerful aid to worship. Jewish people have their symbols and Jesus

would have been very familiar with those of his time – a theme which is brought out clearly in the 'I am' sayings of John's Gospel. He knew the power of symbols, too, and instructed his followers to perpetuate a number of them: bread and wine from the Passover meal, foot-washing after a dusty day, and baptism – using one of the world's most evocative symbols, water.

In our culture we have been rediscovering the value of symbol, a recovery that has influenced much of our worship in the Church. The *Common Worship* Baptism Service draws on some additional (yet traditional) symbols and images that were rejected by some in years gone by, recognizing that, while some would wish to

do nothing that detracted from the symbolic water, others would welcome them as an enhancement of the momentous and life-changing event which baptism signifies.

These are the symbols included in the *Common Worship* Baptism Service:
- Water
- The sign of the cross
- Light (candles)*
- Oil*
- Clothing*

(* These symbols are optional.)

The sign of the cross

There are two different positions for the signing of the cross, and it must be done at least once during the service:
- At the Decision (with or without the Oil of Baptism/Oil of Catechumens). At this point the signing by the minister, marking the

> **Water**
> People are baptized in seas, rivers, swimming pools, fonts, baptisteries or bowls; poorly newborn babies might be baptized with water from a little spoon. Whatever the vessel, however, the symbol of God's abundant grace should not normally be used sparingly. Administration can vary enormously, too, from scooping water with a hand or shell, through pouring from a jug, to completely immersing or submersing the candidate in the water. It has always been the rule that the water should be administered by dipping or pouring. The notes to the *Common Worship* Baptism Service remind us that 'water must at least flow on the skin of the candidate' (Note 12). Smearing with a damp finger or sprinkling a drop or two are not options. Water can also be used as a reminder of baptism (at confirmation or affirmation of baptismal faith, for example, when candidates might be sprinkled by the bishop with water from the font).

candidate as Christ's own, may be followed by the parents, godparents or sponsors also signing the cross on the forehead of the candidate. The accompanying exhortation urges the candidate to 'wear' the mark of Christ faithfully, and the prayer asks for God's protection and guidance.

- After the Baptism (with or without the Oil of Chrism). At this point the traditional meaning of the signing is different from that of the earlier position, so the words to use with it are also different. It should never be done by dipping a finger into the font first; to use water for this is to confuse the symbols.

Oil

The use of oil is entirely optional, but may be used at the points where the sign of the cross is made (see above). If the sign of the cross has been made at the Decision and the candidate is being anointed after the Baptism, a chi-rho shape may be made instead at this point.

Another way of doing it is to use ample oil to pour over the candidate – described as 'sacramental generosity' by some! Many

> **Anointing and light**
> But you are a chosen race, a royal priesthood, a holy nation, God's own people, in order that you may proclaim the mighty acts of him who called you out of darkness into his marvellous light.
>
> *1 Peter 2:9*

cathedrals hold services in Holy Week when the oils are blessed.

Candles

Candles are also optional. A large one may be lit at the Decision, and smaller ones may be lit from it later and presented to the newly baptized. The preferred position for this in *Common Worship* is at the end of the service. In this way the light becomes a symbol of ongoing mission, not simply of personal rescue from darkness.

Clothing

In another optional symbolic act, being 'clothed' with Christ can be symbolized by putting on a white robe or other special garment. If people are thoroughly wet and need to get changed anyway, why not make more of being wrapped about with a large white towelling robe?

> **? DID YOU KNOW** Dipping the candidate in the water is the first option for the mode of baptism in both *The Book of Common Prayer* and *Common Worship*. The only mention of 'sprinkling' was in the Westminster *Directory* of 1645.

> As many of you as were baptized into Christ have clothed yourselves with Christ.
>
> *Galatians 3:27*
>
> Clothe yourselves with compassion, kindness, humility ... clothe yourselves with love.
>
> *Colossians 3:12,14*
>
> To us who are being saved [the message about the cross] is the power of God.
>
> *1 Corinthians 1:18*

CONNECTIONS
Symbols and worship –
pp.40–41, 54–5

Common Worship: the structure of the Baptism Service

When Cranmer put together his 1552 Prayer Book, he needed to include only a service of infant baptism, since in those days it was expected that all babies would be baptized. In 1662 a service for adults was added, but was seen as the exception rather than the rule. The *Common Worship* Baptism Service has a very different starting point. There is basically one service, in order to demonstrate that there is no distinction to be made in the status or efficacy of the sacrament according to the age of the candidate. Where, for practical reasons, there have to be differences, the options for infant baptism are derived from the norm and not the other way round.

Baptism outside the Eucharist

The structure of a baptism outside the Eucharist is much the same as that given above, placing the Lord's Prayer at the end of the Intercessions. The Initiation Services volume works out a number of different variations in detail, so that service leaders cannot go far wrong.

A Saxon font

Baptism at the Eucharist

Service outline	Alternatives for infants and children
Preparation	
Greeting	Thanksgiving prayer for a child ☞
Introduction ☞◉	
(Presentation of the candidates including optional testimony) ✳◉	
Collect ◉	
Liturgy of the Word	
Reading(s) and Psalm ☞◉	
Gospel reading ◉	
Sermon	
Liturgy of Baptism	
Presentation of the candidates ✳◉	
Decision ◉	*Questions addressed to candidate* **through** *their parents, godparents and sponsors*
Signing with the cross ✦	
Prayer over the water ◉	
Profession of faith ◉	
Baptism	
Clothing ☞	
(Signing with the cross) ✦	
(Giving a lighted candle) ☞✦	
Commission ☞	Commission ✶
Prayers	
Prayers of intercession ☞◉✦	
Welcome and Peace ◉	
(Prayers of intercession) ☞◉✦	
Liturgy of the Eucharist	
Sending Out	
Blessing ☞◉	
Giving a lighted candle ✦	
Dismissal	

☞ indicates that the section is optional
◉ indicates that there is a choice of text
✦ indicates that there is an alternative position
✳ indicate that this is not the preferred position
✳ indicates that only the rubrics at the beginning of this section are optional
✶ The Commission at infant Baptism is optional only if the contents are paraphrased at some point in the service – during the sermon, for example.

Seasonal material in the appendices

The appendices of the Initiation Services contain three sets of special material for the major Baptismal seasons – Epiphany / Baptism of Christ / Trinity, Easter / Pentecost, and All Saints. These may be used at other times of the year too, as appropriate.

Cutting the length

When the *Common Worship* Baptism Service first came out, many people were concerned about the length of it. Since then the service has been reviewed and some of the sections which had originally been mandatory subsequently became optional. It is clear from the service outline given here that there are many parts that can be left out if time is pressing, or if the local situation dictates. 'Free-flow' parts of the service can be kept appropriately brief – the sermon, for example (and the notices).

When there are strong pastoral reasons, the shorter questions at the Decision (from the ASB) and a shorter Profession of Faith (similar to the ASB version) can be used.

Perceived length

Very often the problem is not so much the actual length of a service as the perceived length. There are some ideas later in this chapter for making baptism services more engaging. It is also worth drawing attention to the responsive forms of the Prayer over the Water which are also available. When there is a likelihood of people becoming fidgety and bored by a presidential monologue, these could be the answer.

CONNECTIONS
▣ **Engaging the congregation at Baptism** – pp.138–9
▣ **Celebrating the seasons with the Initiation Services** – pp.140–41
▣ **Times and seasons** – Chapter 15

Common Worship: Confirmation, Affirmation and Reception

The three pastoral services of Confirmation, Affirmation and Reception are closely derived from the Baptism Service, each provided as a landmark in a person's life, a landmark on their journey of discipleship first begun at baptism. It is no surprise, then, that these services are of a similar structure to the Baptism Service, nor that we are encouraged to hold baptisms in the same service, to link baptism to the other acts of commitment taking place.

In general...
- The flexibility these services provide helps us to make more sense of the reality we face: there are a number of different paths that people take. Coming to faith, growing in faith, returning to faith and changing church all need to be celebrated in different ways.
- We are encouraged to gather round the font for the Profession of Faith, even when there are not any baptisms.
- We are also encouraged to hold these services in the context of Communion. The welcome into membership of the Church (at baptism or reception) is also an invitation to sit and eat at the Lord's table.
- However, there are also worked-out services and service outlines for confirmation, affirmation and reception outside a Eucharist.
- Whilst being 'public' events, it is not always appropriate to have them all in a deanery or diocesan service. For example, it might be better for an individual to be received into the communion of the Church of England at a local parish Eucharist.

Confirmation – a note about baptism
Since a bishop is the principal minister of baptism in his diocese, he is encouraged to preside over baptisms whenever possible. Confirmations offer the easiest opportunity for this to happen. Some people prefer to be baptized in the midst of their local congregation – so, if the service takes place in another church, let's take the congregation too, if we can.

Affirmation of Baptismal Faith
The affirmation is a very useful pastoral service to use with people who have been confirmed at some point in the past and wish to make a public recommitment to Christ beyond their confirmation. Candidates might include the following:
- People who were confirmed as children or young adolescents, and who wish to make a truly adult declaration of their faith.
- People who have turned their backs on Christ for a period of time and have now returned to the fold.
- People who have taken a significant step in their faith and who wish to register it in a public way.

When and how
- This service is intended to be used sparingly; it marks a significant milestone in a person's life. It is not the same as a congregational 'renewal of baptismal vows' which the whole church might use corporately from time to time.
- The importance of the event is certainly enhanced by the presence of the bishop. However, a priest may preside over an affirmation.

- There is a rubric in the service which encourages the use of water as a reminder of baptism; it is up to us how little or how much we use – but it is important to make a clear distinction between the act of baptism and any other symbolic use of water.
- The president will pray for the candidate and lay a hand on his or her head. This is similar to confirmation, but different words are used.

Reception into the Communion of the Church of England

This service is for people who have been episcopally confirmed in another denomination and who wish to join the Church of England. Again, its significance will be enhanced by the presence of the bishop, although a priest may preside (unless the candidate is a priest himself – when it must be a bishop). In a gesture of welcome and partnership, the president takes the candidate by the hand and receives him or her.

The distinction between those who have been episcopally confirmed and those who have not is a grey area. For example, Roman Catholics and members of the Nordic Churches of the Porvoo Agreement belong to episcopal churches yet may be confirmed by a priest. Nothing is ever straightforward!

Can Nonconformists simply be 'received'?

The Church of England first debarred Nonconformists from Communion in the 1870s, once the practice of confirmation was gaining steam, and Nonconformity became more conspicuous. 'Transfers' from non-episcopal denominations are still required to be confirmed as the way in which they can be received into the Church of England. However, since the Church of England recognizes baptism as complete initiation, and is happy to receive people from episcopal denominations which, historically, have been more deeply estranged, then we must surely add this anomaly to the issues surrounding confirmation which need further consideration.

CONNECTIONS
☑ **Is confirmation essential?** – pp.130–31
☑ **The structure of the Baptism Service** – pp.134–5

The Outline of the Service

With the exception of the optional inclusion of the Gloria, the Preparation and Liturgy of the Word are as for Baptism. This chart begins at the Liturgy of Initiation.

Element of the service	Service includes			
	Baptism	Confirmation	Affirmation	Reception
Liturgy of Initiation				
Presentation of the candidates	●	●	●	●
Decision	●	●	●	●
Signing with the cross	●			
All move to the font				
Prayer over the water	●			
Profession of faith	●	●	●	●
Baptism	●			
Optional symbolic acts**	●			
Declaration for Affirmation			●	
Declaration for Reception				●
Sprinkling/signing with water*		●	●	●
Prayer for faithfulness	●	●	●	●
Confirmation		●		
Affirmation of Baptismal Faith			●	
Reception				●
Commission*	●	●	●	●
Prayers of intercession*	●	●	●	●
Welcome*	●			
Peace	●	●	●	●

From this point, the Liturgy of the Eucharist follows, then the Sending Out, as at Baptism. All of the candidates may be given a lighted candle at the end.

* indicates that the section is optional   ** as at Baptism

Common Worship Baptism: images and impact

Baptism is a momentous event, signifying one of the most important life changes that any of us are likely to experience. It makes sense, then, that our baptism services should not be inconspicuous. The *Common Worship* Baptism Service is impossible to pare down to a mere 10 minutes at the beginning of the parish Eucharist, then to be forgotten. In its recommended form, it weaves its way through the whole of any service, leaving the congregation in no doubt about its importance. It makes sense that we should make the very best of what we do and engage the congregation in the drama of the event.

The ASB Baptism Service heavily emphasized the paschal baptismal imagery of Romans 6. *Common Worship* has broadened the biblical imagery of baptism, incorporating a whole range of biblical pictures to spark our imaginations.

There is also a strong theme of 'journey' running through the service. Some of these images have been brought out in the symbolic actions that we use, while others can be found in the prayers, liturgical phrases and readings.

Making an impact

Whether we worship in a grand cathedral with full choir, much ceremonial and the 'full works' from the Baptism Service, or whether we attend a small church which holds baptisms at the all-age Eucharist and reduces the verbal parts of the Baptism Service to the bare minimum, we can build on these images. We can use them to convey the sense of 'happening' and occasion that baptism surely is. This does not need to take up any more time, and may even make the service feel as though it is passing more quickly. One example is given in the 'Practical tips' box.

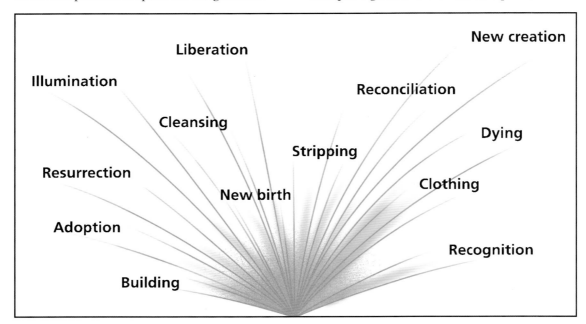

Further ideas...

...Involving others in the service
(children and young people too)

- A godparent or sponsor could say a few well-chosen words to introduce the candidate.
- A group could do a 'reading' from the Dramatized Bible.
- The parents and godparents could sign the candidates with the cross.
- Laypeople might lead the intercessions.
- Members of the congregation could give out the lighted candles.

...During the Prayer over the Water

- Project appropriate visual images onto a screen or screens behind the font.
- Play quiet music in the background ('Come to the waters', for example).

...Music

- Choose and use music creatively to carry the flow of the service.
- Sing a song or a hymn on the way to the font, so that people who are not used to periods of 'waiting' in church services do not have a chance to become fidgety. Or sing half the song on the way there, and the other half on the way back.

...Light

- Hold some Baptisms in the context of an Easter vigil and service of light (such as in *Lent – Holy Week – Easter*). Start before

God's people on the move

The notion of faith as 'journey' is nothing new. In the Judaeo-Christian tradition it can be traced right back to the very roots of our history and the time of Abraham, when God entered into a covenant with him and his household. They were told to pack up and 'go', and God's followers have been on the move ever since. The image of a road, path or way is well known as a picture of faith and life.

In our initiation services we can enact the journey taking place in the life of the candidates. If we have a sufficiently spacious building, we can gather in one part of it (yes, the whole congregation) for the beginning and have the Decision at this point; move into the main part of the building for the Readings and Sermon; move to the font for the Baptism and then over to the holy table for Communion. If there is not quite so much space, then we could still consider moving *en masse* to the font in a grand procession, young and old together. After all, the candidate is on an accompanied journey, and the step being taken at baptism is one into the community which surrounds and supports.

At a Confirmation, Affirmation or Reception service it would also be appropriate to enact a journey, taking the Profession of Faith at the font, whether or not there is a baptism taking place.

dawn, watching and waiting in the darkness with Bible readings about God's history of redemption. Then, as the day breaks, joyfully light candles to signify the light of the risen Christ. The celebration leads into Baptism and Communion, and brings out most vividly the darkness/light and death/resurrection imagery. It certainly will not be forgotten easily.

...Other possibilities

- Pick one of the biblical images on which to concentrate especially. Draw it out in the sermon, in the singing, visually, etc.
- Regularly use large visual images that the whole congregation can see, holding them up or projecting them at the relevant moments: a large drop of water, a cross, a candle, etc.

CONNECTIONS
☒ **Biblical images and the meaning of baptism** – pp.118–19
☒ **Journey and pilgrimage** – pp.128–9
☒ **Symbolic action** – pp.132–3
☒ **Cutting the length of the service** – pp.134–5

Celebrating the seasons with the Initiation Services

A feature of *Common Worship* is that it offers a wide range of seasonal material. This variety extends to the initiation services. Some of these seasonal choices will be found in the main *Common Worship* volume, and the full selection is in the *Initiation Services* volume.

There are three sets of material:

1. Epiphany/Baptism of Christ/Trinity
2. Easter/Pentecost
3. All Saints

Each set contains the following:

- Introduction
- Collect
- Prayer over the water
- Introduction to the Peace
- Prayers of intercession
- Post-Communion prayer
- Blessing

(There are also responsive forms of the seasonal prayers over the water.)

Baptized into Christ Jesus – Easter

By the fourth century, Easter was considered to be the main occasion for baptism, which gave it a particular impact, reflecting the imagery used in the celebration of Christ's death and resurrection on that day. This is the dominant image of baptism in Romans 6.

> Author of life divine,
> in the resurrection of your Son, you set before us
> the mystery of his triumph over sin and death;
> may all who are washed in the waters of rebirth
> rise to newness of life
> and find the promised presence of your abundant grace.
> *From the Easter/Pentecost Prayer after Communion*

> God showed himself to all who have eyes to see
>   and ears to hear.
> The Father spoke from heaven, the Spirit
>   descended as a dove
> and Jesus was anointed with power from on high.
> Here is the door of faith,
> through which we enter the kingdom of heaven.
> *From the Epiphany/Baptism of Christ/Trinity Introduction*

Jesus' Baptism – Epiphany

The feast of Epiphany originated in the Eastern Church and became associated with three themes: the nativity (including the visit of the Magi), the baptism of Christ and the wedding at Cana. The celebration of Christ's own baptism led to Epiphany becoming another normal day for baptism in the Church. It is rare for all three

> As the apostles and prophets, the confessors and
>   martyrs,
> faithfully served you in their generation,
> may we be built into an eternal dwelling for you,
> through Jesus Christ our Lord,
> to whom with you and the Holy Spirit
> be honour and glory, now and for ever.
>
> *From the All Saints Prayer over the Water*

persons of the Trinity to feature at the same time in the Bible; they do so in the narratives of Jesus' baptism, which makes this set of options suitable for Trinity Sunday too.

A great crowd of witnesses – All Saints

The material for All Saints' Day reflects the eschatological themes of the feast day, and we remember those who have run the race before us and the hope into which we are all baptized.

Seasonal Bible readings

There are readings and psalms to accompany the

initiation services in *Common Worship*, although we are not entirely at liberty to use them! They bring out the seasonal baptismal themes, and the notes and rubrics make clear that they are primarily intended for special 'stand-alone' baptism or confirmation/affirmation/reception services, rather than for regular Sunday services. If we have frequent baptisms on Sundays and always use the baptism lectionary, we will be in danger of losing the flow of the Sunday lectionary.

Psalms and canticles

Whilst not strictly 'seasonal', there is also a selection of psalms and canticles which can be sung in procession to and from the font. Not all of us are able to sing psalms from a Psalter, or have psalm-singing choirs who can chant their way to the waters of baptism. It is worth having a look at the suggestions, however, since they also form the basis of some hymns and modern worship songs, which would be ideal to use at this point in the service.

Well worth investigating

It is refreshing to be able to vary the imagery and emphases in baptism services from time to time. Baptism is central to our identity as a Church, and the variation and breadth of biblical views incorporated into the liturgy will help to deepen our understanding of it. This is an advantage to the preacher, too, for there are more biblical models to explore and illustrate. Moreover, we are not obliged to use seasonal material only at the allocated seasons; it can be used at any time of the year as appropriate.

> As a deer longs for flowing streams,
> so my soul longs for you, O God.
> My soul thirsts for God,
> for the living God.
> When shall I come and behold
> the face of God?
>
> *Psalm 42:1–2*

CONNECTIONS
▶ **Times and seasons** – Chapter 15
◗ **Baptism at an Easter vigil** – pp.138–9
▶ **The Sunday lectionary** – pp.236–7

Yet to come: 'Rites on the Way' and Reconciliation

Whilst the major and most essential parts of the *Common Worship* provision were completed by the end of 2000, there was still work for the Liturgical Commission to do, including consideration of two areas closely related to baptism:

- 'Rites on the Way'
- Reconciliation

'Rites on the Way'

The General Synod report *On the Way: Towards an Integrated Approach to Christian Initiation* highlighted the need for services and forms of prayer to surround the baptism of infants and the baptism and confirmation of adults. 'Rites on the Way' is the working title for a collection of these forms which is still in the process of being compiled.

Drawing from tried and tested resources, such as the Roman Catholic Rite of Christian Initiation of Adults (RCIA), the collection sets the initiation services in the context of a series of optional 'staged rites' which reflect the gradual process of coming to faith, now recognized as the experience of most Christians.

The prayers and services fall broadly into four categories:

1. Prayers which can be inserted into a main Sunday service, so that the whole congregation can play a more active part in supporting those who are taking significant steps along the way. For example:
   - a short piece of liturgy in which the congregation prays for parents who are about to embark on the baptism preparation course;
   - a few words and prayers for people who have recently been baptized but, for some reason, not within the gathering of the local Christian community;
   - a 'presentation' of important Christian texts: the Lord's Prayer, the Apostles' Creed, the Beatitudes and Jesus' summary of the law.
2. Material that can be used with a small group, learning about the faith or preparing for baptism.
3. Other prayers that would be more appropriate for use at home with a family – prayers before the baptism, for instance.
4. A set of pastoral prayers surrounding pregnancy and childbirth.

Reconciliation

Reconciliation is a rich theme in the life and death of Jesus, and a ministry which the Church is called to exercise. The Church of England does

not yet have any official liturgy for this ministry other than the regular use of penitential material in public worship. How is the Church to acknowledge and demonstrate reconciliation which falls into the public domain? How do we deal, for example, with the repentant churchwarden who embezzled the collection over a number of years? Or the confession of corporate sin, or the widely revealed misdemeanours of a public figure? The issue is complex and the work is sensitive.

A complex history

From the New Testament we have several glimpses of the way that the first Christians handled sin and forgiveness: 'Therefore confess your sins to one another, and pray for one another, so that you may be healed' (James 5:16; see also Matthew 18:15–20; 1 Corinthians 5:1–5; 2 Corinthians 2:5–11; 1 Timothy 5:20). The early Church had a firm line on discipline. In

Children passing through the 'Rites of Passage'
stone at West Tytherley

Tertullian's time (c. AD 160–220) people were given only one chance for reconciliation. Augustine of Hippo (AD 354–430) distinguished between minor and major sins – the former being dealt with by the individual praying the Lord's Prayer. We know from the *Didascalia* (from third-century Syria) how the local church sorted out quarrels among the congregation. At the Peace, the deacon would ask if anyone had a disagreement with their neighbour and, if anyone did, they would meet on Monday to discuss it. When there was disagreement, there was liturgical provision that could be used. (The Peace in the Order One Communion Service is an apt opportunity for a sincere reconciliatory gesture – not just for a good hug with our friends.) As time went on, formal rites of reconciliation were developed, such as those found in the *Gelasian Sacramentary*.

The Church of England

Cranmer clearly took sin very seriously – as demonstrated, for example, in the inclusion of heartfelt confessions in his services, which he considered to be all that was usually necessary. In his Exhortation to Communion he expected that one-to-one confession with a minister before an open Bible would be a last resort, and he saw no need for public rites of reconciliation. In the nineteenth century the Oxford Movement revived sacramental confession. In the early 1980s, when Ministry to the Sick was going through General Synod, 'rites of reconciliation of a penitent' were thrown out – mainly due to the disputed wording of the absolution. The same dispute continues in the Church today and some have said that getting any rites through General Synod will be a reconciling process for the Church in itself.

With all this in mind, the Liturgical Commission has not rushed into the provision of forms of services. A collection of essays on the subject is the first stage in addressing the issues.

CONNECTIONS
'Staged rites'– pp.224–5

CHAPTER 9

Holy Communion

An unbroken chain

Jesus commanded, 'Do this in remembrance of me,' and the heart of 'this' was to share bread and wine. The Christian Churches have kept this command, sometimes daily, usually weekly, ever since Jesus first commanded his disciples to do so. It is an astonishing unbroken chain of practice down through history, bonding past generations as well as those present with each other through the sharing of the bread and wine.

To be 'in communion' or to be 'excommunicate' is the classic way of describing the membership, or lack of it, of the baptized in the Church of God. A large part of the history of Christian worship is the charting and evaluating of how the disciples of any generation or any confessional family have obeyed Jesus'

command. Anglicanism is no exception and, because many of the controversies of the Reformation – controversies which gave Anglicanism its distinctive identity separate from Rome – were concerned with the Communion service, the history of that service is central to Anglican history.

Never was command so obeyed.
Gregory Dix, The Shape of the Liturgy, *Dacre/Black, 1945*

…we follow his example and obey his command…
ASB and now in Eucharistic Prayer A

What had Paul received?

For I received from the Lord what I also handed on to you, that the Lord Jesus on the night when he was betrayed took a loaf of bread, and when he had given thanks, he broke it and said, 'This is my body that is for you. Do this in remembrance of me.' In the same way he took the cup also, after supper, saying, 'This cup is the new covenant in my blood. Do this, as often as you drink it, in remembrance of me.'

1 Corinthians 11:23–5 – probably the earliest account, around AD 55

Titles of the service

- **The Lord's Supper:** 'When you come together, it is not really to eat the Lord's supper' (1 Corinthians 11:20).
- **Holy Communion:** 'The cup of blessing that we bless, is it not a sharing [or 'communion'] in the blood of Christ? The bread that we break, is it not a sharing [or 'communion'] in the body of Christ?' (1 Corinthians 10:16)
- **Eucharist:** 'when he had given thanks' (1 Corinthians 11:24, etc.). The Greek word here is *eucharistesas*, and *eucharistia,* the name for 'thanksgiving', has come to mean the whole sacramental meal.

The three titles above are used in modern services (see Order One), the first two of them stemming from 1662, the third from wide contemporary usage. Also found are the following:

- **Agape:** 'your love-feasts [*agapais*]' (Jude 12). 'Agape' is generally used of a Eucharist in the context of a larger meal, such as is recommended in *Lent – Holy Week – Easter.*
- **Mass:** this word, so characteristic of Roman Catholic terminology, probably derives from the 'dismissal' in the Latin rite ('*Ite, missa est*') which refers to the sending out rather than to the sacramental agenda. It has no formal place in Anglican terminology.

Holy Communion – the first century

We keep the feast that Jesus gave us because he gave it to us, but there is a rich Old Testament backdrop against which his command is set. The most obvious one is the Passover, and it is clear that Jesus' own 'Last Supper' with his disciples was set in a Passover context and may quite probably have been an actual Passover celebration. The themes of Christ's single historic redemption and our continued rhythmic remembrance echo the significance of the Jewish Passover very closely; and the identification of Jesus as 'the Lamb of God' both reinforces that Passover likelihood and also may account for the lack of mention of a specific slain animal at the Last Supper itself.

Old Testament themes

There are other Old Testament themes too, such as the cross-references in the New Testament to

> **The Passover**
> He said to them, 'I have eagerly desired to eat this Passover with you before I suffer.'
>
> *Luke 22:15*
>
> …our paschal lamb, Christ, has been sacrificed.
>
> *1 Corinthians 5:7*

the manna in the wilderness being typological of Jesus as the bread of life. More generally, it was eating and feasting together which was bonding for both families and friendships, and the various other meals Jesus shared with his disciples draw upon this Old Testament background of trusting hospitality on the one hand and, on the other, of helping us to understand the meaning of the Lord's Supper in the apostolic Church.

The meal

So Jesus came to that Last Supper with his disciples in the upper room on the night before he was crucified. He held a full meal with them, quite possibly a formal Passover meal, though with unique variants. In the course of the meal, he took bread, gave thanks to God, broke it and said as he gave it to them, 'Take and eat; this is my body, which is for you.' After the meal, he took a last cup of wine, gave thanks to God, and said

> **Accounts from the Synoptic Gospels...**
> Mark may well have drawn on Peter's firsthand account, and written his Gospel in the AD 60s. He adds the specific words of Jesus, 'Take and eat this,' and, 'All of you drink of it.' He is then followed by Matthew, who probably wrote in the 70s or 80s. Luke has a slightly odd order. He was a travelling companion of Paul and may also have written in the 60s. Each of these accounts has a slightly formalized style, which probably stems from the use of the account within the weekly celebration of the Supper, so that their description is not based simply upon mental recollections of the original event around AD 30, but just as much upon the live recitation in regular worship at the time of writing.
>
> **...and from John's Gospel**
> John's Gospel has an account of the Last Supper (John 13), but it includes no account of the institution of the Lord's Supper in bread and wine. The major action there is the foot-washing. In the long discourse following the feeding of the 5,000 in John 6, however, Jesus speaks of 'eating the flesh' and 'drinking the blood' of the Son of Man, and these words must, in the last decade of the first century AD, have been highly evocative of the actual weekly celebration which John's first readers were attending.

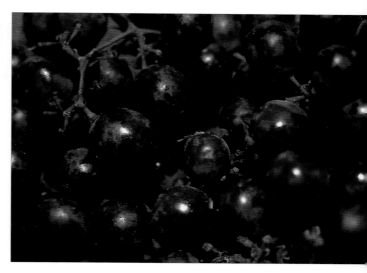

as he gave it to them, 'Drink from this, all of you; this is my blood of the new covenant.'

Paul records that, in respect of both bread and cup, Jesus added, 'Do this in remembrance of me.' This is the actual command which we obey – a command we usually quote as our warrant when we hold or 'celebrate' the Supper ourselves. The evidence is that the command was so obeyed from the start, and thus it is that Paul can say that he received the observance, and the details of it, 'from the Lord' (1 Corinthians 11:23).

What does it mean?
Down through history there has been division over the meaning of the words, 'This is my body … This is my blood…' The wording of the New Testament accounts is unmistakeable – the equation of bread and body and of wine and blood is stark and consistent. This strong, unconditional language is also traceable to post-apostolic authors, and was rarely varied. We obviously cannot drop that language, so we have to ask: What kind of transformation of the elements is meant?

In the accounts of the Last Supper, the source from which we glean Jesus' use of this equation, the words are words of distribution. They were spoken by a Jesus who stood there bodily before his disciples, thus raising a question as to whether he could have meant the words to be taken wholly literally when he spoke them.

After the apostles
There are passing references to the Eucharist in many post-apostolic writings. Probably by AD 100 the service was celebrated every Sunday, with a bishop presiding, and with a Scripture reading and a homily before the sacramental meal. The fuller meal died away, so the second-century scene discloses a sharing of only bread and wine, and the characteristic separate actions with the bread and the cup became assimilated. As the sole components of the meal, they were both taken together; a single thanksgiving, the 'Eucharistic' prayer, was said over them both; the bread was duly broken (we infer) and both were then distributed in immediate succession to each other.

Holy Communion – from the second century to the sixteenth

Two early authors

Justin Martyr of Rome (martyred around AD 165) gives the first full post-biblical account – actually two accounts – of a Communion service. One is a dawn celebration at Easter, when the newly baptized are being welcomed, and the other is a usual Sunday pattern. In both, the meal provides the climax to the gathering, in one case preceded by the baptisms, in the other by the reading of Scripture (with the bishop's exposition), and by corporate prayers (very probably extemporary). At the meal we find a common pattern: the people exchange a kiss of peace, the table is laid, the president leads a prayer of thanksgiving and all say 'Amen'. After the distribution, the deacons take a portion to those who are absent. Elsewhere Justin explains that the thanksgiving (*eucharistia*) transforms the bread and wine so that they are the body and blood of Christ. There are precedents here which have been consciously followed in modern Anglican orders.

Justin gives no actual texts. Fifty years later, a text usually ascribed to Hippolytus of Rome provides a Eucharistic prayer, one to be used by a newly ordained bishop. ('But,' says Hippolytus, 'I do not require him to use this prayer. If he can provide an uplifted and dignified prayer himself, of course he should use that.') The Hippolytan text, because of its antiquity (and Roman Catholic use of it), influenced texts in the ASB, as in Eucharistic Prayers A and B today.

Developments from the second century onwards

In AD 313 the Decree of Constantine legitimated Christianity; in the fifth century the Roman power collapsed and the Dark Ages arrived. The Eucharist saw changes with changing times, and the most far-reaching are mentioned below.

1. The language

Latin was used for worship in Rome from the third century, as it was the language of the people. By the sixteenth century the people did not understand Latin – and its use was now defended as language *not* of the people.

2. Receiving Communion

After the fifth century the reception of Communion fell away, until in the Middle Ages laypeople would receive at Easter only.

3. Sacerdotal language for the clergy

The New Testament does not use the term 'priest' (*hiereus*) for Christian ministers, but only for Old Testament priests, for Christ as our high priest and for the Church as a 'priesthood'. Yet,

from early times, first the bishop and later the presbyter were called a 'high priest' or 'priest'.

4. Sacrificial language for the action

In the New Testament the bread and wine are not offered to God, but in the second century the Eucharist was called an 'offering', in dependence on a proof text (Malachi 1:11) which prophesies that a 'pure offering' will be made one day among the Gentiles. This terminology then ran on – Christians had a priesthood with a sacrifice to offer – and that language soon led to a belief that the priest offers Christ as a sacrifice to the Father as the action of the Eucharist.

5. Transubstantiation

From the ninth to the thirteenth centuries theologians in the West held a kind of devotional auction, bidding up the equation 'This is my body' to its most supernaturalist pitch. Then the Fourth Lateran Council (1215) defined transubstantiation as an article of faith. The people were not receiving Communion at this time, instead focusing their devotion on adoring the uplifted wafer. The cult of the reserved sacrament flourished, and a nun's vision 50 years later led to Corpus Christi Day and its rituals.

6. Ceremonial changes

Over the centuries many ceremonial changes deeply affected the mode of celebration, for example:

- Wafers: from the eighth century the West used unleavened bread, which scattered no crumbs and did not go mouldy. It fitted the changes above.

15th-century monks at Mass

- The 'eastward position': from the tenth century onwards, Communion tables (altars) were attached to the east wall of the church. Tabernacles for reserved wafers were often fixed upon them, and priests came round the front and faced the east wall, elevating the wafer at the words 'This is my body' for the people to see and adore, with bell-ringing and genuflecting.
- Votive Masses: the Middle Ages developed the idea that each Mass, as a sacrifice, has a quantifiable value with God, so that (for a price) one could offer 5, 10 or 500 Masses for a purpose – for a soul in purgatory, for instance.
- The withdrawal of the cup: after the decree on transubstantiation, the cup was denied to the laity on their rare occasions of Communion – lest they spill it. It was taught that Christ's body and blood are both received in the wafer.

The Eve of the Reformation

The Reformers had an open Bible before them. They saw the Eucharist with new eyes. Its totality was very unlike what Jesus had commanded, and the English Reformation ensued.

Holy Communion – from Cranmer to 1662

The Communion service was central to the creation of a separate liturgical programme for the Church of England from Edward VI's reign onwards. This was the work of Thomas Cranmer, Archbishop of Canterbury from 1533 until 1556.

1548

In 1547 the Bible was being read in English and the ornaments of churches simplified. The Parliamentary Act encouraging the reception of Communion frequently and in both kinds led, in March 1548, to *The Order of the Communion,* and the Royal Proclamation which preceded it referred to the intention 'that we be encouraged from time to time further to travail for the ... setting forth of such godly orders as may be most to God's glory'.

This first step was in 1548. It inserted into the Latin Mass after the priest's Communion an English-language approach to the table, and the priest was then to distribute to the people – in both kinds.

1549

In 1549 the English-language Prayer Book contained a full Eucharistic text which followed the outline order of the Sarum rite, and included virtually the whole of the 1548 Order. However, the wording was subtly changed. The 'offertory' kept its title but became an offering of alms; the petitions to God to receive our oblations became requests to hear our prayers; the elevation of the bread and wine during the narrative of institution was forbidden; and the account in the prayer of consecration as to how we obey the Lord's command to 'do this' was greatly toned down. (This is the paragraph called the

anamnesis – the Greek word for 'remembrance'.) The changes that would have been most obvious to the worshippers at the time were these:

- It was all in English, which seemed vulgar to some but conveyed the things of God clearly to others.
- All reverencing or genuflecting to the consecrated elements was now missing.
- Reservation and devotions to reserved elements had also gone.
- Most astonishing of all, when there were no communicants (which was most Sundays), there could be no Communion – the service cut off after the giving of money.

Cranmer already had his eye on the next round and 1549 itself was teed up for that.

1552

During 1550–51 Stephen Gardiner, the traditionalist Bishop of Winchester, claimed that 1549 was 'not far from the catholic faith'. Then Martin Bucer from Strasbourg criticized 1549 as not going far enough. Through these ripples Cranmer was steering his own course towards the 1552 rite. The Act came in April 1552 and the use of the new Prayer Book was enforced from All Saints' Day. The Communion service was completely remodelled. Obvious changes now were these:

- The table stood freely in nave or chancel, probably at right-angles to its altar position, with the priest at the 'north side' clad in surplice and scarf.
- Nothing was sung, except the *Gloria in Excelsis*, and there were no singing clerks.
- The intercessions were removed from the 1549 prayer of consecration and placed in the ante-Communion section, so as to be in use every Sunday, even when there was no Communion.
- In the Communion itself there was no objective consecration. The bread was 'such as is usual to be eaten', not wafers. There was no elevation, no manual acts, no supplementary consecration – and anything left over the minister took home.
- The crucial change came at the point of the instruction to 'do this'. In 1549 the priest then described what we do in remembrance of Christ. In 1552 he actually did it – the distribution of bread and wine was the next item.

- There was therefore much further material to be relocated, from the end of the narrative of institution onwards, including the Lord's Prayer and much of the 1548 material.

Ups and downs

When Mary came to the throne in 1553, Cranmer's Communion service was banned until her sister Elizabeth inherited the crown in 1558. It was later banned again by the Long Parliament in 1645 and was illegal until Charles II's Restoration.

1662

At the Restoration of the monarchy Cranmer's Prayer Book came back. The Communion was almost as it had been, but an objective consecration (including manual acts, supplementary consecration and the consumption of consecrated remains) was imposed on its text. Tiny changes to rubrics were also there. In essence, however, it was Order Two as we find it in *Common Worship* – and that is still the doctrinal norm of the Church of England today.

The dying Henry VIII points to the new era, symbolized by his son Edward VI

CONNECTIONS
- **St Agatha's, 1561** – pp.24–5
- **St Agatha's, 1662** – pp.26–7
- **Cranmer's Prayer Books** – pp.94–5
- **The Restoration of the monarchy and the 1662 Prayer Book** – pp.98–9

Holy Communion in the nineteenth century

The worshipping face of the parishes was transformed in the nineteenth century. It centred on Holy Communion, not so much on the liturgical texts in themselves, but more on the use and ceremonial expression of them.

Introduction and rise of the 8 o'clock Communion

In 1800 most parish churches still followed the received pattern of Communion once a quarter. It was in the context of this infrequent celebration that the '8 o'clock' came to birth – arising, so it is said, from sheer numbers at Islington Parish Church, when the evangelical Daniel Wilson was vicar there around 1828. His 8 o'clock service began simply in order to allow people to come at a different time and thus ease the pressure on the mid-morning service. It may have begun that way, but it soon served another purpose.

The Oxford Movement began in 1833 and centred upon the sacraments, which were asked to carry a heavier doctrinal load than at any time since the Reformation. The movement's leaders taught Christ's presence in the Eucharistic bread and wine in a way which ran close to Roman Catholic doctrine, and they

A monstrance, which displays consecrated bread as a devotional focus for worshippers

emphasized the priesthood of the ordained ministry as giving powers to consecrate the sacramental elements and to offer the Eucharistic sacrifice.

This doctrinal teaching led naturally to the changes in practice in imitation of Rome which marked the middle years of the century. Fasting before receiving Communion reinforced the '8 o'clock', which had begun in other circumstances but now spread rapidly. Non-communicating 'High Mass' became the main Sunday service in many parishes, and the people were warned to come at 8 o'clock if they wished to receive Communion. Chanting of the service was revived (Merbecke's day had come); sacramental hymns were translated from ancient and Eastern rites, or were written afresh – as, for example, for *Hymns Ancient and Modern* (1859); and not only weekly but even daily celebrations of Communion arose in advanced parishes, in the new monasteries and in other 'Catholic' institutions. Exclusion of the unconfirmed from Communion bounded communicants by the high wall of confirmation and silently warned the rest to stay away, or be present only as non-communicants.

Ceremonial

The ceremonial to accompany such 'high' doctrine amounted to a liturgical revolution, even though the 1662 text was still in use. Wafers replaced bread; the priest stood with his back to

> **?** DID YOU KNOW? Clergy went to prison for their ceremonial practices in the 1870s and '80s.

the people in the 'eastward position'; the table itself became a stone altar against the east wall, and often with a great ascent of steps; its coverings became not only a white cloth but coloured frontals; the priest adopted the full Eucharistic vestments of the Church of Rome in matching colours; there were genuflections, elevation of consecrated elements, the ringing of bells, candles on the altar, riddel-posts and curtains surrounding it to the sides; if a cross appeared in the middle of the altar, it was soon replaced by a crucifix; towards the end of the nineteenth century tabernacles and hanging pyxes were introduced onto or above the altars, and, in plain defiance of the Prayer Book rubrics, consecrated elements were reserved in them (the elements were kept locked away and were not actually visible, but the location cried out for devotions towards them). Credence tables arrived, and robed servers assisted the priest with a highly formalized drill. Thuribles, thurifers and incense appeared. Choirboys were brought into the chancels (new church buildings were almost invariably in the 'Gothic' style), and choral chants became integral to the celebration of the Eucharist.

Beyond this revolution with the 1662 service, extreme spirits started to embroider the text itself with borrowings from Rome – the *Ave Maria*, the Canon of the Roman Mass (silent, or additional to the BCP Prayer of Consecration), or other 'devotional' insertions. The Roman service of 'Benediction with the Blessed Sacrament' was also found in daring parishes by the end of the nineteenth century.

Polarization

This account may suggest in total a somewhat extreme 'high church' outlook. It led to a demand for a Parliamentary inquiry. Such practices were certainly polarized from any parishes which remained unaltered through the nineteenth century, as hardy evangelical parishes were inclined to do, but in the light of history, the following long-term impact on the great majority of the parishes, not just on the connoisseur ones, should be noted.

- The whole Church of England became at root a sacramental Church.
- In the process, a considerable latitude for each parish to order its own life without close regard for the law was established.
- From 1850 to 1950 there was a steady adopting as 'normal', in the great sweep of Church of England parishes, practices which originally had been highly partisan – such as liturgical colours, wafers and candles.

The face of the Church of England was changed – and it all centred on the celebration of Communion.

CONNECTIONS
⊞ **St Agatha's, 1867** – pp.30–31
⊞ **The Catholic revival** – pp.98–9

Holy Communion in the twentieth century

As in the nineteenth century, so for much of the twentieth, the 1662 Communion was the only legal service. It provided a background to changes of mood, style and parish policy, whilst actual textual revision came only after 1966.

The false trail of 1927–8

The 1928 Prayer Book failed. The storm-centre was the Eucharist – particularly in relation to permanent reservation of the elements. A short obituary might run as follows: the policy was to broaden the liturgical base of the Church of England in order to legitimate the growing Catholic force in it, but also to set clear limits in order to win acceptance by evangelicals; but both wings were antagonized – evangelicals opposed the broadening and Catholics opposed the limits; Parliament rallied behind an evangelical 'No Popery' cry, but the disillusionment of the Anglo-Catholic party with a book which was supposed to be helping them, but was not enough, probably tipped the scales.

The seminal parish change

Within days of the first, fiery and well-placarded Commons battle in 1927, there occurred on Tyneside an unreported, seminal event which has affected today's worshippers far beyond anything the proposed new Prayer Book was likely to do. On 15 December 1927 the Church of St John, Newcastle-upon-Tyne, changed a non-communicating 10.00 a.m. 'Children's Eucharist' into a new 9.15 a.m. service. This enabled parents (who until then had received Communion at an 8.00 a.m. service) to come with their children; it brought preaching and Communion together, and it was sung. The 9.15 time reflected the 'high' tradition of the parish –

 Sharing the Peace in the Church of England was unknown until 1967.

people could receive Communion fasting, and the 'parish breakfast' after it stems from the same era.

The Newcastle 'Parish Communion' was imitated in various places and grew in popularity. When Gabriel Hebert wrote *Liturgy and Society* (1935), he reinforced the practice with the theology of the Roman Catholic Liturgical Movement. In 1937 he added a practical symposium, *The Parish Communion*, which charted the changes slowly coming to a range of parishes.

After the war the academic weight was greatly increased by Gregory Dix's work, *The Shape of the Liturgy* (1945), and the practical advocacy

Sharing an agapé meal

was furthered by Parish and People, a 'middle-to-high' ginger group. Meanwhile, the Pope relaxed the rule of fasting from midnight the previous night in 1950, and the effect was felt in some parts of the Church of England. The Parish Communion grew accordingly, as the people could eat before they came. The slogan 'The Lord's Service for the Lord's People on the Lord's Day' pressed 'oncers' (people who went to church only once on a Sunday) towards Sunday morning, and in time ran down the once-popular Evensong. In the 1960s questions arose about admitting young children to Communion and allowing more laypeople to distribute the sacrament. An innovation was the 'offertory procession', following Dix's teaching that the bread and wine are brought up by laypeople as symbols of an offering of their lives. The Parish Communion remained a 'highish' movement for decades.

Textual revision 1966–80

This background led to revision of the texts. The legal day dawned in 1966. The Liturgical

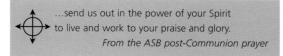

...send us out in the power of your Spirit to live and work to your praise and glory.
From the ASB post-Communion prayer

Commission worked at a draft from 1963 onwards, wanting three readings from Scripture, the Creed as a response to the Word, intercessions which could be properly topical and flexible, a possibility to share the Peace, and a fourfold action of the sacrament. The Eucharistic prayer was consciously modelled on Hippolytus – and Colin Buchanan dissented from the anamnesis text which, like Hippolytus, offered the elements to God. His point was taken seriously.

This new service, Series 2, was agreed by all after some amendment and was authorized in July 1967 for an initial four years. During that time the English language used moved on from Tudor style to a more contemporary approach, addressing God as 'you'. Series 2 got an extension – and eventually got into the ASB, slightly retouched as Rite B (and is in Order One in traditional language today); but new-style common texts appeared from international ecumenical sources, and some imaginative writing emerged from the Commission. Disputes about the anamnesis paragraph and the weight given to the doctrine of the atonement were solved in passing. Thus Series 3, authorized from February 1973, had a polished (and biblical) look which Series 2 never had. It also included a two-year Sunday lectionary.

During the 1970s the aim was to produce a substantial, hardback, modern worship book. Series 3 was revised in 1978–9. Members of Synod put in over 1,000 proposed amendments to the Revision Committee, including the variant on Hippolytus which became the Third Eucharistic Prayer and is Prayer B in *Common Worship* Order One. Three hundred amendments were then handled in full Synod, stepping up the number of alternatives, but also step by step defusing potential opposition. The service finally went through Synod with hardly a voice against it and was authorized in booklet form from 1 May 1980, and within the ASB from 10 November 1980.

CONNECTIONS
⊞ **St Agatha's, 2000** – pp.32–3
⊞ **The aftermath of 1928** – pp.100–103
⊞ **1966: a new strategy** – pp.100–101
⊞ **The first 'alternative services'** – pp.104–5
▷ **The fourfold shape** – p.157

Common Worship Holy Communion: Order One

Part one

The background to the *Common Worship* services of Holy Communion includes Scripture, early Church history, Reformation, recent texts, sacramental doctrine, modern language, calendar, lectionary and pastoral perspectives. All these come together in Order One. As the Eucharist has become central to the life of so many parishes, so it is really the centrepiece of the service book. It will not only provide the ground plan and much of the contents for regular Sunday worship in thousands of parishes, but also the context for a great range of special events from baptisms to anniversaries, from Easter vigils to ordinations. Order One is likely to be the text in view if we speak of the Church of England's Communion service.

It has not dropped fully made out of heaven. Rather it is the fruit of over 30 years of working, celebrating and reflecting with new forms. This is a period in which an ever higher degree of freedom has been given to local parishes to tailor-make the liturgy according to their own pastoral and spiritual needs and in line with their own resources – human, architectural and instrumental. The choice of eight Eucharistic prayers is an illustration of this – parishes may opt for keeping the Eucharist as close as possible to its ASB form, or may major on one favoured new prayer, or may ring the changes from week to week, or season to season, to open further people's understanding of God and his ways. A rich provision of seasonal material also adds to the variety, already enjoyed in the calendar and readings, and in the hymnody and preaching.

That is true of the official provision, so how much more true is it of the home-grown? The door is open for lay leadership of prayers and local creativity in the crafting of prayers. All this gives scope to every facet of our knowledge of God and brings into the liturgy all needs, both local and universal.

Openness to one another

One very obvious trend is an openness to each other. This is expressed in the liturgy, and in turn has been greatly encouraged by it. The worshippers have come to see themselves as the body of Christ with a mutual belonging and a common mission. In many places the bringing of people and table into relationship to each other has

Sharing the Peace

helped this; in some places changed seating has helped; in others interactive styles of preaching and teaching have not only deepened people's understanding of their faith but have also bonded them in common purpose; everywhere the sharing of the Peace (whether by hugs or handclasps) has torn away the liturgical masks and enabled real people to meet each other in Christ. Even the return to 'real' bread, or sheets of wafers which are shared, portrays our meeting with each other. Yes, we are the body of Christ. Yes, he is our peace who has reconciled us in the one body by his cross.

A simple structure

The real clue, however, lies in the liturgical ground plan. The modern Eucharist – very like that of Justin's day in the AD 150s – has a simple structure: the Word, the prayers, the meal. Fit onto that a beginning and an ending, slip in penitence, Creed and hymnody (let alone choir items, kiddies' slots, notices, etc.), and you have it. Jesus said, 'Do this…' and, leaving aside the frills, we do it on that threefold ground plan. All the details fit into that framework. We know the order we are following. That is how we are to approach the celebration.

The importance of 'shape'

A key piece of work was done by an Anglican scholar called Dom Gregory Dix. In his 1945 book *The Shape of the Liturgy* he drew attention to the pattern of actions in the Last Supper and suggested that this pattern, or 'shape', should be the basis for structuring the Eucharist today. He identified a sevenfold shape in the Last Supper which he conflated to a fourfold shape for the Eucharist:

- Taking the bread and cup
- Giving thanks over the bread and cup
- Breaking the bread
- Sharing the bread and cup

The liturgical thinking that has grown out of that book has led to an emphasis on shape and structure in all forms of worship, both within the Church of England and in other 'liturgical' Churches too. The influence of this thinking includes the ASB and *Common Worship* Order One.

The Eucharistic prayer and consecration

History has shown oscillating movements in terms of the role of the Eucharistic prayer as consecratory. It looks as though the original 'giving thanks' was viewed as denoting that the elements were to be viewed as the body and blood of Christ. As doctrine moved towards transubstantiation (1215, Fourth Lateran Council), so the insistence on 'This is my body' as effecting consecration grew. In 1552 the narrative of institution lost this role and gave a simple historical warrant. In Elizabeth's reign there was a return to locating consecration in 'This is my body' (though not accompanied by any belief such as transubstantiation – see the 1571 Articles XXVIII and XXIX). This remains the 1662 concept.

Modern Eucharistic prayers are built on the principle that the whole thanksgiving in its entirety consecrates, and there is no single 'moment' of consecration within the prayers. Thus the petition for consecration (or epiclesis, which since 1980 has included a calling on the Father to send the Spirit) may come before the narrative – as in 1662, Rite A and the new Prayers A, B, C and E – or after it, as in the new Prayers D, F, G and H – for it is the whole prayer which consecrates, a prayer above all of thanksgiving. It is inappropriate to change posture during the prayer, or to overemphasize by ceremonial the words of our Lord's institution of the Supper.

CONNECTIONS
▶ **Epiclesis and the Eucharistic prayer** – pp.172–3

Common Worship Holy Communion: Order One

Part two

The Holy Communion section of *Common Worship* begins with A Form of Preparation. This is followed by a one-page Structure for Holy Communion, which is set out below. A left-hand column has been added in order to show the more basic structure which underlies the order in *Common Worship* and demonstrates its continuity with previous rites.

The cross-headings used in the Order recognizably match the headings in the right-hand column above (though they are not identical with them), so we should know where we are going – and we will discern that receiving Communion is really the climax of the service.

The peaks of the mountains are very clear, so here are some pointers to identify on the way through the valleys, with a view to keeping our direction straight.

Penitence

The text here overlaps with the provision in A Form of Preparation, but this opening place for penitence is now the only place where it is printed within the Order (though the notes permit its use elsewhere).

The Nicene Creed

The Synod and House of Bishops had difficulty in agreeing the translation of the line in the Creed which reads 'was incarnate from the Holy Spirit and the Virgin Mary'. The 'from' governs both because in the fourth/fifth-century original the same Greek preposition (*ek*) governs both. This does not mean, however, that the 'from' has exactly the same meaning in respect of each. (The Filioque issue – whether the Holy Spirit 'proceeds from the Father and the Son' or only 'from the Father' – is dealt with by a text without the 'and the Son' in an appendix.)

Structure of Order One	
Basic Structure	As set out in the rite
Introduction	*The people and the priest:*
	– greet each other in the Lord's name
	– confess their sins and are assured
	of God's forgiveness
	– keep silence and pray a Collect
The Word	*– proclaim and respond*
	to the word of God
The Prayers	*– pray for the Church*
	and the world
The Meal	*– exchange the Peace*
	– prepare the table
	– pray the Eucharistic Prayer
	– break the bread
	– receive Communion
Ending	*– depart with God's blessing*

The intercessions

These give coaching advice for constructing the prayers with sensible structuring rather than insisting on mandatory texts. There are specific forms available in the Supplementary Texts, but any form can be used. Many parishes have intercessors who work creatively at incorporating local needs into the prayers, but it is possible to use a wholly set form on the one hand, or wholly extemporary prayers, with wide contributions from many people, on the other. Unless people can hear each other easily, however, a litany-type approach is usually as far towards congregational response as it is helpful to go. Matters for petition may also be presented visually on a screen or by notice sheets in people's hands. The framework for intercessions suggested in the Order is very helpful, especially for main Sunday worship:

- The Church of Christ.
- Creation, human society, the sovereign and those in authority.
- The local community.
- Those who suffer.
- The communion of saints.

The preparation of the table

This is a subheading which is fulfilled by the first four of the five rubrics below it:

- A hymn may be sung.
- The gifts of the people may be gathered and presented.
- The table is prepared and bread and wine are placed upon it.
- One or more of the Prayers at the Preparation of the Table may be said.

The Prayers at the Preparation, mentioned in the fourth rubric and found in the Supplementary Texts, are varied – some concerning gifts of money (as in the second rubric), some the bread and wine (as in the third rubric), and some of a general sort.

Taking the bread and wine

This comes as the fifth rubric:

- The president takes the bread and wine.

In fact, however, it is the first action of the 'fourfold' structure of the meal, conforming to our Lord's command. Any lifting of the elements at a later point may, perhaps, have devotional or ceremonial value, but is not the dominical 'taking' which comes here.

The fourfold structure

This is continued with the second action (the Eucharistic prayer), then the breaking of the bread and the climax in giving and receiving Communion.

Post-Communion

Here the prayers and dismissal follow a traditional pattern, though with a strong hint that a final hymn comes before the dismissal, not after it.

> **Can't decide what to wear?**
> At the Holy Communion the presiding minister shall wear either a surplice or alb with scarf or stole. When a stole is worn other customary vestments may be added.
> *Canon B8.3*

CONNECTIONS
🕮 **The Lord's Prayer** – pp.70–71
🕮 **Eucharistic prayers** – pp.156–7, 166–77
🕮 **The fourfold shape** – p.157

Common Worship Holy Communion: Order Two

Common Worship breaks new ground in the Church of England's official provision by including both contemporary and Prayer Book services between the same covers. Holy Communion Order Two is largely the Prayer Book service as normally used now and its inclusion, along with Order Two in Contemporary Language, makes some important statements about worship in today's Church of England.

Shape

Firstly, shape is foundational. The ASB divided its Communion services according to the language they utilized. *Common Worship* divides its services according to their shape, with language creating a further subdivision. Order

Two, in both its language forms, has the structure of the Prayer Book service.

Shape is important, and has effects which underpin the content of the prayers used. For Cranmer the initial preparation, including a reminder of the Commandments, led into an encounter with the Word of God and a serious reminder of the sacredness of Holy Communion. Intercession and confession took place from the holy table, leading into a simple narrative of the events of the Last Supper and the reception of Holy Communion.

It was essential to receive Holy Communion immediately. Here Cranmer makes a theological point that Holy Communion depends upon faithful reception of sacramental bread and wine, and where possible worshippers would have gathered around the table to receive these elements. Prayers of thanksgiving or self-offering follow, followed by praise and a blessing. The shape makes its own point.

Tradition

Secondly, our traditions are not static. Generations of worshippers have developed *The Book of Common Prayer* and some of the changes

Structure of Order Two	
Basic Structure	As set out in the rite
Introduction	*The people and priest:*
	– prepare for worship
	– hear and respond to the Commandments of God
	– keep silence and pray a collect
The Word	*– proclaim and respond to the Word of God*
The Prayers	*– prepare the table*
	– pray for the Church and the world
	– confess their sins and are assured of God's forgiveness
The Meal	*– praise God for his goodness*
	– pray the consecration prayer
	– receive Holy Communion
	– respond with thanksgiving
Ending	*– depart with God's blessing*

The Prayer of Oblation
...in Order Two

O Lord and heavenly Father, we thy humble servants entirely desire thy fatherly goodness mercifully to accept this our sacrifice of praise and thanksgiving...

...in Order Two in Contemporary Language

Lord and heavenly Father,
we offer you through your dear Son Jesus Christ
this our sacrifice of praise and thanksgiving...

which have become customary (without challenging the overall integrity of the service) are included here. The Summary of the Law is printed, though the Commandments remain the 'lead case'. Ancient texts like *Kyrie Eleison* and *Agnus Dei* are also provided, and the exhortations have been removed (though the Third Exhortation is in the Supplementary Texts and a short exhortation is retained in Order Two in Contemporary Language).

Language

Thirdly, language has poetic power. *Common Worship* gives the language of the Prayer Book an honoured place, recognizing that its 'feel' goes beyond intelligibility alone. As an example, the Prayer of Oblation has this phrase: '...we present unto thee ... our souls and bodies ... to be a ... lively sacrifice.' The word 'living' could be used, but Order Two preserves the archaism because 'lively' is more dynamic than 'living'. New words are included only where meaning has changed, as in the case of justice being ministered 'indifferently'. We now want our judges to be impartial, not indifferent!

Order Two in Contemporary Language

Order Two thus makes small changes which have developed through time. Order Two in Contemporary Language had a far more difficult task to accomplish. A number of churches

requested a Prayer Book 'shape' but with thoroughly contemporary language. In this case, however, it is difficult to disentangle the shape from the language. Prayer Book texts have remained unchanged for 300 years, with no natural evolution, and it was not obvious to the Revision Committee which contemporary forms would work.

The principles used were these. Where a modern alternative already existed (like the collect for the sovereign), then that would be used. Where the content of the Prayer Book was crucial, then that would be preserved, though with more archaisms removed than in the main Order Two. Where possible, contemporary prayers which echo the Prayer Book's 'feel' are provided as alternatives. It remains to be seen whether this provision will find a ready home, but it does stand in the tradition of the Prayer Book while making its strengths available to those who would be unduly put off by its language.

 One bishop is said to have remarked, 'Water is living. Champagne is lively.'

Common Worship Holy Communion: Supplementary Texts

The ASB introduced many Anglicans to the possibility of choice. Where *The Book of Common Prayer* had little or no variation, the ASB provided some alternative prayers and more seasonal material.

Common Worship continues that development. The Supplementary Texts section provides a wealth of material for all aspects of the service. Most of this is designed for use with either version of Order One, but it is essential to look at each text carefully to decide where it will be used most appropriately.

It is easy to ignore this material, so it is well worth looking closely at what is being offered.

Penitential material
- The Summary of the Law (two versions)
- The Commandments (two versions, one containing glosses from the New Testament)
- The Beatitudes
- The Comfortable Words (two versions)
- An Exhortation

- Four Invitations to Confession
- Six Confessions
- Two Absolutions

Other material
- Seven Gospel Acclamations
- The Apostles' Creed
- An alternative Nicene Creed (without the Filoque clause, for use on suitable ecumenical occasions)
- Five forms of Intercession
- Eight collects to end the Intercession
- Seven Introductions to the Peace
- Twelve Prayers at the Preparation of the Table
- Five sets of Words at the Giving of Communion
- A Form of Supplementary Consecration
- Four Prayers after Communion
- Seven Blessings

All of these are for 'Ordinary Time'. In addition there are 15 sets of Seasonal Provisions, which each include:
- An Invitation to Confession
- A Gospel Acclamation
- An Introduction to the Peace
- A short Eucharistic Preface (in two versions, contemporary and traditional)
- An extended Eucharistic Preface (for use with Prayers A, B & E)
- A Blessing

Why all this choice, and what do we do with it?

1. The main text of *Common Worship* contains only what is necessary for the whole congregation. Too much choice here is confusing, especially for new worshippers.

Many of the Supplementary Texts are for the leader of worship, or are intended only for occasional use. For example, the congregation only need the responses to the intercessions, rather than the whole text.

2. There has been increasing use of prayers for particular seasons of the Christian year. *Common Worship* provides more of these, but it would be foolish to print seasonal texts in the main body of the service.

3. Services differ from one another. A weekday Communion service has a different feel from a major Sunday celebration. Simpler forms of confession may well be needed for occasional use, or a different form of intercession.

4. During Lent more penitential material may be needed.

5. Churches are different. No two churches handle the taking of the collection and the preparation of the table in the same way. The provision of 12 prayers here, with none in the main text, allows for an appropriate prayer to be used.

Life would clearly be simpler if, as with *The Book of Common Prayer*, there was only one way through the service, but immeasurable riches would be lost. The use of some of this material will be easiest and most sensible where a locally produced order of service is used, rather than the main book or official booklets. The desired options can then be printed in that church's main text.

Seasonal colour and vestments

The Christian year provides a rhythm to worship and gives a shape to our living which reminds us annually of the great truths of our faith: Christ's incarnation and revelation, his death and resurrection, the gift of the Spirit, the life of discipleship and our preparation for Christ's coming again. The colours used in churches are a visual reminder of these things. Used well, they deepen our prayer and praise.

The *Common Worship* Calendar gives suggestions for the use of colour. The only major

difference from the ASB is that before Advent red is given as an option. Otherwise purple is still a reminder of preparation, white or gold are for celebration, red is for the Holy Spirit and for the martyrs, and green is for 'Ordinary Time'.

Vestments such as chasubles, copes and stoles, as well as cassocks, surplices and scarves, have no doctrinal significance, according to the Canons of the Church of England. Individual churches will know what they are comfortable with in this respect.

At best they provide an opportunity for our eyes to join in our worship, and where vestments and frontals depict the features of the seasons artistically (perhaps resonating with stained glass or banners), then worship can take place in the beauty of holiness.

Liturgical colours of the Church's year

The following liturgical colour scheme is suggested by *Common Worship: Calendar, Lectionary and Collects*. Words in **bold** indicate each liturgical season and its main colour; other colours mentioned are possible variations for particular days.

Advent – Purple

Christmas – White
Christmas Night and Christmas Day – Gold

Epiphany – White
The Epiphany – Gold
Baptism of Christ – Gold
The Presentation – Gold

Ordinary Time (The day after The Presentation to Shrove Tuesday) – **Green**

Lent – Purple (or blue) or **'Lent array'** (unbleached linen).
Palm Sunday to Wednesday in Holy Week – Red
Maundy Thursday – White
Good Friday – Red or hangings removed
Easter Eve – hangings removed

Easter – White
Easter Day – Gold
Ascension Day – Gold
Pentecost – Red

Ordinary Time (The day after Pentecost to the eve of Advent Sunday) – **Green**
Trinity Sunday – White (or Gold)
All Saints – White (or Gold)
Between All Saints Day and the First Sunday of Advent – Red

Some colours may also be used to mark out other special occasions, for example:

○ **White** – festivals of Our Lord, saints (but not martyrs) and dedication festivals.
● **Red** – saints venerated as martyrs and services which focus on the gifts of the Holy Spirit.

CONNECTIONS
▶ **Times and seasons** – Chapter 15

Preaching at Holy Communion

The sermon or address is probably the least predictable part of the service – the prayers, the songs and the readings may all have been heard before, but the sermon should not have been! While God also speaks to his people through everything else in the service, the sermon should be a unique window affording a fresh view of God's holiness, love and power.

Many faceted

It is reasonable to assume that many of those present at a Eucharist will already have been disciples of Christ for some years. Nevertheless, for some the Sunday sermon will be the only Christian teaching that they receive during the week. While the sermon needs to include a certain amount of teaching about God and the way he wants us to live, however, it also has other aims: it will proclaim Christian truths, it will challenge people to think and live in new ways, it will encourage us and 'warm our hearts', and it will relate to the daily lives of the congregation.

Over the last 50 years the average congregation in many areas has become more highly educated and better informed about the world around. To be credible, preachers need to have their arguments clear and their facts straight.

A stream of words?

In the same period, television and the internet have replaced radio as the dominant broadcast media, and the presentation of printed matter has become more eye-catching. It is important for the preacher to use vivid and pictorial ways of speaking and sometimes to supplement the spoken word with images: a diagram or picture projected on a screen, an object from everyday life (big enough to be seen at the back), a hat or

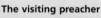

The visiting preacher

The visiting preacher may be in church to fill a gap, to provide some variety, or to share a special message. These are some of the vital points to discuss with the visiting preacher:

- The Bible readings – and the version of the Bible normally used.
- Whether the church is concentrating on one of the readings in its preaching – following through the Moses narratives, for example.
- Whether this sermon is part of a series. It may also be helpful for the preacher to know the subject of the previous week's sermon.
- The length of sermon expected.
- The age range of the congregation.
- The music: have hymns been chosen? Can the preacher suggest something?
- Possibilities for visual aids: e.g. is there an OHP and are people used to it?

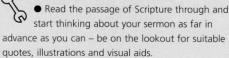

Preparing to preach

● Read the passage of Scripture through and start thinking about your sermon as far in advance as you can – be on the lookout for suitable quotes, illustrations and visual aids.

● Pray about it – what is God asking you to say to this congregation?

● Try to write something at least a few days beforehand; discuss it with a friend, or a group from the congregation, or come back to it yourself with a fresh mind.

● Is there a clear structure?

● What words, phrases or images will your listeners take home with them?

● Do you need to find, make or borrow any visual aids?

● Is there any dead wood that you could trim away to make your message clearer?

● Is there anything you could add to help somebody who is in church for the first time?

a costume … what will the preacher think of next? The acid test is not whether people will remember the visual aid a few days later, but whether they remember the point that it was there to illustrate.

Active engagement

Again, over the last half century, the process of education at all levels has become active rather than passive. More recently, of course, television and the written word have converged in the interactive web-page. Preachers might look for ways to 'activate' the congregation during the sermon. Possibilities include the following:

● Entering into dialogue with the whole group.

● Asking each person to reflect silently on a certain issue for a moment.

● Asking people to talk together in twos or threes, either sharing experiences or discussing a given question.

Preachers may use these devices just to make the sermon come alive for their listeners, but with humility (and courage) they may be able to take on board the feedback they receive and

continue their sermon in a way that they had not planned.

Word and sacrament

In Communion services, Word and Sacrament are twin foci. Since the *Common Worship* lectionary has dispensed with thematic sets of readings, the preacher may find on occasion that the Bible passages lend themselves to a reflection or discourse on part of the service itself – an exhortation to mission, for example, would link readily with the Prayer after Communion and the Dismissal; a reading about reconciliation might raise questions about the way we use the Peace in our services.

Lengthy readings?

And on the day called Sunday, all who live in cities or in the country gather together to one place, and the memoirs of the apostles or the writings of the prophets are read, as long as time permits; then, when the reader has ceased, the president verbally instructs, and exhorts to the imitation of these good things. Then we all rise together and pray, and … when our prayer is ended, bread and wine and water are brought…

Justin Martyr (AD 100–165),
First Apology, chapter 67

CONNECTIONS
⊠ **How to listen to a sermon** –
pp.184–5
⊠ **The *Common Worship* lectionary** –
pp.236–41

Eucharistic Prayers A, B and C

The first three Eucharistic prayers in Order One are drawn from prayers in the ASB Rite A. They each have a discernible family tree, which shows how, as a matter of history, they reached Order One. Each has been marginally retouched in the new Order, but the basic prayer in each case remains distinctly and recognizably itself.

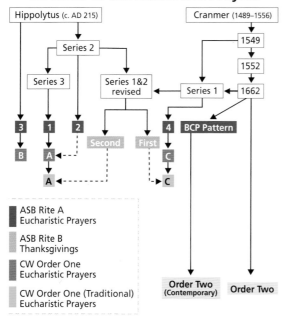

Tracing the influence of Cranmer and Hippolytus on some of the Eucharistic Prayers

These three Eucharistic prayers have many common features. In fact, in the past, there were complaints that the ASB Eucharistic prayers were 'too much like each other'! There are not likely to be such complaints about all eight prayers in Order One. It is, however, worth noting some of the common features of Prayers A, B and C:

- They are all genuinely 'thanksgiving' (which is what 'Eucharistic' means), stemming from the words, 'Let us give thanks to the Lord our God.' The rubrics do not, of course, use the Prayer Book term 'Prayer of Consecration', because the heart of consecration is neither a petition nor a formula but thanksgiving, and because the prayer is seen as effecting consecration through its totality and not through spotlighting a single moment or a specific ceremonial action.

- They all follow the same structure, with a preface (allowing additional seasonal prefaces to be inserted) leading to the *Sanctus* ('Holy, holy, holy Lord') and the optional *Benedictus qui Venit* ('Blessed is he who comes in the name of the Lord'). Then comes:

  1. A link sentence with some recognition of the work of Christ

  2. A petition for consecration (often called an epiclesis)

  3. A narrative of the institution of the Lord's Supper

  4. Congregational acclamations (but these have now been moved down one paragraph to follow no. 5 below in Prayer A)

  5. A paragraph setting out how we respond to our Lord's command, 'Do this…' (often called the anamnesis)

  6. A paragraph seeking the benefits of Communion

  7. An ascription of praise (or a doxology)

  8. The people's 'Amen' (which in Prayer A has the fuller 'Blessing and honour and glory…' leading into the 'Amen')

Some of the similarities came in Rite A within the above structure, with the same responses cued by the same lead-in at the same point in the rite. In *Common Worship: Services and Prayers for the Church of England* these can be found on the sole page which is entitled 'The Eucharistic Prayer' – a page which paradoxically takes the presidential part for granted and sets out only the responses. The acclamations have now been multiplied to four sets, and in Prayer A an additional, repetitive 'To you be glory and praise for ever' may be used at six other points in the prayer.

- They all cover the same central doctrinal themes from creation to eschatology, with only slight variants of emphasis (A has an extra touch of Easter triumph, B has a slightly greater emphasis on the incarnation, whilst C, with its roots in Cranmer's texts, has a strong affirmation of Christ's sacrifice on the cross).
- They all have a similar epiclesis at the same ('Western') position in the prayer – before the institution narrative.
- In principle they are all equally usable by congregations and ministers of any identifiable strand of theological outlook in the Church of England. This was a fundamental principle in their original adoption by Synod in the 1970s and it was reasserted by Commission and Synod in the 1990s.

These three Eucharistic prayers are, in principle, safe and dependable because they are already well tried and widely loved. New prayers have been added specifically because many have wanted the opportunity to try different models and even explore different dynamics between president and congregation. There has been some impatience with the length of monologue and the predictable content of these three, and that has led to a greater spread of style, length and content in the next five. Nonetheless, the more cautious will find in these three prayers great continuity with the pre-2000 Eucharistic worship, and will join with a great company who have valued such prayers at the heart of their Eucharistic celebration.

Prayer A

For he is your living Word;
through him you have created all things
   from the beginning,
   and formed us in your own image.

[To you be glory and praise for ever!]

Through him you have freed us from the slavery of sin,
giving him to be born of a woman
   and to die upon the cross;
you raised him from the dead
and exalted him to your right hand on high.

[To you be glory and praise for ever!]

Through him you have sent upon us
your holy and life-giving Spirit,
and made us a people for your own possession.

[To you be glory and praise for ever!]

Ordinary Preface from Prayer A

And now we give you thanks
because, by appearing in the temple,
he comes near to us in judgement;
the Word made flesh searches the hearts of all your people
and brings to light the brightness of your splendour.

Short preface for the Presentation

CONNECTION
Four sets of acclamations –
pp.170–71

Eucharistic Prayer D

The recognized need

There was a widely expressed need in the Church for the new Eucharistic prayers to include material which was:

- short,
- responsive,
- suitable for both adults and children, and usable when both were together,
- full of vivid, concrete images rather than abstract phrases.

The third point was the most difficult to fulfil. The report *Children in the Way* (The National Society/Church House Publishing, 1981) had identified as a key need a form of Eucharist suitable for when children are present, in the light of the number of churches holding all-age Eucharistic worship, rather than non-Eucharistic all-age services. The Roman Catholic Church had

produced a special Eucharistic prayer for use when children were present – what was the Church of England going to do? Prayer D was written with these needs in mind.

Key features

- **Strong narrative style.** Prayer D tells the story. Story is a form of communication that works effectively in all cultures, especially the audiovisual culture. The Bible itself relates the story of salvation, yet many children and adults no longer know the story of Jesus.
- **Dramatic reconstruction.** This is what makes the past come alive in the present and in the imagination, especially for the young. The early drafts built in the opportunity for children to share in the bringing of the elements and to lead the congregation in stating the reasons for using bread and wine. The aim was to make it possible for children to come around the holy table so that they could see for themselves the drama being acted out. Although not intrinsic to the final form of Prayer D, these elements survive in one of the sets of Prayers at the Preparation of the Table.
- **Short sentences and simple phrases.** The prayer is designed to hold people's attention and not lose them in a myriad of subordinate clauses.
- **Rhythmic response with a familiar cue.** The strong story-telling and dramatic element made it essential to engage the congregation and allow them to look up from the text. The response needed both rhythm and euphony and had to bear repeating.
- **Short.** Tempting as it was to try to cram into the prayer the whole counsel of God, the stages of revision have preserved the original vision for a short prayer – indeed, the final

The crowds came out to see your Son,
yet at the end they turned on him.
On the night he was betrayed
he came to table with his friends
to celebrate the freedom of your people.

This is his story.
This is our song: Hosanna in the highest.

Jesus blessed you, Father, for the food.
He took bread, gave thanks, broke it, and said:
This is my body, given for you all;
Jesus then gave thanks for the wine,
took the cup, gave it and said:
This is my blood, shed for you all
for the forgiveness of sins.
Do this in remembrance of me.

This is our story.
This is our song...

From Eucharistic Prayer D

version is actually shorter than the experimental version tested in many parishes.

His story and ours

The cue line for the response changes part way through, from 'This is his story' to 'This is our story', as the congregation begins to own the

Biblical imagery in Prayer D

- 'Almighty God, good Father to us all.' Jesus never said, 'I am the Shepherd,' because shepherds were distrusted. He had to say, 'I am the good Shepherd.' In a similar way, we cannot take it for granted that everyone's experience of fatherhood is good. As a name for God, 'Father' needs qualifying, not abandoning.

- 'To the city where angels sing your praise.' There are very few positive urban images in our liturgy. Yet the Bible, which begins in a garden, ends with a glorious city. Furthermore, 75 per cent of the world's population live in cities.

- 'With signs of faith and words of hope he touched untouchables with love.' Touch is a powerful image in the Gospels. The sentence also captures the famous 'faith, hope and love' of 1 Corinthians 13 and links it to the miracles (signs) and teaching (words) of Jesus.

- 'To celebrate the freedom of your people.' This phrase captures different levels of meaning: the Passover meal, liberation through forgiveness, the future banquet in heaven.

- 'With opened eyes and hearts on fire.' This offers clear echoes of the Emmaus road experience, when the risen Christ was 'recognized in the breaking of the bread' (Luke 24).

benefits of Christ's passion. The use of the cue and response,

> This is our story.
> **This is our song: Hosanna in the highest.**

was controversial from the start. Some feared resonances with the old hymn 'Blessed assurance, Jesus is mine'. Others valued such resonances. Some, of course, did not know that hymn. There were concerns about whether the words could sustain repetition. At one point the provision of an alternative response was suggested. The feedback from the parishes which used the material experimentally was split down the middle, and few were ambivalent about it: if they disliked it they did so forcefully, but if they liked it they could not bear to see it changed.

Eucharistic Prayer E

Like all the other Eucharistic prayers, this one can be used in almost any setting, but early use at the experimental stages indicated that it might be especially suitable on the following occasions:

- When children are present, as it is short and direct.
- At an evening or midweek Eucharist.
- As the 'standard' Eucharistic prayer in a parish (with seasonal prefaces being used throughout the year to add variety).

Shape
Unlike some of the other new *Common Worship* prayers, Prayer E has a shape familiar from the ASB and similar to Prayers A, B and C. It contains different words and phraseology, however, and – after the opening dialogue common to all the prayers – invites us to do just what we are claiming to do and be more adventurous and fulsome with our praise.

Thirty-eight prefaces!
In the main text of Prayer E there is a short 'default' preface, taking us swiftly through creation and redemption. Alternatively there is a choice of 18 short prefaces or 19 extended prefaces, for different times of the year or special days. These are included in the Supplementary Texts. Recounting God's history, each of these develops a particular theme of praise and helps us to give our worship a strong seasonal flavour.

Distinctive expressions
Prayer E has a number of distinctive phrases, including the following:

It is indeed right and good,
our duty and our joy,
always and everywhere to give you thanks,
holy Father, almighty and eternal God,
through Jesus Christ the King of glory.
Born of a woman,
he came to the rescue of our human race.
Dying for us,
he trampled death and conquered sin.
By the glory of his resurrection
he opened the way to life eternal
and by his ascension,
gave us the sure hope
that where he is we may also be.
Therefore the universe resounds with Easter joy
and with choirs of angels we sing for ever
    to your praise...

Extended Preface of Ascension Day

1. Epiclesis
...send your Holy Spirit
that broken bread and wine outpoured
may be for us the body and blood
    of your dear Son.

The original draft had a much more specific epiclesis, asking the Spirit to fall 'on us and on these gifts'. This was generally felt to be out of line with Church of England Eucharistic prayers, and was changed to the wording we now have in Prayer E.

2. Anamnesis – remembering
So, Father, we remember all that Jesus did,
in him we plead with confidence his sacrifice
    made once for all upon the cross.

'Pleading' was popular with seventeenth-century divines who saw it as a unifying word – it was neither too Protestant nor too Catholic. It avoids any sense of 'repeating'

> Just as I am, without one plea
> but that thy blood was shed for me,
> and that thou bid'st me come to thee...
>
> *Charlotte Elliott*

Seeing the words
Will the congregation want to see the seasonal preface, if you use one? If it is not already printed in a seasonal order of service, it could be put onto the notice sheet, projected onto a screen or printed on a seasonal 'extra' with other special prayers and liturgy for the season.

Christ's sacrifice, yet goes further than merely 'calling to mind' the event.

3. Petition

Lord of all life,
help us to work together for that day
when your kingdom comes
and justice and mercy will be seen
  in all the earth.

Look with favour on your people,
gather us in your loving arms
and bring us with (N and) all the saints
to feast at your table in heaven.

As the prayer moves to its conclusion it expresses an eschatological dimension, of which the Eucharist is a foretaste:

- seeking the coming of the kingdom
- looking to the heavenly banquet

This eschatological dimension was present in early Eucharistic prayers, and was reinforced in the Church of England by the ASB Prayers.

4. Acclamations

There is a choice of acclamations from a set of four (also usable in Prayers A, B, C & G). Each has its own cue line which will soon become familiar and the hope is that regular worshippers will soon be able to come in with the right words without having to look at the page.

Great is the mystery of faith:
Christ has died:
Christ is risen:
Christ will come again.

Praise to you, Lord Jesus:
Dying you destroyed our death,
rising you restored our life;
Lord Jesus, come in glory.

Christ is the bread of life:
When we eat this bread
and drink this cup,
we proclaim your death, Lord Jesus,
until you come in glory.

Jesus Christ is Lord:
Lord, by your cross and resurrection
you have set us free.
You are the Saviour of the world.

CONNECTIONS
▷ Epiclesis and the Eucharistic prayer –
pp.172–3

Eucharistic Prayer F

This beautiful prayer has a more Eastern feel than all the rest because it is influenced by the prayer of St Basil, which is used in the Coptic Church and, in a modified version, in the Byzantine Churches. It has found wide ecumenical acceptance: it is the basis for Eucharistic Prayer IV in the Roman Missal and, in the United States, another variation on this prayer is used by Anglicans, Lutherans and Methodists. Now the Church of England has a version of Basil too.

Trinitarian Structure

What makes the prayer Eastern? In part it is its trinitarian structure which, while weaving the story of salvation throughout the prayer, emphasizes each member of the Godhead in turn. We give thanks to the Father for creation, remember the work of the Son, including the institution of the Supper, and invoke the Spirit on our assembly.

No 'variables'

Prayer F has no provision in its structure for seasonal Proper Prefaces or for one of the four acclamations (such as 'Christ has died, Christ is risen…') which can be used with some of the other Eucharistic Prayers in Order One. However, it does have an optional set of regular short acclamations of its own, reflecting its trinitarian nature:

> Amen. Lord, we believe.
> Amen. Come, Lord Jesus.
> Amen. Come, Holy Spirit.

If they are used they might be said (or sung) first by a deacon or other minister and then repeated by the congregation. This allows the prayer to be used with the responses even in situations where the congregation do not have the full text of the prayer in front of them.

Eastern features

Basil has influenced much of the prayer:

- the beautiful imagery…
  [You] placed us in the garden of your delight.
- the intercessions towards the end…
  Bless the earth,
  heal the sick,
  let the oppressed go free
  and fill your church with power from on high.
- and the poignant description of God's power revealed in both glory and humility…
  Lord God, you are the most holy one,
  enthroned in splendour and light,
  yet in the coming of your Son Jesus Christ
  you reveal the power of your love
  made perfect in human weakness.

Epiclesis and the Eucharistic prayer

The epiclesis in the Eucharistic prayer is the invoking of God or, usually more specifically, the Holy Spirit – for example:

> Father, by your Holy Spirit let these gifts of your creation be to us the body and blood of our Lord Jesus Christ.
>
> *Epiclesis in Prayer F*

During the Middle Ages, the structure which Prayer F unfolds was hotly debated between Eastern and Western Churches. The argument was mainly over the issue of consecration and touched upon this part of the Eucharistic prayer. There were two questions:

● Is there a specific moment when something happens to bread and wine in the prayer, or does the whole prayer effect the consecration?

● If there is a 'moment', is it at Jesus' words of institution, or at the epiclesis, or at some other point?

This argument has mostly been resolved, and the commonly held position is summed up in the following statement:

> The difference from the older view is that there is now no solemnly identified formula or 'moment of consecration'. Rather the whole giving of thanks sets the theological context within which we can confidently assert that this is the communion of the body and blood of the Lord.
>
> *From* The Alternative Service Book 1980, A Commentary by the Liturgical Commission, *CIO 1980*

However, while an explicitly worded epiclesis has become an accepted part of the modern Eucharistic prayer, it continues to be a point of some debate:

● What is the best way to express the presence and work of the Holy Spirit in the prayer?

● Should we pray for the direct operation of the Spirit on the bread and wine, or on the congregation, or should we even be specific at all?

Reception

Anglicans have stressed the importance of the reception of the elements. Thus epicleses are not written in an absolute form, looking only to the consecration of the elements, but also connect the Eucharistic action to the reception of the bread and wine. In the *Common Worship* Eucharistic prayers these questions are addressed in different ways, using a number of slightly different expressions. Proposals to invoke the Spirit directly on the bread and wine have been resisted by General Synod. Some prayers invoke the Spirit on us, and all pray that by the Spirit the bread and wine may be to us Christ's body and blood.

Epiclesis in the Reformation, reformed and evangelical traditions

Invocation of the Holy Spirit can be found in the Reformation, reformed and evangelical traditions. For example:

● During the Reformation Bucer (1539) had an invocation on the congregation:
'Send upon this congregation, now assembled in your name, your Holy Spirit, the Master and teacher, that he may write your law upon our hearts.'

● Hermann (1545) has a slightly more developed prayer:
'Work in us with thy Spirit, that as we have received this divine sacrament with our mouths, so may we also receive and ever hold fast with true faith thy grace.'

● Cranmer introduced an epiclesis into the 1549 Holy Communion:
'With thy Holy Spirit and word vouchsafe to bless and sanctify these thy creatures of bread and wine, that they may be unto us the body and blood of thy most dearly beloved Son Jesus Christ.'

● In 1662 this became a request for fruitful reception:
'Grant that we receiving these thy creatures of bread and wine … may be partakers of his most blessed Body and Blood…'

● An epiclesis was included in the 1637 Scottish Prayer Book, and through the influence of Calvin's Eucharistic theology passed into the reformed tradition.

● Baxter had an invocatory prayer to the Spirit in his *Reformed Liturgy* of 1661, including an invocation of the Father to sanctify the elements and a prayer for the Spirit to soften our hard hearts to enable us to feed on Christ. Such prayers have continued in the reformed tradition and can be found in the Church of Scotland's *Book of Common Order* (1994).

● In the evangelical tradition, the Wesleys' *Hymns on the Lord's Supper* (1745) is a rich compendium of Eucharistic devotion. The theology contained within some of these hymns has led to the epiclesis in *The Methodist Worship Book* (1999).

CONNECTICS
☒ **Eucharistic consecration and the epiclesis** – pp.156–7

Eucharistic Prayer G

This prayer owes its origin to a text published in 1984 by ICEL (the Roman Catholic International Commission on English in the Liturgy) as 'Original Eucharistic Prayer, Text 1'. Extensively redrafted by the group then working on Eucharistic prayers in the Liturgical Commission, it was published in 1989 in *Patterns*

> Zion said, 'The Lord has forsaken me, my Lord has forgotten me.' Can a woman forget her nursing child, or show no compassion for the child of her womb?
>
> *Isaiah 49:14–15*

> How often have I desired to gather your children together as a hen gathers her brood under her wings, and you were not willing!
>
> *Matthew 23:37*

for Worship and eventually went through the Synod revision process, only to be defeated with the other five experimental prayers in February 1996. The July 1999 report of the Revision Committee included part of it, at the request of the Bishop of Oxford, who suggested it might be used as a preface with Eucharistic Prayer F. The Committee responded to the approving noises made by bringing back the whole prayer, with sufficient changes to satisfy the lawyers that they were not reintroducing exactly the same prayer.

In fact, the changes from the 1996 prayer were not many – a much longer ending (everything from 'As we eat…') including three lines of intercession ('Remember, Lord, your Church in every land…') which were originally part of a special section of baptismal material, together with some

> Mother of your people,
> Your celestial breasts give pure spiritual milk.
> You slake the thirst of all who have faith.
> Bridegroom of your people,
> Your celestial beauty inspires us to sing your praises,
> You lift our voices with hymns of everlasting praise.
> *Clement of Alexandria, 'Hymn to Christ'*

standardizing of the narrative of institution, and the resurrection of a clause earlier rejected as too suburban ('He came to supper with his friends').

The main change was the abandoning of two of the features introduced by the Commission into the ICEL prayer. One was the optional congregational acclamation, 'To you be glory and praise for ever!', which could come at the end of almost every paragraph. The other was the rich provision of seasonal and thematic insertions at three points in the prayer. These underlined the prayer's Trinitarian structure, and have been replaced by standard, invariable lines – though the adventurous might have a go at rediscovering the richness of the original. The first point is the climax of the Father's dealings with his people ('When they turned away…'); the second is about the person of Christ ('He offered his life…'); the third is a prayer for the work of the Spirit ('As we eat and drink … form us…').

The main delight of this prayer, however, is in the evocative language, and it was this which persuaded Synod to vote for it. Here are some examples:

- **'All your works echo the silent music of your praise.'** 'Silent music' is paradoxical enough, let alone the idea that it gives an echo, but the imagery echoes our experience of God, who is simultaneously surrounded in the silence and awe of all creation in his presence, and yet is in a heaven which resounds to the shouts and songs of praise of a great company ceaselessly worshipping him. The phrase can be found in both John of the Cross in the sixteenth century and Boris Pasternak in the twentieth century, and evokes Psalm 19.

- **'The crown of all creation.'** Many Eucharistic prayers acknowledge either that God created us or that he created the universe, but it is rare to find a form of words which so neatly and evocatively gives us our place in creation. As the crown of creation, it is our duty to praise our creator – and it is all the more appalling that we turned away from him.

- **'As a mother tenderly gathers her children.'** Some have been alarmed that these lines promote the idea of God being our Mother. The image is biblical, however, coming from Jesus' words over Jerusalem (Matthew 23:37), and simply attributes to God the protective love which is true of a mother.

- **'Form us in the likeness of Christ, and build us into a living temple to your glory.'** These two much-loved metaphors from Ephesians came into Anglican liturgy through the Second Eucharistic Prayer of Rite A in the ASB. They add to the sense of interdependence in the whole business of growth to maturity in Christ.

This is a prayer which needs to be prayed slowly. It can be used for meditation and become part of our devotional life.

> From the beginning you have created all things
> and all your works echo the silent music of your praise.
> In the fullness of time you made us in your image,
> the crown of all creation.
>
> You give us breath and speech,
> that with angels and archangels
> and with all the powers of heaven
> we may find a voice to sing your praise:
>
> Holy, holy, holy…
>
> How wonderful the work of your hands, O Lord.
> As a mother tenderly gathers her children,
> you embraced a people as your own.
> When they turned away and rebelled
> your love remained steadfast.
> *From Eucharistic Prayer G*

Eucharistic Prayer H

The eighth Eucharistic Prayer in Order One, Prayer H, breaks new ground and in particular breaks new ground from the point of view of the congregation. It does not simply include dialogue between president and people, it is dialogue from beginning to end. President and people alternate like table-tennis players, and it is the alertness of the responses which will give flow to the whole prayer. Such a flow is not just alert dialogue, however, it is also prayer, a Eucharistic prayer, a prayer where the president leads and the people respond.

Whilst it is the responsiveness which is most distinctive of this Eucharistic prayer, there are other features worthy of notice and careful reflection.

- It is a short prayer. This is true of the actual count of 44 lines (which is just over half the length of the Rite A prayers, and still considerably shorter than the other new prayers), but the contrast is all the greater in actual use, as a responsive prayer is experienced by the congregation as flowing fast and thus quickly completed, whilst a monologue can seem interminably long. It is in the nature of the prayer that it should keep moving – it is not designed for long pauses, changes of posture or ceremonial excesses.
- It keeps classic Eucharistic prayer features, but presents them differently. There is a recitation of the 'Mighty Acts of God in

Christ', a narrative of institution, a form of anamnesis and an epiclesis. The *Sanctus* is there too, as a climax of praise – but at the very climax of the prayer, not just after the preface.

- It is deliberately drafted for informal and intimate occasions. It is for when 10 people are standing round a dining room table, or for when a PCC wants to have Communion in its warm meeting room instead of adjourning to a less welcoming 'official' church building. That does not mean it cannot be or should not be

Prayer H

It is right to praise you, Father, Lord of all
    creation;
in your love you made us for yourself.

When we turned away
you did not reject us,
but came to meet us in your Son.
You embraced us as your children
and welcomed us to sit and eat with you.

In Christ you shared our life
that we might live in him and he in us.
He opened his arms of love upon the cross
and made for all the perfect sacrifice for sin.

On the night he was betrayed,
at supper with his friends
he took bread, and gave you thanks;
he broke it and gave it to them, saying:
Take, eat; this is my body which is given for you;
do this in remembrance of me.
Father, we do this in remembrance of him:
his body is the bread of life.

At the end of supper, taking the cup of wine,
he gave you thanks, and said:
Drink this, all of you; this is my blood of the new covenant,
which is shed for you for the forgiveness of sins;
do this in remembrance of me.
Father, we do this in remembrance of him:
his blood is shed for all.

As we proclaim his death and celebrate his rising in glory,
send your Holy Spirit that this bread and this wine
may be to us the body and blood of your dear Son.

As we eat and drink these holy gifts
make us one in Christ, our risen Lord.

With your whole Church throughout the world
we offer you this sacrifice of praise
and lift our voice to join the eternal song of heaven:

Holy, holy, holy Lord,
God of power and might,
Heaven and earth are full of your glory.
Hosanna in the highest.

> **?** It is illegal to hold Communion services in private
> homes without the permission of the bishop.
> *(Canon B40)*

used on more formal occasions, it merely means that its central or mainstream use is in the less formal contexts.

- It is not written especially for when children are present. It is incidentally very child-friendly, but it was not written to make special concessions to a particular reading age. Its accessibility for the young (and many older people too) arises from the shortness of the attention span it requires from its participants.

Does it, therefore, trap the worshippers with their heads in a book? The answer to this must be no – no more than a hymn does, and it is a common experience with hymns that, as this or that hymn becomes familiar through being used several times in a year (but by no means every week), so people keep a book open but refer to it less and less. When the Revision Committee crafted this prayer, they deliberately sought to make the two-line responses fairly memorable, such that they could not only be acclaimed confidently in worship, but should also, by catching in the memory, carry a message into each participant's private life and personal spirituality. If you have been using this prayer, you might well check the impact the responding couplets have had on you.

> **Exclusive use of Prayer H**
> Should this prayer become the only use of a parish? No. For all its merits and usefulness, it does not include any regard for seasons of the year or changes of mood. It is a matter of pastoral discernment to judge when it should be employed in main Sunday Eucharists and when not. If its distinctive character proves so popular that people do not want to use other Eucharistic prayers, then there will be a need for further official alternative Eucharistic prayers written on the responsive principle.

CHAPTER 10

Services of the Word

'What should the Church do when it meets on Sundays?' If this was a vox pop question, what might the answers be?

'Take a collection.'
'Sing some hymns.'
'Have coffee.'
'Have Communion.'
'Spend time praying together.'
'Read the Bible.'

Other things might come to mind, such as praying for healing, doing some church business, planning for the church's mission, sorting out how to repair the roof, and deciding who is going to get involved in a particular piece of community action.

The basic agenda still revolves around those four things which the Church did immediately after the Day of Pentecost: 'They devoted themselves to the apostles' teaching and fellowship, to the breaking of bread and the prayers' (Acts 2:42).

When the Liturgical Commission discussed the future shape of Morning and Evening Prayer in the 1980s, a question was raised about whether the contents could be reduced to just a few words. The result of this may be seen in the instructions for A Service of the Word in *Patterns for Worship*:

- This may be a service on its own or lead into the Holy Communion.
- There should be a balance between the four main ingredients:

    word – prayer – praise – action.

This basic pattern emerged through the Synod process as A Service of the Word, first authorized in 1993. It is simply a set of instructions, with notes, showing how to put a Word service together. As the note at the beginning of the service says, 'It provides a structure for daily prayer, for Sunday services and for services of an occasional nature.' It is from this authorized structure that the other services in this section of *Common Worship* flow, as well as other services such as Family Services, put together with the aid of *Patterns for Worship* or the computer programme *Visual Liturgy*.

Word and sacrament

Another possible function of A Service of the Word is to be the first half of Holy Communion. In the three ancient strands of worship, the Word service was the first part of Holy Communion. It was, therefore, natural for the Liturgical Commission, in producing the first (Synod) edition of *Patterns* in 1989, to argue that we should 'regard word services of different structures as an interchangeable first part of

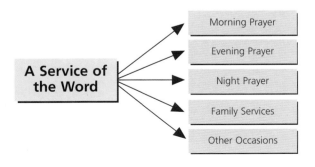

Holy Communion'. The flexible service (Rite C) of that book has been replaced in *Common Worship* with 'A Service of the Word with a celebration of Holy Communion'. This is even more flexible and carries the warning, 'Not normally to be used as the regular Sunday or weekday service'.

Word services for Sundays

As well as the modern offices of Morning and Evening Prayer on Sundays deriving from A Service of the Word, this section of *Common Worship: Services and Prayers for the Church of England* also includes a form of the 1662 services of Morning and Evening Prayer, and contemporary and traditional language versions of Night Prayer. This popular, late-evening service, often called Compline, is one in which we commend ourselves and one another to God at the end of the day before going to bed. As the introductory note says, it works best if it really is the last thing before bed, and not followed by more chatter! In this section there are also other resources such as the Litany and Prayers for Various Occasions.

CONNECTIONS

▷ **Three ancient strands of worship –** pp.180–81

Word services in the early Church

When the earliest Christians went together day by day, as the Acts of the Apostles says, to the Temple in Jerusalem for prayers, the ingredients of the daily worship probably included prayers, psalms, readings from the Scriptures and explanations of them. There is a debate as to how far the Jewish synagogue pattern of daily prayer at morning, afternoon and evening influenced the early Church, because the Jewish evidence largely comes only from ninth-century texts.

Three strands

The pattern of Christian daily prayer evolved into three strands:

1. **The Word service.** Justin Martyr writes in the middle of the second century of a service in two parts. The second part is what we would today call the 'liturgy of the sacrament'. The first part majors on readings from the prophets or memoirs of the apostles, 'read for as long as time allows', followed by a discourse and common prayer.
2. **Daily prayer.** Hippolytus' Apostolic Tradition emphasizes the times of prayer. To the early core of fixed psalms, hymns and songs, with intercessions, are added many introductory prayers, the continuous recitation of the Psalter, readings from the Scriptures and other Christian writings.
3. **The teaching.** This focuses on instruction in

the Word of God, a Bible study with no particular liturgical shape.

Thomas Cranmer

In the Middle Ages, the daily prayer pattern predominated. When Thomas Cranmer became Archbishop of Canterbury in 1533, he realized that much of what ordinary people knew about

The sleeping congregation (Hogarth)

> If we offer the sacrifice of praise unceasingly and prayer without intermission, every day is a festival to the Lord: our prayer ascends like incense in the morning; the lifting up of our hands like an evening oblation.
>
> *Origen, Homily on Numbers 23*

God they learned from wall paintings and stained glass, with a mixture of stories from lives of the saints and the Bible. The services were all said or sung in Latin, according to very complicated rules (see the Preface to the 1552 Prayer Book).

When Cranmer made his skilful amalgamation of eight Latin medieval services into the two Word-based services of Morning and Evening Prayer, the expectation was that everyone would come every day to church: that was why the parson had to ring the bell to summon the congregation. It did not work, however, and Morning and Evening Prayer were used on weekdays by the clergy and on Sundays by the whole Church.

The Book of Common Prayer – ASB

It was these services (enshrined in the Prayer Book of 1662) which lasted for well over 350 years. There have been few attempts to change the pattern. The 1872 Act allowed abbreviated services for daily use, and for a 'third service' on Sundays. The 1928 proposed Prayer Book included the old services of Prime and Compline in its Appendix. In 1968, the interdenominational Joint Liturgical Group produced *The Daily Office*, which influenced the services of Morning and Evening Prayer in the ASB. While the structure remained broadly as it had been since 1549, there was now a wider range of seasonal material, a new way of reading through the Psalms regularly and some modern canticles and collects.

Shorter Morning and Evening Prayer in the ASB provided a more accessible option for some and, whilst based on the work of the Joint Liturgical Group, were not quite the same as the services descended from 1549.

Cranmer's Preface to the 1552 *Book of Common Prayer*

It is more profitable; because here are left out many things, whereof some are untrue, some uncertain, some vain and superstitious; and nothing is ordained to be read, but the very pure word of God, the holy Scriptures, or that which is agreeable to the same; and that in such a language and order as is most easy and plain for the understanding of both the readers and hearers. It is also more commodious; both for the shortness thereof, and for plainness of the order, and for that the rules be few and easy.

CONNECTIONS
▣ **Cranmer's Prayer Books** – pp.94–5
▣ **'Third' services and Family Services** – pp.182–3
▣ **Further detail of Cranmer's daily offices** – pp.196–7

All-age worship and the 'directory' approach

The 'third' service

The 1851 Religious Census revealed the need for changes in the rules about worship if the Church of England was going to reach the 'unchurched millions'. This led to the 1872 Act of Uniformity Amendment Act, which allowed Morning and Evening Prayer to be shortened and permitted a 'third service' on special occasions, so long as it contained only the words of the Bible and the Prayer Book, plus hymns. Under pressure, the Convocations in 1892 allowed the use of other material 'substantially in agreement with Scripture and the Prayer Book'.

The twentieth century

This, together with the blossoming Sunday School movement at the end of the nineteenth century, paved the way for special services for 'children's churches' from the 1930s onwards, and the development of 'Family Services' from the 1960s. In the last three decades of the twentieth century there were said to be far more people worshipping in Family Services, which were scarcely recognizable as falling within the provisions of the 1872 Act, than there were at the statutory services. Some of the reasons for the popularity of the Family Service were recognized by the Liturgical Commission in *Patterns for Worship*:

- It provides a place where those unfamiliar with formal worship can begin to feel at home.
- It can be a bridge, reflecting local culture more easily than the rest of the Church's worship.
- People welcome the excuse to accompany their children, and then find they understand teaching which is simple and visual.
- It is a place where genuine intergenerational

In 1857 at St John's, Portsea, in a former circus building, experimental services were held in which: 'After singing two verses of the National Anthem, the more instructive and generally interesting portions of the newspapers were read ... A hymn is then sung, and a portion of the Bible read and expounded. Another hymn is sung, and a prayer offered ... The meeting concludes with a doxology.'

W.N. Yates, Buildings, Faith and Worship, Clarendon Press, 1991

activity takes place, with adults and children learning from each other in worship.
- It provides an opportunity for people to grow and use their gifts by sharing in planning, leading and contributing to worship.

Q: Who can lead A Service of the Word?

THE LAW AND **A:** Any suitable person who is invited to do so by the minister, says Canon B11.1: 'Readers, such other lay persons as may be authorized by the bishop, or some other suitable lay person, may, at the invitation of the minister of the parish … say or sing Morning or Evening Prayer.' A Service of the Word is the authorized alternative to these services, and also to the first part of Holy Communion.

an outline service (which made clear which parts of the service were essential and where authorized material had to be used – the Creeds, for example) and a wide variety of resources.

The result was the production of *Patterns for Worship* in 1989, eventually commended by the House of Bishops and published in 1995. Significantly, the working title until a year before publication was 'The Directory', dropped because it was a bit too close to the Westminster *Directory* of 1645, another set of instructions for public worship. But the idea of producing outlines, instructions and resources was simply a development from the Commission's earlier seasonal resource book, *Lent – Holy Week – Easter.*

A Worship Action Group

Some churches encourage different people to be involved in preparing worship by having a Worship Action Group. The title implies activity, which 'Worship Committee' might not, and WAG reads better than WC. Based on *Patterns for Worship*, possible terms of reference might be:

- To review and evaluate all aspects of worship including:
  - structures and patterns of worship on Sunday
  - the relationship between the worship, the preaching programme and the rest of the life of the church
  - the use of music and drama
  - the place of children and other groups.
- To be responsible for the planning and preparation of Sunday worship. This might be every week or once a month.
- To ensure that the varied gifts of the congregation are being used in worship.
- To plan developments and to prepare for regular PCC discussion of worship.

The Directory

There were, however, anxieties being expressed about whether such services might be in danger both of departing from the Anglican doctrinal norm and also of creating an individualistic or pietistic Family Service culture, which failed to provide a bridge to anything that was recognizably Anglican in worship. The Commission suggested to the House of Bishops that the best way of handling the problem of combining common prayer with local freedom, both with all-age services and in meeting the needs of the inner urban areas, would be to produce a 'Directory', containing instructions for

CONNECTIONS
☒ The Westminster *Directory* – p.27

The structure of A Service of the Word

The basic structure of A Service of the Word is very simple and very ancient. Worship begins with the gathering of a group of people who intend to worship. This is recognized in some kind of invitation and response between leader and people, a call to worship which may be echoed in hymn or introit. The service moves on to focus on the Word of God, but to prepare for that there will sometimes be prayers of penitence, to clear the way and to make our hearts ready for hearing what God is saying. The proclamation of the Word is followed by a response which may take the form of an expression of faith and commitment, prayer and praise, or penitence if that has not come earlier.

The service ends with a dismissal, a 'sending forth' or a blessing, any of which express the need to carry with us into the world the challenging and comforting presence of the God who is in our midst.

How to listen to a sermon

So there you are, sitting in the quiet oasis of the church sermon. What do you think about? Review the past week? List things to do? Panic about Sunday dinner? Get diverted by other distractions – those around you, or the preacher's annoying style of delivery? Learning from continuous talking is not easy, so try this:

1. Before
- Pray for the preacher.
- Believe that God has something to say to you; expect him to meet you.
- Be open to the Spirit.

2. During
- Don't try to remember everything: work out one point to take away from church with you. Not all the congregation will take the same point away.
- Try to get hold of the structure of the sermon: look for the links between the different points.
- Don't think about how good this message is for Sarah-Jane: focus on how it links with your own experience and expectations.
- If the preacher is expounding a Bible text, it may help to have the text in front of you, either in the Bible or the printed service sheets some churches use.

3. After
- Turn the point of a sermon into a prayer and a commitment: what does God want me to do?
- Make use of the way in which the theme of the sermon links with the prayers and worship which follow. Sometimes the minister can helpfully underline the main point of the sermon in the first part of the blessing which concludes the service.
- Share and discuss the theme of the sermon with others who heard it, or tell it to others, perhaps those at home who did not hear it. Discuss the sermon, not the preacher.

How it works

The authorized introduction to the service stresses the need for careful choices and planning: 'The primary object in the careful planning and leading of the service is the spiritual direction which enables the whole congregation to come into the presence of God to give him glory.' Those planning the service need to have a firm grasp of the structure, laid out in the following chart, amplified by explanatory notes:

The Preparation	
Greeting	Note 1 suggests different ways of starting the service.
Prayers of Penitence	These must be authorized, and may come here or in the prayers.
(A song, or a set of responses)	If the service is similar to Morning Prayer, the *Venite* might be sung; if it is part of the Holy Communion, *Kyrie* or *Gloria* come here.
Collect	Either here or in the prayers

The Ministry of the Word	
Readings from Holy Scripture	Note 5 allows for readings to be reduced to one, and allows them to be dramatized or sung.
A psalm, or scriptural song	
A sermon	Note 7 says this includes the use of drama, interviews, discussion, audiovisuals and the insertion of hymns between parts of the sermon.
Creed or Affirmation of Faith	Must be an authorized text.

The Prayers	
Intercessions and thanksgivings	
The Lord's Prayer	

The Conclusion	
Liturgical ending	Note 10 says there must be a clear ending, which might be the Peace, the Grace, or a suitable ascription or blessing.

 Notes for lesson readers

- Give the page number if there are Bibles in the pews (specifying Old or New Testament, if the numbering starts from the beginning in both).
- Announce the reading in this order: book, chapter, verse.
- Read a little louder and more slowly than you would in normal conversation.
- Try to catch the mood of the passage as well as the message. Different parts of Scripture suggest very different treatments to express the descriptive, the poetic, the dramatic and the intimate.
- End simply, with 'This is the word of the Lord', to which the congregation responds, '**Thanks be to God**.'

CONNECTIONS
⊠ History of
A Service of
the Word –
pp.180–81
⊠ Using A
Service of
the Word –
pp.188–9

Morning and Evening Prayer on Sundays

...in traditional language

One of Cranmer's skills in compiling Morning and Evening Prayer, while using ancient texts and structures, was to invite the participants to take part in a spiritual conversation. We listen to God speaking – in the opening sentence, the invitation to confession and the readings; and we respond – with confession, a prayer that God will open our lips, and the canticles and Creed after the readings, one canticle suitable for the Old Testament, one for the New.

This to-and-fro movement in the liturgy is very basic and simple, but one that engages our attention. Those who construct more modern 'all-age services' sometimes talk in terms of 'presentation' and 'response' units as the building blocks for worship. Cranmer did it first, so it is good that his services, in traditional language, are there as part of the Church's *Common Worship*.

Simple to use

Early in the discussions about *Common Worship* it was decided to include services in both modern and traditional language, thus gathering the worship of the Church into one volume. The format and style of the Prayer Book is often difficult for visitors and newcomers to follow, and so BCP-style Morning and Evening Prayer are presented in the way that they are most frequently used. The spoken words are the same as in the Prayer Book. The text is as clear and simple as possible. Headings and short rubrics make the structure of the services stand out, and the texts are printed in short lines for clarity and for ease of saying aloud. Lesser-used options are signalled by rubric, but have been taken out of the main text.

...in modern language

These orders for Morning and Evening Prayer on Sundays are designed to be flexible outworkings of A Service of the Word. They are suitable for a wide range of contexts, from a simple form of prayer for individual or small-group use to a principal service playing a key part in the Christian formation of the congregation. They carry worshippers through three main phases – preparing for worship, hearing God's Word and

praying for God's world – and then conclude with a blessing, the grace or the peace. As principal services they can be very full, with confession and absolution, a psalm and two readings, a Creed or affirmation of faith and a sermon, together with hymns and songs. On other occasions – providing the essential movement of Preparation, Word and Prayer is followed – they may be pared down to much more simple forms.

Dialogue and response

The important thing is to follow the essential movement of Preparation, Word and Prayer and to allow the interweaving of Word and response to take place. It is this interweaving that gives the services their traditional 'office' feel of a continuing dialogue between God and the people.

The people pray for forgiveness, God forgives. God's Word is proclaimed, the people praise and pray. The people who gather to worship are then sent out into the world with God's blessing.

This ancient pattern has been developed in at least two distinctive ways in these services:

- The first is the simple encouragement to use the time following the readings creatively, as an opportunity to respond to God's Word in different ways. This space for the Spirit to ignite the Word in our hearts is then caught up in the traditional climax to the readings in the office – the Song of Zechariah (*Benedictus*) in the morning and the Song of Mary (*Magnificat*) in the evening. And remember that songs are best sung! There is a great range of musical settings for these great scriptural praises available today and, of course, metrical versions can also be used.

- The other distinctive way in which these services encourage response to God's Word is through a number of Thanksgivings that can follow on after the readings. Again very flexible, they can be used simply as different endings to the service or more fully as opportunities for testimony, rededication, ministry of healing or commissioning for evangelism and other acts of Christian mission.

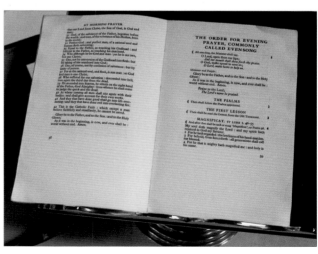

CONNECTIONS
☒ The influence
of religious
communities –
pp.108–9

Using A Service of the Word on Sundays

A Service of the Word has certain elements that are mandatory and several basic structures that can be used as the skeleton for the service. Beyond that there is a lot of scope for improvising and customizing. Here are some ideas to start with, based around the four constituent elements of the service:

- Word
- Prayer
- Praise
- Action

Some of the following appear more suitable for all-age worship than for an adult Service of the Word – planners will need to be discerning – though many so-called 'all-age' features work well in adult services too.

Word

- A Bible reading can be dramatized by being acted out – usually this requires quite a bit of rehearsal.
- A narrative passage can be read by different people taking each of the characters, plus someone as narrator.
- If the passage has a structure that lends itself to being spoken by several different voices, people can be placed around the building (see the example from Genesis 1).
- A group can perform a simple dance or mime to accompany the reading of a passage by one person.
- Music played quietly underneath the reading of a passage can be effective.
- Pictures can be projected onto a wall or screen to accompany the reading of the passage.
- Sermons can include testimony, visual material, drama and discussion groups (if preaching on a healing miracle, why not interview a doctor from the congregation, someone who has been ill, or someone who has experience of healing?). *Patterns for Worship* offers other ideas too.

A Christingle service can be based
on A Service of the Word

Genesis 1 for several voices
Reader 1: *God said, 'Let there be light,' and there was light.*
Reader 2: *And God saw that the light was good, and God separated the light from the darkness.*
Reader 3: *God called the light Day and the darkness he called Night.*
All: *And there was evening and there was morning, the first day.*
(Or you could have a different person read each 'day' of creation, with the congregation responding each time, 'And there was evening…')

Prayer

- Intercessions can be led by two people or a group.
- There are many examples of responsive intercessions available in the various *Common Worship* resources, and it is also possible to write your own. (If there is a response in the intercessions, people need to be told what it is, as well as what the cue phrase is, or it needs to be printed – on the notice sheet, for example.)
- Begin by inviting suggestions for intercession topics – this needs careful leading to stop it becoming the notices! It also needs a leader who can weave the suggestions into meaningful intercessions.
- A sung response (e.g. a Taizé chant) can be used.
- Pictures, photographs and other visual material can be used as an aid to prayer.
- Ask the congregation to break into groups for prayer if people are used to that.
- End the intercessions with the Lord's Prayer or a collect, if it is appropriate.

Praise

- Remember that praise can be sung or spoken.
- There might be a block of singing at some points in the service.
- Thanksgivings and acclamations can be used.
- A short acclamation can be used repeatedly throughout the service, as a kind of theme song. It would not need to be printed out each time – teach it once and use it at appropriate moments unannounced – children and adults will soon get the hang of it.

Action

Action can either feature on its own, or accompany other parts of the service. Some examples:
- Sharing the Peace.
- Moving in a procession, with a purpose (buildings that are too large for the regular congregation are especially good for this because there is room to move and somewhere to go).

> **Example of a short acclamation**
> This is the day that the Lord has made!
> **We will rejoice and be glad in it!**
>
> This could be used at the start of the service, at the Peace, as part of the blessing, in a block of praise material, etc.

Sharing the Peace

- Writing on pieces of paper things we are sorry about, carefully collecting the papers and burning them.
- Drawing pictures and cutting out pictures from newspapers to make a 'prayer collage' on a big board.
- Asking everyone to write their name on a paper 'brick'; these are then built into a 'church' on a board (see 1 Corinthians 3:9).
- Creating an Easter garden as part of a Good Friday all-age service.
- Making a Christingle, as an integral part of a Christingle service.

Remember to make sure:

1. that the action is safe (especially if candles, etc., are involved).
2. that the action is appropriate and does not feel demeaning or trivial.

CONNECTIONS
◉ The structure of A Service of the Word – pp.184–5
◉ The four main ingredients of A Service of the Word – pp.178–9
◉ Prayers, Litanies and Thanksgivings – pp.192–3

Affirmations of faith and Penitential Prayers

Credal statements

The requirement for candidates for baptism to confess their faith, beginning with the simple 'Jesus is Lord' of 1 Corinthians 12:3 and later developing into the Apostles' Creed, led to creeds being part of worship early in the life of the Christian Church. When Councils of the Church defined further statements of faith in opposition to heretics, these statements too found a place in worship by the early sixth century. In our worship today, they are not so much a test for heresy as an opportunity to respond to the Word of God in readings and sermon and to praise God for who he is.

The Apostles', Nicene and Athanasian Creeds are all authorized for use in the Church of England. The Affirmations of Faith section of *Common Worship* contains different versions of these Creeds, such as:

- the question and answer version of the Apostles' Creed – the version used in the Initiation Services
- a responsive version of the Nicene Creed, with the responses getting shorter towards the end as it moves towards a climax.

There is also a short alternative affirmation of faith, now brought into line with the alternative profession of faith in the Initiation Services.

A credal hymn

We believe in God the Father,
God almighty, by whose plan
earth and heaven sprang to being,
all created things began.
We believe in Christ the Saviour,
Son of God in human frame,
virgin-born, the child of Mary
upon whom the Spirit came.

Part of Timothy Dudley-Smith's hymn based on the Apostles' Creed, first published in Patterns for Worship

From the Athanasian Creed

We proclaim the Church's faith in Jesus Christ

We believe and declare that our Lord Jesus Christ, the Son of God, is both divine and human.

God, of the being of the Father,
the only Son from before time began;
human from the being of his mother,
   born in the world;
fully God and fully human;
human in both mind and body.

As God he is equal to the Father,
as human he is less than the Father.
Although he is both divine and human
he is not two beings but one Christ.

From a translation of part of the Athanasian Creed

Q. Can we use a credal hymn instead of the Creed?

THE LAW AND **A.** Not unless it has been authorized.

In both A Service of the Word and Holy Communion the Creed may be omitted on weekdays, so it clearly does not make the service invalid in any way. On Sundays, however, there is no provision for omitting the Creed and using a credal hymn instead, other than the authorized one by Timothy Dudley-Smith or one of the texts of Scripture. Where an unauthorized credal hymn is used on a Sunday it might well follow one of the shorter affirmations of faith.

- Some new pieces of writing explore the penitential themes in Psalm 51, Isaiah 6, Hosea 6 and Luke 15.
- Some are responsive, like a litany of confession.
- The absolutions are roughly designed to match the confessions in style and theme; so the word 'heal' is in both the first confession and the first absolution, the fifth one of each is trinitarian in theme, and so on.
- Some of the absolutions have 'us', some 'you' in the declaration of forgiveness, in each case printed in italics to show that they can be changed. This recognizes that many services are taken by laypeople and that many priests now want to include themselves by using 'us'.
- Instead of one of the set confessions, the *Kyrie* ('Lord, have mercy') may be used, with penitential sentences between the responses.

In addition to baptismal and conciliar Creeds, there is a third kind of ancient Creed, the credal hymn. Probably the first example of this is Philippians 2:5–11, and this is joined in *Common Worship* by a number of other thematic and seasonal texts from Scripture. The Commission had discussed the possibility of authorizing one or two more modern credal hymns as part of its proposals, but concluded that even something like Newman's 'Firmly I believe and truly' was too far away from the text of any of the Creeds. So the hymn 'We believe in God the Father', a metrical version of the Apostles' Creed, was specially commissioned, and Bishop Timothy Dudley-Smith wrote it in August 1989.

Confessions and absolutions

Sixteen different forms of confession and absolution are provided in the supplementary material for A Service of the Word. Drawn largely from *Patterns for Worship* and *The Promise of His Glory*, they break new ground in a number of ways:

Father,
we have sinned against heaven and against you.
We are not worthy to be called your children.
We turn to you again.
Have mercy on us,
bring us back to yourself
as those who once were dead
but now have life through Christ our Lord. Amen.
A confession based on Luke 15

Prayers, litanies and thanksgivings

Prayer in church is different from praying on our own. It helps us to have some kind of structure to enable us to pray together. One way is to have set prayers, with an 'Amen' (literally 'so be it') at the end to show that the congregation agree. Another alternative is a litany, where the leader mentions a matter for prayer (a 'bidding'), followed by silent prayer and a short sentence to sum up the prayer, which leads into a united response from the congregation. There are prayers of both these sorts in the main volume of *Common Worship*, both in the section called Prayers for Various Occasions and in the intercession index to the Holy Communion services. Sometimes such prayers are constructed so that they can be said without any break or response, as one continuous whole.

There are several advantages to a litany form:

- It is more flexible, and therefore it is easier to include local or topical items.
- People can use the spaces for saying their own prayers, either silently or out loud, for example by mentioning people's names.
- It provides an opportunity for continual checking up that the congregation are in agreement with the prayer (and keeping awake!) by allowing them to join in the response.

A new petition in the Litany

Bring your joy to all families;
strengthen and deliver those in childbirth,
watch over children and guide the young,
bring reconciliation to families in discord
and peace to those in stress.
Lord have mercy.

How the General Thanksgiving was used in one north London church during the 1861 revival

'It would be difficult to exaggerate the extraordinary visitation of supernatural power, which brought the most hardened to their knees, pouring forth a torrent of supplication which astonished experienced Christians.'

Morning Prayer on Sunday saw 'the introduction, Sunday after Sunday, into the General Thanksgiving, of numerous clauses, some of them most touchingly worded, from those who desire to praise God for the great spiritual mercies vouchsafed to them.'

The structure of a collect

Collects usually follow this pattern:

- **Who?** The address to God ('Almighty God…')
- **Why?** Something about God on which to base this request ('by whose grace we are … called')
- **What?** A definite request ('strengthen us by your Spirit'), sometimes with a reason ('that…')
- **How?** The ending ('through Jesus Christ…') explains how we dare to expect God to answer prayer, and everyone says they agree ('Amen').

The 'state' prayer

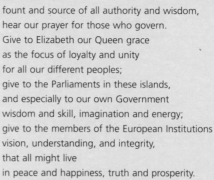

Eternal God,
fount and source of all authority and wisdom,
hear our prayer for those who govern.
Give to Elizabeth our Queen grace
as the focus of loyalty and unity
for all our different peoples;
give to the Parliaments in these islands,
and especially to our own Government
wisdom and skill, imagination and energy;
give to the members of the European Institutions
vision, understanding, and integrity,
that all might live
in peace and happiness, truth and prosperity.
Through Jesus Christ our Lord. Amen.

Litanies

The chanting of litanies in procession is said to have been started by St Chrysostom in Constantinople as a counter-attraction to heretical Arian processions at the end of the fourth century. By the mid fifth century these praying processions were known in Gaul as 'rogations', hence our 'rogation days'. Our Prayer Book Litany was compiled by Cranmer in 1544 (and slightly retouched in subsequent years), drawing on the Litany of Gregory the Great and those from Sarum and York in use in this country. It was this Litany which the compilers of the ASB took and amended. Both the sixteenth-century and the twentieth-century versions are in *Common Worship*, with one or two changes made to the ASB version (see 'A new petition in the Litany').

Preparing for a litany

- Make sure that the phrase at the end of each summary section is the same, or is followed by an identical phrase in each case, so that the congregation know when to make their response.
- Introduce the litany by echoing the first line: 'We pray to the Lord (of the harvest, etc.), saying… (give the words of the cue and response, which can then be repeated with the congregation joining in the response part)'.
- Explain to the congregation how to use the silences for prayer.

General Thanksgiving

The General Thanksgiving in *Common Worship* is from *The Book of Common Prayer*, written in 1662 by the writer of popular devotional material, Edward Reynolds, Bishop of Norwich. The Liturgical Commission both wrote and considered modern alternatives, but felt that none could stand comparison with the 1662 prayer in terms of language, compactness and all-embracing concern for spiritual reality.

CHAPTER 11

Daily prayer

Morning and Evening Prayer

Light and darkness, day and night, are part of the world we experience all the time, but we really only become aware of them at their moments of passing. Times of change or transition are important to us as human beings and we need to respond to such moments in a concrete way. In the rhythm of daily life, morning and evening can be moments of change in which our hearts naturally move towards God in praise, in confession and in the renewal of our love. The Christian tradition of Morning and Evening Prayer has its roots in this Godward response at the great moments of dawn and dusk.

An ancient custom

Daily prayer has always been an intrinsic part of the life of the Church, but not always as we know it now. From the earliest days the baptized 'devoted themselves to the apostles' teaching and fellowship, to the breaking of bread and the prayers' (Acts 2:42). The tradition stemmed from synagogue worship and the domestic pattern familiar to Jewish people. From the Gospel accounts it can be seen that the disciples had longed for Jesus to give them guidance for their prayers (Luke 11:1). His reply beginning, 'When you pray…' is one applicable to a culture in which prayer was the usual pattern of life. Such a pattern was then continued by the early Christians as they rejoiced in their access to God the Father through Christ his Son.

Hours and offices

Services of prayer and praise, said at specific times of each day, came to be called 'services of the hours' or 'offices' (from the Latin *officium*, meaning service or duty). From early days these would have incorporated prayer with Psalms and Christian hymns.

Complexity

Daily prayer developed throughout the centuries and, by the sixteenth century, some complex and demanding patterns had taken shape, as represented by the monastic offices in England, which were said several times a day in Latin. Cranmer's intention at the Reformation was to make the daily offices accessible to laypeople in the hope that they would make them part of their pattern of prayer. He reduced them from eight to only two – Morning and Evening Prayer – drawing from five of the old services. They were written in English so that everybody could understand. Morning and Evening Prayer revolved around continuous and systematic Bible reading and psalmody, supported by canticles, prayer and the Apostles' Creed.

From the very beginning of the Church of England, ordained ministers have been charged with saying daily prayer, both morning and evening, and with making such prayer not only a feature of their own life but part of the worshipping life of the people of the church in which they minister.

CONNECTIONS
⊞ Morning
and Evening
Prayer in
traditional
language –
pp.186–7
▷ More about
Thomas
Cranmer's
daily offices –
pp.196–7

Beginnings and buildings

The first Christians were Jews and they continued in a pattern of daily prayer familiar to them from Judaism, following a style of corporate prayer and the reading of Scripture that was well known from home, the synagogue and the Temple. Here lie the roots of individual and corporate Christian prayer.

The early Church

Hippolytus (c. AD 170–236), an important leader of the Church in Rome, gives us a glimpse into early habits of prayer: 'Let every faithful man and woman, when they have risen from sleep in the morning, before they touch any work at all, wash their hands and pray to God, and so go to their work.'

If Christians were at home they were to pray aloud or, if they were elsewhere, secretly, also at the third, sixth and ninth hours (9 a.m., 12 noon

and 3 p.m.), before they went to bed, at midnight with their spouses, and at cockcrow – quite a tall order! In addition to these seven times of private prayer, the church met for corporate prayer in the morning and at the lighting of the evening lamps. Christians were encouraged by Hippolytus to be present at these times.

House of prayer

The New Testament reveals that early Christians living beyond Jerusalem met in synagogues, if they were accepted, as well as in their homes. Temple worship was not essential and St Paul even went so far as to say that each believer is the temple of God, where the Spirit dwells as he calls them to lead holy lives. The first Christians were also expecting the imminent return of Christ, and had no reason to build their own places of worship. As time went on, the oppression of Roman government would have squashed such plans flat in any case.

The conversion in AD 312 of the Emperor Constantine (c. AD 274–337) led to a dramatic reversal in the Church's fortunes. No longer persecuted, growing in numbers and officially supported by the state, the Church built splendid and imposing churches and cathedrals in which Morning and Evening Prayer became the regular public services.

Thomas Cranmer and the Reformation

Although Cranmer was influenced by the continental reformers, his work on the daily offices was quite

The cathedral is the mother church of a diocese and, as such, houses the bishop's throne (the Greek word for which is *cathedra*). In the early centuries the bishop's throne was placed centrally in the apse, with seats for presbyters on both sides. In Northern Europe in the Middle Ages, a series of chapels were built at the east end of cathedral churches and the *cathedra* was brought to one side of the sanctuary or chancel. 'Quire' or 'choir' was the term used to designate this area for the clergy. Under the influence of the Oxford Movement and in an attempt to enhance the singing in worship, robed (musical) choirs were moved into the (architectural) choir. 'Quire/choir dress' – the appropriate attire for the clergy in this area – also became the attire of the musicians. Hence the practice began of choirs wearing surplices.

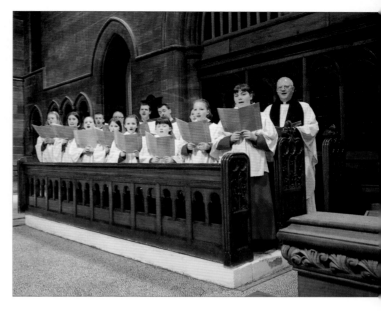

unique. He fused material from five of the medieval offices from the Sarum Breviary into his Morning and Evening Prayer.

How Cranmer reformed the medieval services

- Eight daily services in Latin became two daily services in English, incorporating and combining material from the old services of the hours.

Cranmer's Orders of Service and their monastic roots

Morning Prayer	from	Evening Prayer	from
Lord's Prayer	**Matins**	Lord's Prayer	**Vespers**
Versicles	**Matins**	Versicles	**Vespers**
Gloria	**Matins**	Gloria	**Vespers**
Venite	**Matins**	-	-
Psalms	**Matins**	Psalms	**Vespers**
OT Lesson	**Matins**	OT Lesson	**Vespers**
Te Deum	**Matins**	Magnificat	**Vespers**
NT Lesson	**Lauds**	NT Lesson	**Compline**
Benedictus	**Lauds**	Nunc Dimittis	**Compline**
Kyrie	**Prime**	Kyrie	**Vespers**
Creed	**Prime**	Creed	**Vespers**
Lord's Prayer	**Prime**	Lord's Prayer	**Vespers**
Precis	**Lauds**	Precis	**Vespers**
Collect of the Day	**Lauds**	Collect of the Day	**Vespers**
Collect for Peace	**Lauds**	Collect for Peace	**Vespers**
Collect for Grace	**Prime**	Collect for Aid	**Compline**

- Consecutive reading of the Bible was introduced, so that the Old Testament was read once and the New Testament three times each year.
- Psalms were repeated on a daily basis, and the whole Psalter was covered each month.
- The services were in English, with clear structures and simple rules to follow.

Cranmer was also very gifted at editing, translating and rewriting material, from the Latin rites (the *Te Deum*, the second and third collects, for example), Greek sources (the prayer of St Chrysostom in his 1544 Litany was included in Morning and Evening Prayer in 1662, for example) and from continental reformed services (the absolution, for example), as well as composing some beautiful new prayers himself (the General Confession, based on Romans 7:8–25, for example).

It says much for the enduring quality of Cranmer's work that his Evening Prayer, in particular, continues to be much loved by many and that much of the 'traditional' language in *Common Worship* is Cranmer's work, still valued by English Christians today.

CONNECTIONS
◁ The monastic offices – pp.194–5
◙ Three strands of early Christian daily prayer – pp.180–81
◙ Cranmer's Prayer Books – pp.94–5

Renewed interest in daily prayer

The latter years of the twentieth century saw a swing back towards corporate Christian daily prayer. Many Christians struggle to pray alone and find the discipline of meeting with others to pray a tremendous encouragement and help. A major challenge remains to find the best times to suit those who would like to pray. *The Alternative Service Book 1980* followed *The Book of Common Prayer* in expecting daily prayer during the week to be the same as Morning and Evening Prayer on Sundays. This has proved to be unworkable or inappropriate for many, however, and a number of alternatives have emerged.

This renewed interest in daily prayer is reflected in the wide range of publications and influences which have come to the fore. Here are some of the resources which have greatly enriched the prayer of the Church.

J.S Bach's family share in morning prayers

Celebrating Common Prayer
The Daily Office SSF is the daily prayer book of the Franciscan communities. When it was published in 1994 as *Celebrating Common Prayer* it received a very warm welcome from many who were looking for a more substantial and varied diet than that provided by Morning and Evening Prayer in *The Alternative Service Book*. It has become widely used, and some of its material has been incorporated into *Common Worship*.

The main offices are Morning and Evening Prayer, with additional orders for Midday and Night Prayer. There is a vast range of alternative canticles and other resources, and a scheme of seasonal material to enhance the celebration of the Church's year.

Celtic prayer
Characteristics of Celtic prayer include:
● a holistic approach to life, faith and environment

> **A Celtic prayer for protection**
> Be the eye of God dwelling with you,
> The foot of Christ in guidance with you,
> The shower of the Spirit pouring on you,
> Richly and generously.
> *From* Threshold of Light, *ed. A.M. Allchin and Esther de Waal, Darton, Longman and Todd, 1986*

- a deep sense of the rhythms of life
- an awareness of God's action in the ordinary things
- a wonder at creation and God's glory shown through it
- the need for God's protection and guarding in a world shot through with danger.

The latter part of the twentieth century saw renewed interest in the spirituality associated with Celtic Christianity, echoing as it does the concerns of many in the Church today.

Taizé

Extended chanting of short, harmonized phrases, lengthy silences, a chairless space, creative lighting, icons and symbols ... all are characteristics of Taizé worship. Taizé is a monastic community in France, welcoming thousands of young (and not so young) people to stay every year and to join the brothers in daily prayer. Much of the impact of their meditative worship lies in the contemplative repetition of simple chants, interspersed with solo verses and accompanied by simple yet soaring instrumental arrangements. The words are sung over and over until they penetrate the whole personality. The founder of the community explains it like this: 'Nothing is more conducive to communion with the living God than a meditative common prayer with, at its high point, singing that never ends and that continues in the silence of one's heart when one is alone again' (Brother Roger, *Prayer for Each Day*, Cassell, 1998).

Whilst it is hard to emulate that sense of community, which undoubtedly contributes to the tremendous impact Taizé has on those who visit the brothers, many have used the meditative style of worship to great effect in parish churches. Having versatile lighting and flexible furniture all lend themselves to a recreation of the Taizé environment, although even a single chant interspersed throughout the intercession or during the administration of Communion can raise our worship heavenwards.

Daily Prayer from the Diocese of Durham

This neat pack of little booklets was initially produced in the Durham diocese to assist the daily prayer of both clergy and laity, both individually and collectively. Having been well received, it was published with a commendation from the Bishop of Durham in 1998 to make it more widely available. The services are relatively straightforward to use, whilst drawing on a rich store of texts from the Bible and the Church's tradition, as well as offering seasonal variety. There is a separate booklet for each season of the Christian year, plus others containing supplementary material for additional times of prayer, material for saints' days and holy days, and readings to carry when travelling (it is lighter than a Bible, after all). A key feature of this provision is that it is meant to be particularly 'laity friendly', with an option for praying only one office in a day. In a Morning and Evening Prayer pattern, we would miss half the dose if we used only one.

Other patterns of daily prayer

Prayer at night

The popularity amongst some Christians of the late-evening service of Compline shows that bedtime is now a more significant time than dusk, since the advent of electricity and light at the flick of a switch has blurred the meaning of 'evening'. The day is over, and prayers are offered as Christians entrust themselves to God's care and protection through the night. This can be marked symbolically by candles being extinguished at the end of the service and a quiet dispersal of the group. There are a number of forms of night prayer in circulation, and an order for Night Prayer (Compline) is also included in *Common Worship*.

Quiet time

Praying on one's own is just as much a feature of Christian prayer as praying with others. On many occasions Jesus went away to a quiet place

to pray alone, and when we follow his example we find the opportunity to draw close to God at our own pace and with our own agenda, not one that has been fixed by a set form, or by other people. We can speak and listen, and find God in the stillness.

Whilst the traditional 'quiet time' has been rejected by some as an unworkable regular pattern for them, it is still held to be essential by many others as a source of basic spiritual nourishment. The conventional time for personal Bible study and prayer has been in the early morning, so that each new day begins with the awareness of God. For those who have no peace or space at this time of day, however, there may be other points of the day which will be more appropriate – maybe 20 minutes at lunchtime, after returning home from work, or just before the ending of the day.

A 'quiet time' does not have to be free-form and unstructured; in fact, it is probably better

for it to have some shape and rhythm, and forms of corporate prayer can also be used in a personal daily pattern. The Daily Prayer booklets from the Durham Diocese and *Celebrating Common Prayer* are both examples of resources that can aid and inspire us to pray when we are on our own.

Bible reading

If we are to be steeped in the Scriptures and know them through and through, then we will need to be reading the Bible regularly and systematically. There are several schemes that we can use. A careful look around any good Christian bookshop will reveal many different books and booklets, offering a variety of Bible reading plans (including the *Common Worship* weekday lectionary). Some are more challenging than others, some will take longer to use than others, and some will have notes, exercises, games or pictures to help in our exploration of the biblical text and in our search to hear God speaking. Some finish the reading for each day with a sentence or short paragraph to be prayed in response to the reading.

> **DID YOU KNOW?** Compline, the traditional name for worship at the end of the day, takes its name from the Latin *completorium*, which means 'completion'.

The Weekday Lectionary

Long before Jesus read from the lesson appointed for the day (Luke 4:17) there have been patterns for reading the Scriptures. *Common Worship* provides three lectionaries, which churches are encouraged to use flexibly according to need. These are currently available in annual editions, and are initially authorized from Advent 2000 to 27 November 2004. Eventually they will be coupled with other daily prayer material and published together in one volume.

Altogether, on a typical day six readings from the Bible are provided, along with a number of psalms.

The Eucharistic Lectionary

The Eucharistic Lectionary is designed for use at a daily celebration of Holy Communion, and has semi-continuous short readings on a two-year cycle. It is familiar from the ASB, but now complements the Sunday Lectionary more appropriately.

The Office Lectionary

The Office Lectionary provides two readings which cover most of the Bible in two years. The readings are appropriate to the seasons of the Christian year, and this lectionary will most appropriately be used by a group (or individual) praying daily on a regular basis. Its format is similar to the Morning and Evening Prayer Lectionaries in the ASB.

The Second Office Lectionary

The Second Office Lectionary envisages a situation where a group needs readings which will 'stand alone' because the members do not meet every day: you do not need to come back tomorrow to hear the end of the story! Such a group may be at a weekday Communion service, and so a Gospel reading is always provided. It would also be appropriate for a choral Evensong at a cathedral. Readings cover much of the Bible, but the lectionary is not exhaustive.

Which Office Lectionary should we use ?

If a church has both Morning and Evening Prayer, then the Office Lectionary is intended for the morning and the Second Office Lectionary for the evening. If a regular group of people meet only once daily, then the Office Lectionary would be most suitable (whatever the time of day), with its semi-continuous readings. However, situations differ and there is no prescription. What is offered may look confusing, but it is richer than before, and a little planning will yield a rich harvest!

CONNECTIONS
▶ **Using the Psalms in church –**
pp.248–9

Future daily prayer in the Church of England

Daily prayer during the week is part of the second phase of *Common Worship* and so, at the time of writing, it is still under construction. In the meantime, A Service of the Word legitimizes most contemporary forms of daily prayer. However, a number of features of the new provision are already clear.

A structured form

It will seek to build upon the contemporary appeal of structured forms of daily prayer and Bible study and, in particular, upon the success of *Celebrating Common Prayer* (CCP). At the same time it will learn from some of the excesses of CCP, notably its tendency to be rather complicated to use and its heavy reliance on the seasons to give flavour – some would say too much – to each day.

A fourfold provision

Similarly, it will take and adapt CCP's pattern of a fourfold office. Morning, Evening and Night Prayer will be provided, though Morning and Evening will remain the pre-eminent 'hours' for prayer. Rather than devising a straightforward form of Midday Prayer, the new office book will provide a form of prayer which can be used at any time of the day. This will be very flexible, suitable for those requiring a simple, meditative prayer, perhaps for use in the middle of the day.

A Service of the Word
When A Service of the Word was first authorized in 1993, it covered non-Eucharistic Sunday services, including Morning and Evening Prayer. However, its strict requirements for prayers of penitence, sermon and creed meant that it could not easily be used as authorization for the weekday offices. In the *Common Worship* Service of the Word, these requirements have been adjusted to take account of the different needs of weekday services, so that A Service of the Word now embraces all daily prayer. This allows us much more freedom of choice when we come to pray in the week and we are not restricted to using only one set form. Many forms of daily office which – though previously unauthorized – have been proving to be very popular are now brought within the bounds of legality. Since all forms of daily office are covered by the authorization of A Service of the Word, the Sunday version of Morning and Evening Prayer in contemporary language did not need separate authorization in 2000.

But it will also serve those who are looking for a simple structure and some basic texts around which their more concentrated reading of the Bible can be built.

Personal and corporate prayer

This creative new development is a good example of the aims of the future daily prayer material. It hopes to support the two classic forms of daily prayer that have developed in the life of the Church. One, more naturally done in company, focuses on praise of God and prayer for the world. The other focuses on a deep engagement with Scripture, leading to prayer of a more internal, personal sort, and is quite easily done alone.

Liturgists often describe the first as the people's prayer and trace its origins to urban centres in the fourth century when believers, many of them new to the faith, gathered to pray in the emerging worship centres of the time. The second is often referred to as monastic prayer. It was developed at a similar time by those seeking a more demanding spiritual life, involving

withdrawal from the world and deeper absorption in the Word of God.

Flexibility

Of course, both ways of meeting with God on a daily basis are right and true, and although some people may be attracted to one more than the other, every help should be given to enable them to embrace both patterns. Hence the new provision will encourage individuals and communities to use the forms of daily prayer and the accompanying lectionaries in ways that suit their particular needs and rhythms. For example, some may wish to treat Morning Prayer essentially as an offering of praise and prayer at the beginning of the day, freeing them to concentrate their more systematic reading of and meditation on Scripture in a simple 'Prayer During the Day', or, if they prefer, at Evening Prayer. Others will want to develop different configurations. The new material will lend itself to a range of possibilities, all of which are designed to give God's people maximum help to structure prayer, praise and engagement with Scripture into their daily lives.

CHAPTER 12

Pastoral Services

Taking their collective name from the biblical image of a shepherd tending the flock, the Pastoral Services are an expression of God's care and nurture, through the liturgy of the Church, at times of particular need or significance. In a general sense, all worship has the potential to be pastoral – reminding us of God's redeeming love for the whole world, and of our part as a community to demonstrate that love to one another and to the stranger.

Some worship might be thoroughly 'pastoral', whilst actually belonging to another group of services. Confirmation and Affirmation of Baptismal Faith, for example, are both useful pastoral rites – providing a corporate and public means of expressing a personal milestone in a person's journey of faith. Similarly, services of Reconciliation – which are yet to take shape and work their way through the General Synod – could be described as services which meet a pastoral need.

More specifically, the material in the *Common Worship* Pastoral Services book comprises:

- Wholeness and Healing
- Marriage
- Emergency Baptism
- Thanksgiving for the Gift of a Child
- Funeral

Rites of passage

It will be immediately obvious that each of these services recognizes an important transition or transformation in a person's life (or a passing from life

> **A mission opportunity**
> Christians are not the only people who feel a desire to turn to God for help and blessing at these life-changing points. This presents the Church with an enormous mission opportunity. As people from all backgrounds approach their local church for a service, we have the privilege of listening to their story and sharing God's story with them.

to death). These are typical 'rites of passage' which, as human beings, we have an inbuilt desire to mark and to remember. These are also occasions when we are likely to feel that the event in which we have been involved has a wider significance in the universal scheme of things, and

we yearn to bring our fears and/or joys into the presence of our creator.

Considering the stages

For instance, the birth of a child is a momentous event. We might well define the actual delivery of the baby as the moment of transition which needs to be marked, but life is not all that simple. For some, conceiving the child in the first place might be the greatest cause of anxiety and distress, whilst for others, circumstances after the birth may indicate a need for prayer. Certainly, pregnancy and parenthood are rarely as idyllic as the dreamy images we are given by the advertising media.

Spreading out the prayer

Therefore, because big events are so often surrounded by other significant steps along the way, *Common Worship* provides us with a wealth of material (often described as 'staged rites') to surround all of these major life transitions. All are useful tools to assist the Church in caring for and expressing God's care to a fragile world.

CONNECTIONS
◉ Confirmation, Affirmation of Baptismal Faith and Reception into the Communion of the Church of England – pp.136–7
◉ Reconciliation – pp.142–3
◉ Rites of passage and 'staged rites' – pp.224–5

Wholeness and Healing

Originally part of the initiation continuum, Wholeness and Healing has first been published with the Pastoral Services. The provision incorporates a revision of the material first published in 1983 in *Ministry to the Sick*, and goes much further in offering the Church liturgical resources for healing ministry, for the increased interest in both healing services and prayer ministry for healing is reflected in the range and flexibility of the material in *Common Worship*. This material has been prepared in consultation with other groups involved in the healing ministry, taking into account the provisional conclusions of a House of Bishops' working party on the healing ministry, subsequently published in *A Time to Heal* (2000).

There are five basic sections:
- A celebration of wholeness and healing, especially suitable for diocesan or deanery occasions, which can lie within a Eucharist or stand alone.
- Laying on of hands with prayer and anointing at a celebration of Holy Communion, intended for occasional use as part of the regular life of a parish.
- Prayer for individuals in public worship. This is a set of notes giving guidance about good practice.

In addition there is material for the following:
- Ministry to the sick. This is concerned primarily with the celebration or distribution of Holy Communion to people who are ill at home or in hospital, or are housebound. Forms of Communion follow Order One in both contemporary and traditional language, whilst ministers wishing to use Order Two are

> Are any among you sick? They should call for the elders of the church and have them pray over them, anointing them with oil in the name of the Lord.
>
> *James 5:14*

directed to the form in the Sunday book. For distribution of Communion only, an outline is provided for both Order One and Order Two, and there is a full sample service for each, as well.
- Prayers for 'protection and peace', to use with individuals who are 'suffering from a sense of disturbance or unrest'.

The two services, while providing frameworks, recognize local diversity and allow much freedom. There are texts printed in the two main services, but the rubrics often allow for suitable

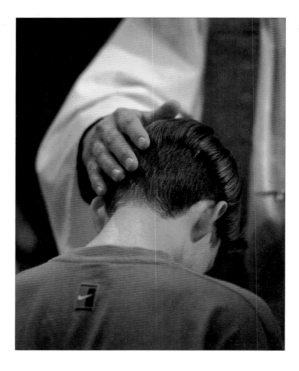

Ministry teams

One effect of charismatic renewal has been the growing belief that when we meet God in worship, he might actually do something to us. The influence of John Wimber's teaching was to convince many that this kind of an encounter was normal, and that it could be facilitated by personal prayer ministry from trained members of 'ministry teams', who would be available to pray with people over some area of response to the sermon, for healing or deliverance, or for any other need. The 'healing service', which in some churches had been a quiet, dignified affair, was replaced more and more by a sometimes noisy and dramatic 'ministry time', which might include people falling to the floor, weeping or laughing under the power of the Spirit. The so-called Toronto Blessing, which broke out in 1994, served to make these ministry times even more prevalent.

Prayer ministry continues, both within and outside charismatic churches, but many Anglicans are rediscovering ways of handling ministry much more in continuity with their heritage: the use of oil for anointing, and understanding the Eucharist as a healing sacrament are growing significantly.

Holistic approach to personhood and healing

The Old Testament concept of shalom expresses the harmony intended and desired by God for both the community and the individual. Christ fulfils the promise of shalom by being the Prince of Peace in our midst.

Ethically the concept is embodied in the Ten Commandments which, if obeyed, ensure right relationship and peace with God, family and society. This is a holistic view encompassing the whole of life. Jesus' summary of the law underlines and intensifies this understanding (Mark 12:29–31; Matthew 22:37–9).

You shall love the Lord your God...
with all your heart – your will, emotion and commitment,
with all your soul – your very essence of being,
with all your mind – your intellect, thinking and
    decision-making,
with all your strength – your physical self,
    your activities and your energy,
and you are to love your neighbour as yourself –
    doing unto others as you would have them do to you.

Jesus came to establish God's rule and kingdom. He demonstrates its coming, restoring health and wholeness in heart, mind, soul, strength and society. He ministers in every kind of brokenness: emotional, spiritual, psychological, physical and sociological, touching the lives of the hurt, lost, disturbed, sick, and those who are marginalized and shunned. All this is seen as fulfilment of the Old Testament hope and promise (e.g. Luke 4:18–19; 7:22, echoing Isaiah 61:1–2; 29:18–19; 35:5–6). Healing is re-establishing the lost shalom, although it will only finally be realized in death as our eternal life, in him and through him, is fulfilled.

alternative words to be used. Suggested readings are listed in the supplementary texts. There are likely to be more prayers and resources compiled and commended for use with these services in due course.

Anointing with oil

Anointing with oil was first officially recognized in the 1983 provision *Ministry to the Sick*. *Common Worship* now provides prayers of thanksgiving and consecration for the oil, and makes the anointing the central feature of the first two services mentioned above. The oil is to be administered by 'authorized ministers' –

although the term is left undefined. The category most certainly includes priests, and might also cover appropriately trained and authorized laypeople.

Laying on of hands

This is another central feature, though clearly distinguished from the anointing with oil. For this ministry no authorization is required, but there is helpful advice suggesting that those involved in this ministry should be offered appropriate help in preparing for the task.

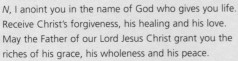

Anointing

The minister says

N, I anoint you in the name of God who gives you life.
Receive Christ's forgiveness, his healing and his love.
May the Father of our Lord Jesus Christ grant you the riches of his grace, his wholeness and his peace.

From Wholeness and Healing

CONNECTIONS
Ministry to the Sick, in the ASB and beyond –
pp.106–7

Thanksgiving for the Gift of a Child

This service was originally intended to be part of a collection of services and prayers, supporting and surrounding both adult and infant initiation. The collection began to take shape in *Rites on the Way* (a Liturgical Commission report from July 1998, largely drafted by Michael Vasey before his death) and included prayers for conception, a form of blessing during pregnancy, prayers after birth and also after death, miscarriage and stillbirth. The draft introduction to this collection captures the flavour of this bringing together of the wonder of human creativity with an openness to God.

A versatile service

Originally designed for family use, at a private celebration of a birth or adoption, at home or in church, with only family and close friends present, the service was changed during the Synod revision process for use on more public occasions, for example the public celebration of the birth or adoption of a number of children, either in church on a Sunday afternoon or as part of the main Sunday service. This explains some elements which are more personal and direct than the equivalent service in the ASB. So, for instance, 'supporting friends' are encouraged to stand with the parents for the Thanksgiving, and may say 'informal words' as well as responding to the questions:

Do you receive these children as a gift from God?

> The reception of a child into the human community is an important moment. It is appropriate both for the child, for the parents and for the community that it should be marked in significant ways. The creation of a new human being within the relationship of two people is a wonder of creation. However baptism is not a birth rite but the application to an individual of the life-changing coming of Jesus Christ into the world. Baptism is not simply a beginning, it is a reality into which we grow through all our lives. The forms of service that follow are not replacements for baptism; they are intended to enable families to bring the mystery of life into the presence of God and to enable them, where they so wish, to grow into the new reality that God has made known to us in Jesus Christ and declares to us in the sacrament of baptism.
>
> *'Towards an Introduction',*
> *Rites on the Way: Work in Progress*

Do you wish to give thanks to God and seek his blessing?

As a more public service, it will not only help parents who have doubts about infant Baptism, yet wish to acknowledge their child as a gift from God, but will also provide the right kind of opportunity for many others, often not members of the Church at all, who recognize that something has happened for which they wish to give thanks to God.

A simple structure

The structure is very simple: Introduction; Readings and Sermon; Thanksgiving and Blessing; Giving of a Gospel; Prayers. The additional prayers include one for the father and another for grandparents, as well as a prayer after a difficult birth, one when a child is adopted and another when a child has special needs.

> ### A mission strategy
> One church has regularly used a similar service as part of its strategy for reaching young families. Using contacts through its weekday range of under-fives' activities, and also training church members to be on the lookout for new babies down the street, it holds four or five major Thanksgiving Services a year, on Sunday afternoons, with lively music and a visual sermon, followed by tea over which those who come can meet church members responsible for Christian Basics courses or home groups.

When a child has special needs

Living God, creator of us all,
We thank you for entrusting *N*
into the special care of *N* and *N*.
Give them and all who surround them
wisdom and understanding, courage and patience;
give them grace to put aside fear and anxiety
and to fulfil your purposes;
fill their hearts with your unfailing love,
that *N* may grow up secure in giving and receiving love
and in the enjoyment of your presence,
to enrich our lives and the lives of others
in ways beyond our imagining,
in Jesus Christ our Lord. **Amen**.
A prayer from Thanksgiving for the Gift of a Child

For the father

Heavenly Father
you entrusted your Son Jesus,
the child of Mary,
to the care of Joseph, an earthly father.
Bless [*this man*]
as he cares for his family.
Give him strength and wisdom,
tenderness and patience;
support him in the work he has to do,
protecting those who look to him,
as we look to you,
for love and salvation,
through Jesus Christ
our rock and defender. **Amen**.
A prayer from Thanksgiving for the Gift of a Child

CONNECTIONS
Services surrounding Baptism – pp.138–9

Marriage in the Bible

There is much about marriage in the Bible. Stories of the patriarchs in Genesis recount lengthy and significant episodes heavily interwoven with marriage and family ties, prophets use nuptial images to bring home their messages, Jesus performed his first miracle in John's Gospel at a wedding, and Paul gives advice to Christian married couples.

The precise details of the wedding ceremonies that people went through are not quite so easy to identify. We can pick up hints here and there about what happened at Jewish weddings, but there are no descriptions of marriage services as such and, as we shall see, there was no specifically Christian marriage service for some time after the beginning of the Christian Church.

Marriage in the Old Testament

There were two parts to Old Testament marriage:

1. Betrothal: here the dowry was paid to the father of the bride, sometimes as a cash payment, sometimes in the form of goods and

sometimes in years of service working for the bride's father (as was the case with Jacob in Genesis 29). This payment was intended to provide security for the bride and, after the betrothal, the couple were regarded as being under the same restrictions as husband and wife (which is why Joseph considered divorcing Mary after she became pregnant).

2. Marriage: the ceremony included two processions, the first when the bridegroom and his friends went to collect the bride from her home and the second when, after their return, the guests escorted the bride and groom to their future home. (We can find hints of this, and the couple's adornments, in Isaiah 61:10 and Psalm 45:14–15.)

After this there was the wedding banquet, ending with the bride being escorted by friends to the nuptial chamber (and it seems that the bride remained veiled, which is how Jacob was deceived into marrying Leah and not Rachel in Genesis 29:23).

Marriage in the New Testament
The Jewish marriage customs outlined above can be seen in Jesus' parable of the wise and foolish virgins and in the story of him attending a wedding at Cana. Beyond this, the New Testament material on marriage is ethical teaching rather than descriptions of what happened in the service. Jesus emphasizes the teaching found in Genesis 2 about a man and a woman leaving their families and the two becoming one flesh (see Matthew 19:5). Jesus also spoke about divorce (Matthew 5:31–2). Paul writes about marriage being 'in the Lord' (1 Corinthians

Adam and Eve in the Garden of Eden

7:39), as well as often including advice about marriage and family in the ethical instructions in his letters.

Early Christian teaching on the permanence of marriage is particularly important given the context of the world in which the first Christians lived. By the time of Jesus, in the Jewish religion women had come to be seen as the possession of their father or husband and had no legal rights. A wife could not divorce her husband, but he could divorce her and often he could do so in a surprisingly simple way.

In the Greek world, too, divorce was easy and extramarital relationships for men were commonly accepted. Married women did not have such opportunities. Against such instability in married life, the early Christian Church called on its members to return to the pattern of permanency and fidelity outlined in the creation stories.

Early Christian marriage
There is no Christian marriage service mentioned for quite some time after the New Testament period, although there are hints in some early writers such as Ignatius that Christians should have some sort of specifically Christian ceremony involving the bishop. Tertullian recommends that the wedding ceremony should be in the context of the Eucharist. It seems very likely that Christians got married according to the local secular custom and that very keen Christians also had a specifically Christian ceremony. The Letter to Diognetus in the second century says, 'Christians marry just like anyone else,' which might mean that there was no specifically Christian marriage service when the author was writing.

By AD 866, however, there was a full Christian marriage service. In that year Pope Nicholas wrote about it in a letter to the Bulgarians. By then it was certainly becoming more common for Christians to have a specifically Christian marriage ceremony – but history does not tell us clearly how this ceremony evolved.

The history of marriage in England

The Middle Ages

The year is 1350 and Godfrey is a merchant with a small but profitable business just down the hill from the cathedral in Durham. He is marrying Sarah at his local church, St Mary the Less. Nearly everybody gets married in church nowadays, though this has not been the case in previous centuries.

On the day of the wedding Godfrey and Sarah meet at the church door, where the first part of the ceremony takes place. Here they assure the priest that they wish to get married and are free to do so. Everyone knows that they are not married to anyone else already, because Durham is a small place and you could not keep that sort of thing quiet for long.

The ceremony moves into the church, where vows are taken (the only liturgy in English) and a ring is given to the woman. The priest blesses Godfrey and Sarah in their new relationship and the service moves on to the Eucharist (though none of the congregation receive the bread and wine, as was normal in the Middle Ages).

After the church service, Godfrey and Sarah are escorted to their new home where there are further prayers. These include the blessing of the bedchamber, in which the group of friends present are reminded that Sarah had promised in church that she would be 'buxom in bed'.

The Book of Common Prayer

Giles and Anne also live in Durham and are also getting married at St Mary the Less, but the year is 1664 and they are using the newly reintroduced *Book of Common Prayer*.

This time the whole service takes place in the church and does not finish with a Eucharist, though Giles and Anne are encouraged to be in church the following day for the regular Sunday celebration of Communion. They still exchange vows (in which the wife promises to obey her husband), a ring is given and there is a long exhortation at the end of the service about biblical teaching on marriage. After the service the priest stays at the church – there is no trip to provide a blessing of the bedchamber.

The Prayer Book service gives three reasons for getting married, in this order:
- Having children.
- Sexual relations.
- Mutual support.

The service also implies that sexual union is a kind of concession allowed because of human weakness, rather than a joyful feature of married life.

One thing has not particularly changed since the Middle Ages: the bride is still treated as the inferior partner and almost as a possession, being given away by one man (her father) to another (the groom).

The nineteenth century

William and Catherine are a third couple getting married at St Mary the Less, this time in 1835. Unlike our previous two couples, they would rather be getting married somewhere else. William and Catherine are both faithful members of the small Methodist congregation in Durham. They do not know anyone at the parish church very well and would dearly like to have a wedding ceremony at their own church. The problem is that the law recognizes only Church of England weddings, although Jews and Quakers may hold their own ceremonies. Everybody else has to go to the parish church and have a Church of England wedding service – even if they are practising members of another denomination.

The twentieth century

It is 1986 and Roger and Kate are going to a wedding at St Mary the Less. They are Methodists and are already married – they were able to marry in the Methodist church they both attend, since English law was eventually changed in the nineteenth century to remove the insistence that everybody must get married in the parish church.

Roger and Kate are going to Chris and Debbie's wedding. Kate and Debbie are both students in Durham. St Mary's is no longer a parish church and has become a college chapel. The service will be conducted by the college chaplain and he will use the relatively new ASB Marriage Service.

Debbie will not be promising to obey Chris in this service – the ASB provides two sets of marriage vows and the promise to obey comes in only one of them. The preface which the minister reads at the start of the service has rearranged the three reasons for getting married from the Prayer Book so that now mutual support comes first, followed by sexual union and the procreation of children. As with the Prayer Book, the whole ceremony takes place in church and very few people (even practising Christians such as Chris and Debbie) will include Communion as part of the service – though the notes in the service do allow this.

Marriage: from ASB to *Common Worship*

The emphasis of the *Common Worship* Marriage Service is on marriage as a gift and blessing from God, rather than a legal contract. In the Pastoral Introduction, which is intended to be read by the wedding guests as they wait in church for the bride to arrive, a wedding is described as, 'one of life's great moments, a time of solemn commitment as well as good wishes, feasting and joy,' and marriage is spoken of as 'a creative relationship as [God's] blessing enables husband and wife to love and support each other…' This is an occasion not only to make serious promises but also to celebrate God's gift of love and his blessing on marriage.

What's new in the *Common Worship* service?

The ASB marriage service worked well and the *Common Worship* service is basically very similar.

However, there have been a number of adjustments and some new features.

- **Entrance** – If the bride does not wish to be brought in by her father (or another relative) a note allows for the bride and groom to enter the church together.
- A new **Preface** (the long explanation of what marriage is all about) has been provided, whilst the Supplementary Texts contain an alternative based on the ASB version.
- The question at **The Declarations** can be put to the bride before the bridegroom (the bride may say her vows first, as well).
- **Parental roles**. As in the ASB, there is nothing about 'giving away' the bride in the text of the service. The Notes, however, refer to it as an optional traditional ceremony, make clear that it is not restricted to the bride's father, and provide a form of words which avoids the bride being 'given':
    Who brings this woman to be married to this man?
Alternatively, parents of the couple may demonstrate their support in a different way. Once the couple have declared their intent to marry, the minister may say:
    N and N have declared their intention towards each other.
    As their parents, will you entrust your son and daughter to one another as they come to be married?
Both sets of parents respond:
    We will.
- **A congregational pledge of support** is an integral part of the service. Once the bride and groom have made their declarations, the minister says:

- The bride and groom are the *ministers* of the marriage and the person taking the service is the *registrar*.
- In English law you can only get married between 8 a.m. and 6 p.m.
- Anyone who objects to the wedding going ahead in the service itself has to guarantee to pay any extra costs incurred by the couple if their allegations prove groundless.

Will you, the families and friends of *N* and *N*, support and uphold them in their marriage now and in the years to come?
We will.

- **The Collect, Readings and Sermon** sections are printed in the *Common Worship* service immediately after the Declarations; permission to place the Reading(s) and Sermon after the Blessing of the Marriage 'if occasion demands', comes only in a note.
- **The Vows.** Ever since Series 1, the bride has had a choice over whether or not to promise to 'obey'. In *Common Worship* the (sometimes offending) word is found only in a form of vows in the Supplementary Texts, and the ASB's corresponding promise on the part of the groom to 'worship' has been cut. Alternatively, the couple may use *The Book of Common Prayer*'s version of the vows, which is provided as a further option in the Supplementary Texts.
- **When the couple exchange rings** they may say their words simultaneously.
- **'Asunder'** has made a return ('Those whom God has joined together let no one put asunder').
- **Prayers** for the couple are printed in the *Common Worship* service both as a list of suggested concerns and as a form of intercession with congregational response. There is also a wealth of alternative forms and prayers in the Supplementary Texts, some recognizing the variety of relationships which may have preceded or still surround this

marriage, for example: 'For the healing of memory', 'For an existing family' and 'For the families of the couple'.

Clarity

The service structure is in two clear parts:
- Introduction
- Marriage

There is also provision for holding the ceremony in the context of a Communion Service, which has a fivefold structure:
- The Gathering
- The Liturgy of the Word
- The Marriage
- The Liturgy of the Sacrament
- The Dismissal

Within a Eucharist, the components of the 'Introduction' are distributed between The Gathering and The Liturgy of the Word.

User-friendly

The aim of the language in the service and of the structure is to be as 'user-friendly' as possible, while not detracting from the solemnity of the occasion. Many people in the congregation at weddings (and often the couple too) are not regular churchgoers and so those planning and leading the service need to bear in mind the need for clarity and accessibility in the way the service is presented.

Finding your way through the Marriage Service

The Marriage Service	
Mandatory Material	**Optional Material**
The Introduction Welcome	Sentence Prayer Hymn
Preface (what marriage is about)	
The Declarations (that the couple may legally marry, and that they both wish to do so)	
The congregation pledges its present and future support of the marriage.	Parents entrust the couple to each other.
The Collect **Readings** **Sermon**	
The Marriage	Hymn 'Giving away'
The Vows **The Giving of Rings** **The Proclamation** (that the couple are married) **The Blessing of the marriage** **Registration of the marriage**	
Prayers (concluding with Lord's Prayer)	Hymn
The Dismissal Blessing of the congregation	Hymn

Preparing for the service

Since there are a number of choices to be made from the *Common Worship* marriage material, the couple will need to have the opportunity to sit down with the minister and have various choices laid before them, so that they can decide for themselves which options to use at specific points in their wedding.

Here is an indication of the most significant points at which alternative texts are available:

- Hymns
- The Preface
- The Declarations
- The Readings
- The Vows
- Prayers – at The Giving of Rings, at The Blessing of the Marriage, at The Prayers

The couple may also be invited to consider including some of the other optional features.

Frequently asked questions

Can our children be involved in the service?

Often nowadays couples have children already, either together or from a previous relationship. They can be involved in reading lessons, carrying the rings, leading prayers or as bridesmaids/ pageboys. There are also two prayers in the appendix which focus on an existing family.

Can the bride still be 'given away'?

There is a long-standing tradition that the bride's

father 'gives her away' and, while some people consider this to be anachronistic, many still value this symbolic action. Although not in the ASB, it has been brought back as an option before the vows. As another option, the couple may be 'entrusted' to one another by their parents.

Can we get married in that pretty church I pass on the way to work?

The law at present is very strict about the church buildings in which couples may marry. Basically a couple can be married only in the parish in which one of them lives, or at a church where one of them regularly worships.

Before the wedding

There are many ways in which the local church can support a couple who come to be married. Here are a few ideas:

- When the banns are called, the couple can be prayed for and maybe the minister or others can lay hands on them in prayer – there are prayers for the calling of banns in the supplementary texts.
- Many parishes offer marriage preparation. This may offer the opportunity to explore the changes that marriage will bring over the years, as well as planning the day itself. There can be teaching on marriage and prayer for those to be married. Some parishes hold day conferences for all the couples getting married at their church that year. These days

are ideal opportunities for including some worship relating to marriage.

At the wedding

The service itself can be enhanced by extra items not in the official order of service:

- Musical items performed by the choir or by friends of the couple – a piper, a brass band, an opera singer, etc.
- Garlands of flowers, carried, displayed or presented as 'crowns'.
- A guard of honour – one bride walked up a path lined with her Brownies as she approached the church porch.

After the wedding...

...the marriage begins! The local church can provide help, including someone impartial to talk to in time of need. There are also prayers available for the following:

- A new home.
- A service of thanksgiving for marriage – on the anniversary of a wedding, or a general service for many couples at the same time.
- Making a new start when a marriage is improving after a bad patch.
- Blessings of replacement wedding rings (yes, even the happiest of couples get burgled or lose a ring down the drain).

All of these liturgical resources can be found in *Common Worship Pastoral Services*.

 Some points to consider when staging the service
- Will the couple enter the church together? How is this entry to be organized?
- The couple will probably need seating during the reading and sermon.
- If the parents are 'entrusting' the couple to each other, where will they stand and will they need the text of their words in front of them?
- When will the congregation stand and sit? The text of the service does not provide the answers!

CONNECTIONS
◀ 'Giving away the bride' – pp.214–15

A brief history of funerals

Pre-Christian Roman customs

In ancient Rome five things made up the funeral:

1. The ceremonies at home, including the last kiss (to catch the dying person's soul), the washing and anointing of the body and the placing of a coin in the mouth.
2. The funeral procession, at night, with torches, and wearing black clothes, called *lugubria*, from which the word 'lugubrious' comes.
3. The actual burial or cremation.
4. The ceremonies of purification for the relatives and the dead person's house.
5. The funeral feast.

In the early Church

Early Christian funerals take on some of the same elements, simply because of what has to be done physically. The preparation of the body, the procession, the burial or cremation and the

> For she, when the day of her death drew near, did not crave that her body might be sumptuously adorned, or embalmed with spices, nor desired she any choice monument.
>
> Nor did we think fit to celebrate that funeral with weeping and loud-voiced cries, because with such demonstrations of sorrow men are wont to lament who think on death as a misery or even as utter destruction. But she died not miserably, nor indeed did she die utterly … And behold, the corpse was carried forth, we both went and returned without tears…
>
> *Augustine, on the funeral of his mother Monica in AD 387*

funeral feast, together with the movement from one place to another, give the Christian service its structure. The whole atmosphere changes, however. Christian funerals are held in daytime, with mourners in white, and pagan crying and wailing are replaced by psalms and hymns. The

bodies of the dead are treated with respect and not as dirt, and yet the other extreme of lavish clothing for the grave is avoided. Here, as the catacombs outside Rome bear witness, are people for whom death is not the grim ending of life but an occasion for joy, as Christians, sure of the resurrection, go to be with their Lord. The excesses of the funeral feast were replaced by the celebration of the Holy Communion of all the faithful, both at funerals and on the anniversary of the death.

Medieval developments

The five elements in early Church funerals – preparation of the body including the *viaticum* (giving Communion to the deceased), procession with psalms, Bible reading and prayer at the graveside, and the Eucharist – are not only developed but transformed in atmosphere during the medieval period.

Gone are the joy and triumph, the waving of palm branches and shouts of 'alleluia'. The mourners are in black. The psalms are penitential ones: we get our word 'dirge' from the opening word of the second part of the office of the dead, '*Dirige*'. A deep consciousness of sin and judgement has swept away the glad confidence of a Church sure of the resurrection. Prayer for the dead is no longer a joyful communion together in Christ, but a desperate pleading for release from punishment – as in the York Use in England: 'Loose him, and deliver him from the cruel fire of the boiling pit.' The tendency for the worship of the Church to be overwhelmed with keeping anniversaries of the dead and praying for them led by the early thirteenth century to the growth of the observance of All Souls' Day.

Reformation

What Cranmer did at the Reformation was a severe reaction against the purgatory-dominated pattern of the Middle Ages. Some of the medieval elements are kept (the sung processional sentences and the words from 'Man

Comparing the funeral structure

Secular Roman	Medieval	1549	1552
Home	**Home**		
Last kiss	Dying		
Coin	Viaticum		
Procession	**Procession**	**Procession**	**Procession**
	Church	**Church or grave**	**Graveside**
	Office	Sentences	Sentences
		Burial	Burial
		Psalms	
		Reading	Reading
	Mass	Prayers and responses	Prayer
	Absolution	(Communion)	
	Procession		
Burial	**Burial**		
Purification			
Feast	**Feast**		

born of a woman…'), but the whole service is truncated and the flavour is different. The reading is 1 Corinthians 15 on the resurrection, and the commendation is a thanksgiving, full of hope in the resurrection. In the radical 1552 revision it all takes place at the graveside, and every trace of prayer for the departed has gone. It was this service, with a very few changes (two psalms were inserted again), which was reissued in the 1662 Prayer Book and has served the Church for over 400 years.

Funerals and the Eucharist

Graveside funeral feasts degenerated into debauched and lavish banquets, and were banned in the Church by the end of the fourth century. They were replaced by the celebration of the Eucharist – both at funerals and on the anniversary of the death. Hence the words of this fourth-century writer:

'Do you according to the Gospel, and according to the power of the Holy Spirit, come together even in the cemeteries, and read the holy scriptures, and without demur perform your ministry and your supplication to God, and offer an acceptable eucharist…?'

Apostolic Constitutions

From ASB to *Common Worship* – what's the difference?

The *Common Worship* Funeral Service is radically different from that in the ASB, with some new features and a new structure, linked to developments in the way people think about death and dying. The ASB service majored on being positive and proclaiming the resurrection; it began to meet the need for a modern service for crematoria, and provided alternatives for the funeral of a child, as well as enshrining a compromise between Anglo-Catholics and evangelicals over the vexed question of prayer for the departed. But it was still possible (as with the 1662 service) for a minister to lead the whole service without mentioning the name of the dead person. Those compiling the *Common Worship* service looked afresh at some of the basic questions, including that of prayer for the departed.

What is the funeral for?

In 1964 the Liturgical Commission Report on the Burial of the Dead answered this question as follows:

1. To secure the reverent disposal of the corpse.

2. To commend the deceased to the care of our heavenly Father.

3. To proclaim the glory of our risen life in Christ here and hereafter.

4. To remind us of the awful certainty of our own coming death and judgement.

5. To make plain the eternal unity of Christian people, living and departed, in the risen and ascended Christ.

The report commented that 'it would, perhaps, be natural to add a sixth point, namely the consolation of the mourners', but argued that this would happen automatically if the other five

things were done. Since 1964 there has been the beginning of a new openness in talking about death, of which the growth of the hospice movement and of bereavement counselling or listening are both symptoms and causes. This has been aided rather than hindered by the media portrayal of the nation's reaction to some major disasters, including the death of Diana, Princess of Wales. An increasing number of those coming to arrange funerals now want to say something – or have something said – to celebrate the life of

---

Some psalms used at funeral services

Psalm 23 – 'The Lord is my shepherd'
- God is our shepherd, he looks after us.
- He is strong enough to help us (with rod and staff).
- He will bring us to feast with him in heaven.
- So we need not fear the valley of the shadow of death.

Jesus said, 'I am the good shepherd. I know my own and my own know me … I lay down my life for my sheep'
(John 10:14,15b).

Psalm 90 – 'Lord, you have been our refuge'
- The eternal nature of God.
- The shortness of a human life, by contrast.
- A prayer (v. 12–16) for three things with three results.

Psalm 121 – 'I lift up my eyes to the hills'
For those desperately wanting to know where they can go for help.
- The psalmist is sure the creator God helps him.
- God does not sleep (if we are awake at night, he is too).
- He knows about our going out and our coming back home (and he will be there even if no one else is).

Psalm 130 – 'Out of the depths have I called to you, O Lord'
- God hears us.
- God forgives and redeems us.

the one who has died. So we might want to add an extra point to the list above: 'Celebrating a life; enabling people to talk about their loss, to God and to one another; marking a stage in the grieving process.'

New features

The new features include the following:

- Seeing the funeral as part of a longer process.
- More openness to grief and sadness as well as resurrection.
- An opportunity for words to be said (a 'tribute') about the dead person.
- Allowing for symbols of the dead person's life and faith to be placed on or near the coffin.
- A fuller form for the Burial of Ashes.
- An authorized Outline Order for Funerals, to provide more flexibility.
- A brief pastoral introduction printed at the beginning of the service.

Why are we here?

We have come here today
to remember before God our *brother/sister N*;
to give thanks for *his/her* life;
to commend *him/her* to God our merciful redeemer and judge;
to commit *his/her* body to be *buried/cremated*,
and to comfort one another in our grief.

Introducton to the Funeral Service

Tribute

Remembering and honouring the life of the person who has died, and the evidence of God's grace and work in them should be done in the earlier part of the service, after the opening prayer, though if occasion demands it may be woven into the sermon or come immediately before the Commendation. It may be done in conjunction with the placing of symbols, and may be spoken by a family member or friend or by the minister using information provided by the family.

Note 4 to the Funeral Service

CONNECTIONS
▶ **Praying for the departed** – pp.226–7
▶ **The grieving process** – pp.224–5
▶ **The Psalter** – Chapter 16

The structure of the Funeral Service

Both theology and pastoral need determine the structure of the *Common Worship* Funeral Service. The opening sentence, 'I am the resurrection and the life…', puts down a clear marker for the resurrection. In the ASB this is the main emphasis, boldly stated in the opening prayer: 'Heavenly Father, in your Son Jesus Christ you have given us a true faith and a sure hope…' The *Common Worship* service begins on a more incarnational note, acknowledging both the process of grief and the humanity of the person who has died.

Gathering and celebrating

The beginning of the service – 'The Gathering' – is when we recognize the different groups that make up the funeral congregation, with different relationships to the dead person, and gather for a common purpose: 'We have come here today to remember…' This is immediately followed by a prayer acknowledging our own grief, reminding the mourners that Jesus himself was moved to tears at the grave of his friend Lazarus.

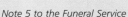

The Sermon

The purpose of the Sermon is to proclaim the Gospel in the context of the death of this particular person.

Note 5 to the Funeral Service

Then the focus moves to the dead person. We need to say who they were to us, and that we will miss them. This is the point, early in the service, when a tribute may be made. At some funerals, a number of people may wish to read something out, or to place some symbolic object on or near the coffin. Having something tangible to do may be very helpful, and often happens at a child's funeral. Next comes an opportunity for penitence. This is nothing like the heavy medieval pleadings for forgiveness for the dead person, but simply a recognition that, confronted with death, we all need to get straight with God and sometimes we are conscious of our failure, or the words of reconciliation we did not have time to utter before the person died. The words in the service say, 'We are mindful of all that we have failed to do'.

Moving on

It is only when the human-focused, incarnational celebration and remembering of the person's life has been openly stated that the service can then move on to the other themes of resurrection, heaven and glory, set by the reading or readings from the Bible. So the Funeral Service moves from the human to the divine, from earth to heaven, from the different groups of people who gather here to the communion of the saints in heaven, from the celebration of the life of the person who has died to the celebration of the life

of eternity. The service moves through eternal truths in the reading of Scripture, the sermon and the prayers, before reaching its climax in the Commendation and the Committal.

This human–divine axis is even more obvious when the service moves on into Holy Communion, when the underlying structure of the service is that of the Eucharist. Most funerals, however, will not include Communion.

One service for everyone

Some people argue that there should be one very Christian service, full of assurance, for church members, and another kind of service for those who are less sure. The Commission says, 'We believe that it should be possible to have the

> **The Structure of the Funeral Service**
>
> **The Gathering**
> (Sentences – optional)
> Introduction
> (Prayer – optional)
> (Prayers of Penitence – optional)
> The Collect
>
> **Readings and Sermon**
> **Prayers**
> (Holy Communion – optional)
>
> **Commendation and Farewell**
> **The Committal**
> **The Dismissal**

same basic rite for all, and not one service for church members and one for others.' To do otherwise would involve invidious judgements about who should receive the 'second-class' service.

Endings

The final point to note about the structure of the service is the variety of possible ways to end it, including some familiar texts such as the Song of Simeon and 'God be in my head', and the prayer with which the ASB service opened, proclaiming our 'true faith and a sure hope', a fitting conclusion to which this gospel journey might lead us.

> **Cremation: when to have the Committal**
> It is obvious that when the body is being buried, the Committal happens at the point of burial. But what happens when there is a cremation? Canon Law says every minister has a duty 'to bury ... the corpse or ashes of any person deceased' within the parish. So the words in the Burial of Ashes Service may form the Committal, and at the crematorium or church the minister may say, 'Now, in preparation for burial, we give his/her body to be cremated'. It is also possible to use words of Committal at the crematorium or church if necessary.

CONNECTIONS
⬛ Tribute –
pp.220–21

The funeral journey

Many of the *Common Worship* Pastoral Services, like the Initiation Services, have a 'journey' motif, marking the stages of a process through which people are moving. Sometimes people call these 'staged rites' – because they mark different stages, not because they are good drama!

The grieving process

As grieving is a process marked by different stages, so the Funeral Service makes links with some of that process. The Gathering, for instance, recognizes that for some of the mourners the early part of the service will be a recapitulation of those stages since the death in which they have not been able to participate fully. The service has a clear function in underlining the fact of death and its finality, helping people to move on. Some of the optional prayers can pick up other stages of the grieving process, including anger, denial and depression.

An impossible task?

It would be a tall order for the minister to lead all of the many opportunities for prayer with the family before and after the funeral. While the funeral itself ought normally to be taken by the minister, or one of the increasing number of Readers trained for this ministry, saying some prayers the night before the funeral or on the morning of the funeral is done in some parishes by one of a team of bereavement visitors, trained to stand alongside the bereaved family and to visit them afterwards. Again, in some provinces of the Anglican Communion there are 'Life Celebrants' – laypeople trained to draw out from the family what should be said and done in the tribute. Alternatively, a Christian family member or friend might take on these responsibilities.

Within every congregation there will be some on another grieving journey, for some other loss, who can be helped in their reflection by what is done and said at this funeral.

While the Funeral Service stands perfectly well on its own, it is part of a longer continuum,

CONNECTIONS
🔲 **Staged rites –** pp.204–5

providing the richest set of liturgical resources around dying and funerals that the Church of England has had since the Middle Ages. This continuum begins with ministry to the sick and moves on to ministry at the time of death, through the possibility of prayers in the house after someone has died, prayers either in church or at home before the funeral, through the funeral itself, to some prayers at home after the funeral, a later Memorial Service and the provision for annual memorials. The bereaved will need to be able to say different things to God and to one another at each of these different stages.

Planning the funeral

Some families have a funeral book, where they set out the options they want for their own funeral, including hymns and who is to take part. Some churches encourage people to plan in this way.

'Staged rites'

This is the phrase used to describe a series of services or prayers which take people through various stages in a process. It is often used for 'rites of passage' which mark life-changes through which people go. It can be helpful to think of these rites in three stages:

- Preliminal (*limen* is Latin for threshold, the crossing of which from one stage of life to another is the central point of the event). This stage is about separation from the past, with an eye on some purpose for the future.
- Liminal. This symbolizes, sometimes through some symbolic action, the change which is taking place, focusing on the isolation and disintegration of crossing the threshold, for example from one community to another in baptism.
- Postliminal. A celebration of arrival in the new state, acceptance and reintegration into community.

Sometimes a rite of passage, such as a funeral, can be broken down into a series of separate stages on different occasions. Receiving the body into church, for instance, can happen in a truncated form at the start of the funeral service, or in a more extended form, perhaps with a vigil, on the afternoon or evening before.

Walking the lonely road

Risen Lord Jesus,
draw near to us as we walk this lonely road.
Pierce our weary sorrow
and gladden our heavy hearts as you go with us,
and bring us in the end to your heavenly table. **Amen.**

A prayer based on Luke 24

Here are some points of connection between liturgy and pastoral care, provided for in *Common Worship*:

Ministry at the Time of Death
 – Prayer when someone has just died

Before the Funeral
 – At home before the funeral
 – For those unable to be present at the funeral
 – On the morning of the funeral
 – At church before the funeral
  – receiving the body
  – a funeral vigil

The Funeral Service (Is it within the Holy Communion?)

After the Funeral
 – At home after the funeral
 – Memorial service

The Burial of Ashes

What do Christians believe about death?

Undeniably, human beings die. As such we simply take our place in the dying of all things. But Christians believe that, in Christ, God has entered into the reality of our death and overcome it. God's promise to save the world is fulfilled in Christ, whose rising from death signals the end of the old life lived in the shadow of death and the beginning of the new life lived in the light of eternity. The gift of the Spirit to the followers of Christ marks our share in this new life.

Now, or not yet?

We know, however, that we live in the 'in-between times'. We know that we are in between Jesus' triumph over evil and the eradication of evil. We know that we are in between our experience of God's forgiveness and healing and our transformation into the holy people that God intends us to be. We know that the new creation has burst into life through Christ, but that it is still to come fully when Christ returns and makes all things new. What happens in this in-between time to those who die in Christ?

In their enthusiasm to affirm that those who die in Christ are, in Paul's words, 'with the Lord'

(1 Corinthians 5:8), many Christians have implied that the 'faithful departed' have entered into the fullness of salvation now. Although very good at expressing the biblical conviction about the assurance of salvation, this view tends to downplay other biblical convictions about the Last Judgement, the *parousia* (Second Coming) of Christ and the re-creation of the world. It also fails to take the Christian belief in the resurrection of the body with full seriousness.

Resurrection of the body

The resurrection of the body – rather than the immortality of the soul – connects the fullness of my salvation to the material order of creation. God's purposes for me are tied to God's purposes for everything that God has made. To put it bluntly, my resurrection body will be part of God's new creation that is still to come. This is why 'creation waits with eager longing for the revealing of the children of God' (Romans 8:19) – and we must remember that creation *waits* for the children to be revealed. The fullness of my salvation is bound up with yours. God's purposes will not be complete, Christ will not have returned the kingdom to the Father (1 Corinthians 15:24), until the last enemy of death has been overcome for us all.

Waiting

We are saying, then, that ultimately one person's salvation cannot be isolated from the salvation of others, nor abstracted from the renewal of creation. This means that, alongside our assurance that nothing, not even death, can separate us from the love of God in Christ (Romans 8:38–9) and that those who die are 'with the Lord', we can place an expectation that

> The apostles too have not received their joy: they likewise are waiting for me to participate in their joy. So it is that the saints who depart from here do not immediately receive the full reward of their merits, but wait for us, even if we delay, even if we remain sluggish … For you will wait, just as you are awaited.
>
> *Origen (c.185–254), Sermon on Leviticus 7:1–2*

the dead are also waiting for the kingdom to come in its fullness. The Spirit who was poured out on them in life sustains them through death and yet still yearns for the fulfilment of God's promises for them to share in a new heaven and new earth. Of course, their experience of time may be very different from ours, but it will still intersect with ours at the point at which God, through the coming again of Christ, fully establishes his rule and reign.

Prayer for the departed

As well as thanks for the life of the departed and confidence that they are safe in the arms of Christ (Luke 23:43), Christian prayer for those who have died in faith may also express the common hope for the coming of the kingdom that binds the living and the dead together in the communion of saints. This is why the *Common Worship* Funeral Service prays:

> Bring all who rest in Christ
> into the fullness of your kingdom
> where sins have been forgiven
> and death is no more.

and:

> May God in his infinite love and mercy
> bring the whole Church,
> living and departed in the Lord Jesus,
> to a joyful resurrection and the fulfilment
> of his eternal kingdom.

> We meekly beseech thee … that, when we depart this life, we may rest in him, as our hope is this our brother doth; and that, at the general Resurrection in the last day, we may … receive that blessing, which thy well-beloved Son shall then pronounce to all that love and fear thee, saying, Come … receive the kingdom prepared for you from the beginning of the world.
>
> *From the collect in the Prayer Book's service of Burial of the Dead*

CHAPTER 13

The Ordinal

A continuous pattern

The Church of England, like all historic Churches, has a pattern of ordained ministers, and ordinations are conducted by bishops. This pattern is traced (albeit with less than total certainty) back to the first century AD, and it is a pattern which in broad principle was retained through the Reformation. Thus the Archbishop of Canterbury is bishop of a diocese founded when Augustine, who led the mission to Kent in the spring of AD 597, was ordained bishop later that same year to become the first occupant of the see – and the continuity has been sustained ever since.

At the back of an ordinary *Book of Common Prayer* are the three services for ordaining deacons, priests (also called 'presbyters') and bishops (in that order). The services together are known as the 'Ordinal' and technically comprise a separate book, even though – like the Psalter – they are usually bound up with the BCP. They are introduced by a short preface, always called the 'Preface to the Ordinal', which Cranmer wrote for the first English-language Ordinal in 1550. According to the rites in the Prayer Book, the three orders are each conferred within a 1662 Communion service: deacons after the Epistle, priests after the Gospel and bishops after the Creed. The sermon comes at the beginning of the rite; there is an exhortation about the duties of each order, then an interrogation and a litany before the laying on of hands. At the laying on of hands, there is a kind of injunction but not a true prayer, and after the laying on of hands there is a presentation of a New Testament to deacons and a Bible to priests

Women bishops at the 1998 Lambeth Conference

and bishops. All understandings of ordination in the sixteenth and seventeenth centuries included the separation of the ministers from all secular employment and their total commitment to 'full-time' service (with some provision also for a stipend to keep them alive and in action).

Issues surrounding ordination

The following issues have been contentious in recent years, and some of them impinge upon the future shape of ordination services:

- Is episcopal ordination essential to the very being of a Church?
- Is there any distinctive 'priesthood' of the presbyterate?
- Should there be a 'permanent' diaconate? If so, should those who currently become 'transitional' deacons for up to a year be ordained instead 'direct' to the presbyterate?
- Are women proper persons to be ordained? Can women be bishops also?
- Can (and should) 'catholic' ordination be restricted by limited licences for those being ordained to 'local' ministries?
- Can presidency of the Eucharist properly be delegated to laypeople or deacons?

'Tentmaking' ministry

In the twentieth century there developed the practice of ordination to a non-stipendiary (or 'tentmaking', from Acts 18:3) ministry and, more recently (though only in some dioceses) a 'local' ministry, in which both selection and deployment have in view a ministry in the congregation from which the candidate (non-stipendiary) comes. Yet all non-stipendiaries being ordained are still placed within the same order of ministers as the stipendiary ministers. They also conform to the strongly held policy of the Church of England only to ordain those who, being duly qualified, selected and trained, now have a 'title' – an identifiable post or place within which to exercise their ministry.

ASB

A new Ordinal appeared in the ASB, to be used within an ASB Holy Communion service. The sermon comes, as in any other Eucharist, after the Gospel reading and the ordination follows the sermon. The rite of ordination is not unlike the shape of 1662, but the ordination itself – i.e.

It is evident unto all men diligently reading holy Scripture and ancient Authors, that from the Apostles' time there have been these Orders of Ministers in Christ's Church; Bishops, Priests, and Deacons ... to the intent that these Orders may be continued, and reverently used... [The rites following must be employed from now on...]
From the Preface to the Ordinal, 1550, 1552, 1662

Receive the Holy Ghost for the office and work of a Priest in the Church of God, now committed unto thee by the imposition of our hands.
The first part of the formula accompanying the laying on of hands on those being ordained priest, from the Book of Common Prayer, 1662

Absolutely null and utterly void.
The judgement of Pope Leo XIII on Anglican Orders in Apostolicae Curae, 1896

the laying on of hands with prayer – is effected in the context of a weighty prayer, a considerable contrast with the BCP. Because the rite comes within a modern Eucharistic service, the ordination and giving of the Bible are followed immediately by the Peace, with all the welcome in Christ and mutual adherence which that implies.

2000–2005

As no new ordination rites were produced in 2000, the ASB material has been re-authorized for five years. The time is being used for a thorough review of the ASB services with a view to having new forms authorized by 2005. In the process some very big questions have to be addressed.

In the meantime, the *Common Worship* 'Rules to Order the Service' allows a variation in order: 'the presentation to the Bishop ... may occur after the greeting, the presentation to the people after the declaration, and the giving of the Bible and other symbols as part of the concluding rite'.

 Thomas Aquinas asserted that you did not need to be confirmed to be ordained.

CHAPTER 14

Calendar, Lectionary and Collects

Cycles of life

Holidays are part of life for most people – whether it is a break from work or just a chance to get away from over-familiar surroundings for a day. In the past, holidays were 'holy days' and enabled people to celebrate religious festivals (often with considerable enthusiasm!) and to go to church.

When Moses passed on God's commands to the people of Israel, about to cross into the Promised Land, he told them to celebrate the first harvest not simply with thankfulness but also with a generous spirit (Deuteronomy 8 and 26). These ancient peoples recognized a pattern in the God-given seasons of the year. In the northern hemisphere it is not surprising that festivals – not only Christian or Jewish festivals – have been associated with the darkness of winter, the coming of warmth and light, the lengthening of days (Lent), and so on.

Christian festivals

Take, for instance, the annual celebration of the birth of Christ. No one knows the date of the initial event, and its celebration is one of the more 'recent' Christian festivals, catching on only between the fourth and sixth centuries. It was attached to the pagan Roman festival of the unconquered sun; the giving of presents derived from the festival of Saturn earlier in December; the greenery and lights from the Roman New Year; and there were Celtic, Germanic, Scandinavian and New World influences too.

In addition to this 'natural' annual cycle is the pattern of almost datable Christian events, revolving around the great festival of Easter – or, as it is called in almost every other language, Passover (*Pasg* in Welsh, for instance). The celebration of the great three days of our redemption is both a reminder of the cross, the tomb and the resurrection, and a renewal of the believer's experience of dying and being born again in Christ. Easter illustrates the crucial difference between merely observing dates in a calendar and using the celebrations to deepen faith. In the early years of the Christian era, this celebration of the three days of Christian

---

Sundays

All Sundays celebrate the paschal mystery of the death and resurrection of the Lord. Nevertheless, they also reflect the character of the seasons in which they are set.

Principal Feasts

The Principal Feasts which are to be observed are:
   Christmas Day
   The Epiphany
   The Presentation of Christ in the Temple
   The Annunciation of Our Lord to the Blessed
      Virgin Mary
   Easter Day
   Ascension Day
   Pentecost (Whit Sunday)
   Trinity Sunday
   All Saints' Day

Other Principal Holy Days

Ash Wednesday, Maundy Thursday and Good Friday are Principal Holy Days.

Excerpts from 'Rules to Order the Christian Year'

Passover was extended (as a period of preparation for baptism) into what we call Holy Week, then further extended (into Lent) and, similarly, the celebration of new life in Christ was extended to the Ascension and Feast of Pentecost.

Seasons of the Church's year

The earliest festivals

The foundation of the Christian year is the regular celebration of Jesus' resurrection by the earliest Christians every Sunday, the 'first day of the week' (see Acts 20:7; 1 Corinthians 16:2). By the end of the first century this had been renamed 'the Lord's Day'. It is not unlikely that the very first generation of Christians also celebrated the festival of Easter, and we know that Easter, Pentecost and Epiphany were the key marker dates of the earliest Christian calendar.

Hot debate

Christians have long argued over the date of Easter. When should Easter be celebrated – on the Jewish Feast of Passover or on Resurrection Sunday? The debate became acrimonious, until it was agreed at Nicea (AD 325) that it must fall on the first Sunday after the spring full moon, but never on the Jewish date of 14 Nisan. Even using the same formula, however, the Eastern and Western Churches sometimes come up with dates as much as five weeks apart. There are moves between representatives of all parts of the Church to try and bring the date of Easter closer to a set time each year: watch this space in a century's time!

A moveable feast

The celebration of Easter is, therefore, both the heart of the Christian year and the reason why the calendar – and lectionary – can seem so complicated. If you imagine the year as a circle, the Ash Wednesday to Pentecost segment (about a quarter of the year) moves considerably each year (in 2008, for example, Easter falls on 23 March and three years later on 24 April).

The *Common Worship* year – longer seasons

In the *Common Worship* Calendar, the two major cycles, associated with the two great seasons of Christian celebration and experience, have been extended. The first, the 'Incarnation' season, beginning on Advent Sunday, runs on until the Presentation of Christ (2 February), when the tone alters as we look forward to the Passion. The second, 'Eastertide', continues to the Day of Pentecost, which is its culmination.

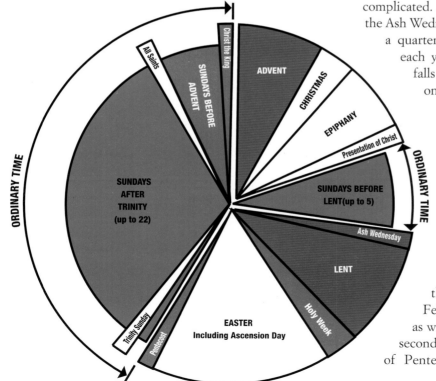

Between these two great seasonal cycles are two periods of what we might call 'flexitime' (Ordinary Time), because these periods vary in length.

The yearly cycle

The Incarnation cycle begins on the First Sunday of Advent (at the end of November or early December), runs on through the Christmas and Epiphany seasons, then arrives at the first period of Ordinary Time – which is very short if Easter is early, and longer if Easter is late. This period winds up with the Sundays before Lent. The 'death and resurrection' cycle falls between Ash Wednesday and the Day of Pentecost, running through the season of Lent in

preparation for the Passion, Easter, Ascension and the celebration of resurrection life in the Holy Spirit.

A long period of Ordinary Time follows through the summer, finishing off with a period of Sundays before Advent (unofficially known as the 'kingdom season'). This begins on the Sunday closest to All Saints' Day (1 November) and culminates in the Festival of Christ the King, which rounds off the year.

A new feature is the use of the Second Sunday before Lent as a 'creation Sunday', a focus which is reflected in the readings in all three years, and in the collect. This effectively replaces the ASB's Ninth Sunday before Christmas, with its Creation theme.

Sundays belong to the seasons

All the Sundays, except in the long summer season of Ordinary Time (which the *Common Worship* Calendar refers to as 'Sundays after Trinity'), are called 'Sundays of (*a season*)'. This is because the Sundays reflect the tone of the seasons. We find this not only in the readings but also in the other seasonal resources provided in *Common Worship*.

The Collects

The *Common Worship* collects derive almost entirely from the working group of the four national Anglican Churches of the British Isles. That group brought together the best of a large selection of prayer material drawn from throughout the Anglican Communion and elsewhere, together with some new writing. Where appropriate, the *Common Worship* collect matches the collect of *The Book of Common Prayer* on any given Sunday.

For each Sunday and festival a collect and Post-Communion Prayer are provided. A set of *Common Worship* collects in traditional language is also provided. Where a collect is based on a Prayer Book original, the Prayer Book form is substituted. Prayers written in contemporary language have been 'Cranmerized'.

CONNECTIONS
▷ Celebrating the saints – pp.234–5
▷ Using the Lectionary and Collects – pp.238–9

Celebrating the saints

Heroes of the faith have had their stories recounted throughout history, as we know from the narratives in both the Old and New Testaments. The book of Hebrews delights in telling the stories of the people of God who have kept the faith and calls us to be inspired by their example.

So we, too, look to great Christian examples for encouragement and inspiration. The *Common Worship* Calendar gives us a framework to follow and is the most recent of a number of approaches which have evolved during the 2,000 years of Christian history.

Early Christian martyrs

The persecutions of the Church in the Roman and Persian Empires led to suffering and martyrdom. In time the anniversary of the death of a martyr was marked by the local Christians with prayers and, normally, a celebration of the Eucharist around the tomb. Later, some of the tombs were enclosed by church buildings, such were their importance. These local anniversaries formed the beginnings of a calendar of saints' days and, as various saints gradually gained recognition by the wider Church, the calendar took shape.

The categories widen

With the absence of state persecution in the Roman Empire after the conversion of Constantine, remembrance was extended to

Archbishop Janani Luwum, who was martyred in 1977 during Idi Amin's regime

Therefore, since we are surrounded by so great a cloud of witnesses, let us also lay aside every weight and the sin that clings so closely, and let us run with perseverance the race that is set before us, looking to Jesus the pioneer and perfecter of our faith.

Hebrews 12:1–2

other holy people. At first these were often bishops and monks, punished for their faith by exile or imprisonment. Later significant theologians such as John Chrysostom and Basil found their way into the calendars, as did biblical heroes of the faith such as the apostles.

Reformation

By the time of the Reformation there were a number of issues relating to saints. A cult of relics had developed, along with pilgrimage to shrines. Saints were now invoked as intercessors

? Elizabethan changes to the Calendar in the Prayer Book led to the distinction between the major saints, who were printed in red, and the minor saints, who were printed in black. This is the origin of the phrase 'red-letter day'.

and there were so many that working out which saint was being celebrated, and which readings and prayers to use, had become an extremely complicated daily task. Cranmer did not abolish the remembrance of saints, but simply reduced the number of saints to include only those in the Bible. This was changed in the time of Elizabeth I, with the restoration of a number of other saints. Intriguingly, however, there was no principle of how to recognize or canonize a saint.

The Alternative Service Book
Modifying the system of categories for festivals, the ASB introduced a large number of new

 The Church of England has no mechanism for 'creating' new saints.

names, including people who had died since the Reformation. Indeed, the ecumenical nature of the twentieth century led to people being included who had been persecuted by our Anglican forebears. People were also included for a wide range of reasons, from martyrdom to social reform, and there were a few more women in evidence.

Common Worship
Common Worship has further extended the list of saints and has recategorized them, dividing those celebrated into three categories of observance: festivals, lesser festivals and commemorations. The extent to which each person is celebrated liturgically depends on the category into which they fall. Some of the saints' days which were during Advent or Lent, or in the early days of Christmas or Easter, have been relocated so as not to detract from the season.

The Church of England does not 'canonize' and has clear qualifications for inclusion among the lesser festivals: the person concerned must have been dead for at least 50 years, except in the case of a martyr, who may be included sooner.

Creative celebration
The lists of saints and heroes in the *Common Worship* Calendar provides the Church with an extensive resource which, if used creatively, can be a compendium of Christian history, thought and faith as well as an inspiration to the Church today to follow Christ in these heroes' footsteps. There are several anthologies of saints and inspirational Christians – collections of their writings or biographies of their lives. Their stories can inform our own and illustrate the way in which the good news of Jesus has challenged and directed believers throughout the centuries. They can also play a role in our daily prayers.

 Guy Fawkes Day had a specially provided service in *The Book of Common Prayer* until 1859.

The Sunday Lectionary

What is a lectionary?

Imagine trying to do an enormous jigsaw puzzle of the Bible. It has 10,000 pieces but you have no picture to work from. You begin with the pieces you recognize – bits of someone eating an apple, a plant on fire, a stable door, some thorns, a white sheet, a dragon's head – and then you do the edges. What you don't do is pick up pieces at random and place them anywhere on the board; instead you devise a scheme by which to compile the whole picture. A lectionary is such a scheme, by which we see how the different parts of the Bible come together. It will help us to make sense of the Bible as we read it week by week, placing together the different parts of the Bible jigsaw into recognizable patterns and shapes.

Piecing together the biblical story

Reading the Bible in church every Sunday by the thematic method, as in the ASB Lectionary – grouping pieces of the same colour from different parts of the picture – helps a congregation to learn the themes (and that is important for the major themes, of course), but it leaves them without any help about how the pieces fit together.

The *Common Worship* Lectionary gives various opportunities to read in a 'continuous' way, helping worshippers to build up one area at a time and follow the plot week after week.

What did the early Christians do?

No one knows exactly what pattern of Scripture readings was employed by the synagogues in the time of Jesus and the first Christians (see Luke 4:16–21; Acts 13:15), but there was clearly a pattern. In the course of time, the writings of the New Testament became part of the established

pattern of Bible reading in the worship of the Church. No doubt there would have been those then, as there are today, who reject any system for reading the Bible in public worship and leave it to the local leadership, but the overwhelming majority of Christians down the ages have recognized that this can be disastrous for long-

> The Anglican Church is the greatest Bible-reading church in the world. In no other church anywhere is the Bible read in public worship so regularly, with such order, and at such length, as in the Anglican fellowship of churches.
>
> *Bishop Stephen Neill, Anglicanism, Penguin, 1958*

term understanding of God's ways. Anglicans follow the time-honoured principle that a systematic reading of the Scriptures according to a planned scheme is the best way to bring worshippers into contact with the living Word of God.

Where did the Lectionary come from?

The *Common Worship* Lectionary is not entirely new. At its heart is the ecumenical 1992 *Revised Common Lectionary*, which itself began life as the 1969 Lectionary of the Roman Catholic Church.

In 1992 a group of liturgists from the Anglican provinces of England, Ireland, Scotland and Wales began to work on a new calendar of the Church's year and the adaptation of the new lectionary. Amongst other minor changes, they added optional Old Testament lessons for Eastertide, and provided alternative shortened psalms. A number of other denominations world-wide have also adopted the *Revised Common Lectionary*, so it is both pan-Anglican and ecumenical: you may well be able to visit a church in another part of the world and find a recognizably similar lectionary being used.

Using the *Common Worship* Lectionary

The *Common Worship* Lectionary seeks to protect the week-by-week pattern of readings by using the same lectionary for the same congregation each week, regardless of whether the service is a Eucharist, Morning Prayer, Family Service…

What is in it?

For every Sunday, principal feast, holy day and festival, there are three cycles of readings, each of a distinctive character:

● The Principal Service lectionary provides an Old Testament reading, a psalm, a New Testament reading and a Gospel reading for each service. Those who have overall responsibility for planning the worship decide

which readings, if any, are to be omitted. In this cycle, the psalm is a meditation on the Old Testament and, if used, must be alongside the Old Testament reading.

● The Second Service lectionary is for whatever is considered to be a church's 'second' service at an earlier or later point in the day, bearing in mind those who attend more than one service. Again, this lectionary can be used with any form of service.

● The Third Service lectionary is provided for any 'third' service, but is particularly appropriate for Morning or Evening Prayer, since it generally includes more psalmody and the New Testament is not necessarily taken from a Gospel.

Each of these cycles runs for three years, Year A beginning on the First Sunday of Advent in all years whose date is exactly divisible by three: 2001, 2004, 2007, 2010. In Year A, the bulk of the Gospel material is drawn from Matthew, in Year B it comes from Mark and John, and in Year C from Luke. John is also used significantly in the pre- and post-Easter seasons in all years.

CONNECTIONS
▷ **Fitting it all together** – pp.238–9
▧ **Challenges and implications** – pp.240–41
▧ **The Weekday Lectionary** – pp.200–201

Fitting it all together

The first thing that needs to be done before any lectionary readings can be chosen is that the 'principal service' of the church needs to be identified; this will be your main service. It may be the mid-morning Sunday service, or it may be at 6.30 in the evening. Whichever it is, the 'Principal Service' lectionary cycle needs to be used consistently, regardless of the type or patterns of service.

Seasons

During the special seasons of the liturgical calendar, putting together the readings and collects for the principal service is a relatively straightforward task. The only choice that needs to be made is how many readings there are going to be in the service, and which ones are going to be omitted if necessary. The readings and collects each bear the same Sunday title as the Sunday itself. Thus on the Second Sunday of Advent, for example, the readings and collects of the Second Sunday of Advent are used.

At Christmas there are three complete sets of readings to choose from; this is exceptional and recognizes that a church may have more than one principal service on or around this day.

Choices in Ordinary Time

For a significant part of the year – the Ordinary Time between Trinity Sunday and All Saints' Day – churches can opt to follow the 'Continuous' or the 'Related' approach to the Old Testament (see below). Either way, the same pattern must be adhered to throughout the season. (The word 'continuous' really means 'semi-continuous', because it is impossible to read everything.) The Gospel and New Testament readings are the same in both patterns.

How does it all work?

In the related pattern, the Gospel (which more or less just keeps working its way through the book) sets the theme for the Old Testament reading and psalm. In the continuous pattern, the Old Testament (with its psalm) is read semi-continuously, independently of the Gospel. In both patterns, the New Testament is read semi-continuously.

Readings and collects are unhitched

The readings in Ordinary Time are unhitched from the collects, and belong to dates and 'Proper' numbers, rather than to Sunday names. At the same time, the collects (which work on a one-year cycle) always belong to the same Sunday each year. Thus, for example, the collect of the Tenth Sunday after Trinity will always be the same:

> Let your merciful ears, O Lord,
> be open to the prayers of your
>   humble servants;
> and that they may obtain their petitions
> make them to ask such things
>   as shall please you;
> through Jesus Christ your Son our Lord…

The readings, however, will vary from one Year A, B or C to another, because the date of Easter and therefore also of Trinity Sunday varies.

Free choice?

As an alternative to using the *Common Worship* Lectionary all the time, churches now have the option to devise their own reading schemes and sermon series during specific periods of Ordinary Time. During the seasons, however, they should adhere to the Lectionary.

It is possible to piece together the correct readings, collect and prayer for each day from the 'master' volume, *The Christian Year: Calendar, Lectionary and Collects*, but the complexity described above makes it inadvisable!

Help is at hand!

Someone has already done the hard work! Each year there are booklets published, in which the lectionary readings have been matched with the calendar dates. Finding the right collect is not so difficult.

Why are the collects distinct from the readings?

The collects in the BCP were intended primarily to provide a devotional 'prayer of the week'. The ASB collects were offered as 'theme prayers' to introduce the theme which linked together the Bible readings for that Sunday. The new collects seek to recover the ancient understanding of them as 'gathering together' prayers, collecting up the silent prayers of the people at that point in the liturgy. In Ordinary Time they no longer hold a theme and have no need to accompany specific readings. It is only around the major festivals and seasons that they could be seen to perform this function.

United benefices and the Lectionary

United benefices may find the continuity of the *Common Worship* Lectionary hard to appreciate when the churches of the benefice have a Sunday service only two or three times a month, and at different times of the day. The worship planners will need to choose the readings that make the best sense for their situation, consider the demands on the (often) itinerant preacher(s) and take the continuity of their congregations into account more than the time of day at which they meet.

CONNECTIONS
The Sunday Lectionary –
pp.236–7

The Lectionary – challenges and implications

The *Common Worship* Lectionary presents some new ways of approaching worship. Here we explore some of the implications.

Advance planning

The fact that we now have a greater number of choices to make from the Lectionary, especially during Ordinary Time, means that a preacher or leader cannot leave it until Saturday evening before deciding what to do; there needs to be a longer-term plan of readings and an agreement within the leadership as to which readings will be the focus for the sermons.

Liberation from themes

As we plan services, we may find that themes will still emerge from time to time, but now they will emerge from our own reading of the passage; this is the advantage of allowing the Bible to speak for itself into our own time and community. Freedom from imposed themes will also give us more scope

Planning ahead

Having long-term schemes makes it far easier for other people to share in the planning and preparation for worship. If we do not do so already, this is an ideal opportunity to draw a number of key people together to study the Scriptures that will be read, and to plan the services as a whole. It will mean that preparation may take more work, but a wider involvement can bring tremendous benefits. The group may spot in advance, for example, the week when the narrative of Naaman the Syrian and Jesus' healing of 10 lepers will be read. This would leave time for a member of the Leprosy Mission who also happens to be one of the congregation to put together some striking pictures on OHP slides which can be used during the intercessions.

The widespread use of the Lectionary has prompted a vast range of resources to accompany it: selections of hymns and songs for each week, prayers of intercession, background notes for preaching, and so on. These can be immensely useful, giving inspiration and encouragement to planners and participants alike.

for considering the shape of our worship and to choose items to fit the point in the service rather than the overall theme of the day.

Sermon series

We all know Anglican churches that have devised their own sermon series for years (and chosen suitable readings of their own). Now we are officially allowed to do this, within certain boundaries. The opportunity in the long summer Ordinary Time for tackling a biblical book, character or set of issues allows potential for a gripping sermon series (as long as everyone is not on holiday).

Of course, we can also devise a sermon series, and give it a title, using the semi-continuous readings from the Lectionary at this time of the year.

A planning group in action

Integrated listening and learning

Amongst the abundance of lectionary-related resources is material to help us to integrate our children's work with our adult and all-age services. There is a wealth of resources to support the reading and teaching of the Scriptures for all age groups in the Church.

> **?** **DID YOU KNOW?** Churches can depart from the Lectionary, as permitted during certain parts of the year, only by the agreement of the minister and PCC. The boundary to this freedom depends on whether the service is Holy Communion or a Service of the Word. For Holy Communion, freedom corresponds with Ordinary Time. For Services of the Word (which are not combined with a Eucharist), lectionary-linked periods do not have to be so long: the Third Sunday of Advent to the Baptism of Christ, and Palm Sunday to Trinity Sunday. When a monthly pattern of services combines both of these forms, then the Holy Communion guidelines would be best followed, for the sake of continuity.

> **Attentive listening**
> The *Common Worship* Lectionary may help us to recover an understanding that the readings are there not merely to introduce or support the sermon. Often consecutive passages from two or three books will be read over a succession of Sundays. Congregations can be helped to understand that, while one of the readings may be taken up in the sermon that follows, we can also hear and receive the Word of God in the public reading of Scripture.

Using the collects

The recovery of the ancient understanding of a collect as a 'gathering prayer', collecting up the silent prayers of the people at that point in the service, challenges us to use them as such. Many congregations will need a bit of practice before growing used to a different way of doing things and will be helped into a time of silent prayer by a short bidding, giving some guidance – for example: 'In a few moments of silence, let us pray for…'

CONNECTIONS
Ordinary
Time – pp.232–3

CHAPTER 15

Times and seasons

Think about the way in which the secular year works, with birthdays, bank holidays, New Year, Valentine's Day and even the arrival of Beaujolais Nouveau! Each is celebrated in a distinctive way by family and community. Institutions such as schools and colleges have their own yearly cycles which might include a commemoration of the founder, the staff pantomime, sports day and prize-giving. Recognizing rhythms and marking milestones are part of the way we function as human beings.

From the very earliest times, Christians have kept certain days and times of the year as special

times of worship. Sunday, the first day of the week, was regularly celebrated as both the day of resurrection and of creation, for example. It is recorded as far back as the New Testament as a day of meeting and breaking of bread. Easter is also an ancient festival – some claim that there is evidence to its origins being in apostolic times. Other special days and seasons have developed over the centuries, as have associated liturgies and symbolic acts.

By the Middle Ages, the Church's liturgy emphasized certain seasons in two ways:

- By providing seasonal services that were different from the normal pattern of Eucharist and daily office.
- By providing seasonal prayers and inserts (called Propers) which could be used as part of the normal services.

When Thomas Cranmer revised the services provided for the new Church of England, he swept away nearly all this seasonal material. The 1662 Prayer Book ends up with no special seasonal services and very few Propers (there are only five Propers for the Eucharistic prayer).

The Alternative Service Book 1980 increased the amount of Proper material by including the following:

- Seasonal sentences from Scripture for use at the beginning of services.
- More Proper prefaces to insert in the Eucharistic prayer.
- Seasonal blessings.
- Post-Communion sentences which are often seasonal.

The ASB did not provide special services for different parts of the year, but expected ministers to adapt the normal Sunday service by using the Proper material. This was not enough for many churches and, if they wanted a special service for Advent Sunday or for Good Friday, they had to make up their own or use one from another Church (often the Roman Catholic Church).

To help fill this gap, after the publication of the ASB further books were published which provided much more seasonal material:

- *Lent – Holy Week – Easter*: This provided material for this part of the year, including services for Ash Wednesday, Palm Sunday, Maundy Thursday, Good Friday and the Easter Vigil.
- *The Promise of His Glory*: This is a 'winter season' book offering material from All Saints' Day right the way through Advent, Christmas and Epiphany, up to the Presentation of Christ in the Temple (2 February).
- *Patterns for Worship*: An extensive collection of material of all sorts, for occasions all through the Christian year.

In addition to these official Church of England publications, some members of the Liturgical Commission also published some more seasonal material in *Enriching the Christian Year*. This book includes provision for Mothering Sunday, Ascension, Pentecost and Trinity Sunday and more.

Beyond 2000

Recognizing the popularity of the seasonal material published since 1980, *Common Worship* continues to meet the need for distinctive worship to mark special festivals and events. In the Holy Communion Service, for example, there are sets of seasonal material for no less than 19 different feasts, festivals or seasonal periods. In the Initiation Services there are seasonal variations for each of the major baptismal seasons. And in the selection of confessions authorized under A Service of the Word there are also some seasonal forms from which to choose.

More to come

This *Common Worship* seasonal material is contained in the various *Common Worship* volumes. In due course there will be further official publications containing even more seasonal provision incorporating the best of those post-1980 seasonal publications, and new material, too. There will be a volume which has been given the working title *Times and Seasons*. This organizes prayers and liturgy according to season, much as does *Lent – Holy Week – Easter*, for instance. There will also be a completely revised version of *Patterns for Worship*.

CONNECTIONS
Calendar, Lectionary and Collects – Chapter 14

Making the most of seasonal material

Prayers, prefaces, introductions and symbolic acts that are associated with specific seasons are all intended to enhance our worship, making some aspects of God's saving history more noticeable by emphasizing them especially on particular days. Using these liturgies can help us to grow into the rhythms of the Church's calendar, too, as we repeat them year by year and recount the stories of God's marvellous deeds.

There are no hard-and-fast rules for using the seasonal material, but here are a few ideas.

An Advent Eucharist
At St Zacchaeus the Tax Collector they have produced an Advent Communion booklet for

use at their Sunday and midweek Eucharists. It is basically Order One in contemporary language, with material from *The Promise of His Glory* included. In outline, this is how it works:

- The Advent candles are lit at the start of the service (after the hymn), using prayers from *Promise* – children are usually involved in doing this and in leading the prayers. This leads into:
- The prayers of penitence: the *Kyrie* form is used with appropriate Advent inserts.
- The sermon and hymns all reflect the Advent theme, as do the collect and readings, of course.
- The intercessions follow a standard format over the weeks of Advent, using a form from *Promise* with its response: 'Come, Lord Jesus.'
- Eucharistic Prayer E is used with the Advent extended preface replacing the first part of the prayer, and with the acclamations, 'Christ has died; Christ is risen; Christ will come again.'
- Seasonal material for the Peace and the blessing is taken from the Advent page of the Holy Communion supplementary texts.

A Palm Sunday Service of the Word
On this Sunday, the congregation gathers in the school just down the road from the church, and there they hold the first part of the service, taken from *Lent – Holy Week – Easter*. This includes the prayer over the palm crosses and the reading of Matthew 21:1–11. Nothing has been printed out except for the hymns which they will all sing on the procession up the road to the church – the congregation know the few responses well enough not to need any text in front of them.

When they get to the church, they continue with an all-age Service of the Word, following a

How to use seasonal material with a congregation

There are a few basic options:

- Create a special 'one-off' service (e.g. Christmas Carols).
- Insert seasonal material ('Propers') into the normal Sunday service.
- Make each of the different seasons distinctive by carefully choosing an appropriate set of choices from all the options and sticking with it throughout the whole season, repeating it at the same time each year.

Whatever we do, we will not find the seasonal services all laid out for the congregation, ready to use, in any of the *Common Worship* volumes. So how do we actually produce the goods for the congregation to use? Nowadays there are many options. Below are a few ideas. Each will require at least some effort and time, and some will depend on the equipment available locally.

Inserting seasonal parts into regular services

- Put all the seasonal material on the notice sheet or a separate 'seasonal insert' to be used alongside the normal service book.
  Advantages: This is fairly easy to do if the church has a notice sheet anyway; everyone has just what they need in front of them.
- Put the whole service onto the notice sheet or order of service.
  Advantages: As above, and everything is all together in one place.
- Print a seasonal booklet – for example, an Advent Eucharist.
  Advantages: It can look more permanent, especially with a card or laminated cover; it helps the congregation to grow used to a set of options; carefully worded rubrics can still allow for some further variation – 'The president introduces the Peace', for example.
- Project the variable bits onto a screen, or as many screens as necessary for clear visibility.
  Advantages: the congregation can hold their usual book and just look up at the variable points, without searching for that little piece of paper that has fallen underneath the pew.

One-off specials

- Print an order of service just for this occasion.
  Advantages: Everything that the congregation needs can be presented clearly in one booklet.
- Project everything in the service onto a screen or a number of screens.
  Advantages: This saves on printing; the congregation do not bury their heads in a book, nor do they have to worry about finding their place.

pattern similar to most such services in this church. Material for congregational use is projected onto a large screen, but there are a few large-print copies on paper for people who find it hard to see over a distance. The Palm Sunday theme is picked up in the intercessions and the blessing, as well as in hymnody, the other reading and the talk.

CONNECTIONS

▣ **Initiation Services, seasonal options** – pp.140–41

▣ **The Eucharist, seasonal material in the supplementary texts** – pp.162–3

CHAPTER 16

The Psalter

The importance of the Psalms

The Psalms, dating from centuries before the birth of Jesus Christ, have had a place in Christian worship from the earliest days of the Church. The Psalms were clearly important to Jesus, who quoted from them and sang them with the disciples (see Matthew 26:30). Jewish Christians saw no reason to stop singing them, and indeed believed them to look forward to

Psalm 23:1–4 Old English

Our Lord gouerneþ me, and noþyng shal defailen to me; in þe stede of pasture he sett me þer. He norissed me vp water of fyllyng; he turned my soule fram þe fende. He lad me vp þe bistiȝes of riȝtfulnes for his name. For ȝif þat ich haue gon amiddes of þe shadowe of deþ, y shal nouȝt douten iuels; for þou art wyþ me.

West Midlands Psalter,
c.1350

Christ, just as the prophets did. Neither were the Psalms only a feature of Jewish Christianity. Paul, the apostle to the Gentiles, mentions them especially, encouraging the Colossians to 'sing psalms, hymns, and spiritual songs to God' (Colossians 3:16).

Taking root in daily worship

As the Church became established, the Psalms took root in daily worship. The growth of monastic communities from the fourth century onwards led to a number of patterns of saying or singing the Psalms. Often huge numbers were said or sung each day, requiring many hours for their recitation. Some later medieval communities and cathedrals made sure that all the psalms were used every day. Certain psalms became associated with particular seasons of the Christian year, or accompanied particular readings from the Bible.

The Church of England is therefore not unique in giving an honoured place to the Psalms. However, their regular use, and the encouragement for a psalm to be used in every act of Sunday worship (or a psalm-based song in a Service of the Word), shows that one of the marks of Anglican worship is a willingness to engage with the Psalms, and use ancient words of praise in twenty-first-century worship. There were English versions of the Psalms hundreds of years before the Prayer Book, and the version in *The Book of Common Prayer* dates from 70 years before the Authorized Version of the Bible. Cranmer ensured that all 150 psalms would be said

> **Psalm 23:1–4 Jerome's Latin version – The Vulgate (390–405)**
> *Canticum David*
> 1. *Dominus pascit me nihil mihi deerit*
> 2. *in pascuis herbarum adclinavit me super aquas refectionis enutrivit me*
> 3. *animam meam refecit duxit me per semitas iustitiae propter nomen suum*
> 4. *sed et si ambulavero in valle mortis non timebo malum quoniam tu mecum es virga tua et baculus tuus ipsa consolabuntur me.*

> **Psalm 23:1–4 Coverdale (1539)**
> 1. The Lord is my shepherd : therefore can I lack nothing.
> 2. He shall feed me in a green pasture : and lead me forth beside the waters of comfort.
> 3. He shall convert my soul : and bring me forth in the paths of righteousness, for his Name's sake.
> 4. Yea, though I walk through the valley of the shadow of death, I will fear no evil : for thou art with me; thy rod and thy staff comfort me.

> **Psalm 23:1–4 Scottish Psalter (1650)**
> The Lord's my shepherd, I'll not want;
> he makes me down to lie
> in pastures green; he leadeth me
> the quiet waters by.
>
> My soul he doth restore again,
> and me to walk doth make
> within the paths of righteousness,
> e'en for his own name's sake.
>
> Yea, though I walk through death's dark vale,
> yet will I fear none ill;
> for thou art with me, and thy rod
> and staff me comfort still.

or sung at Morning and Evening Prayer each month, and they have remained as a heartbeat of Anglican worship ever since.

Singing the Psalms

Through the centuries the Psalms have been sung in different ways. The Reformation saw a flowering of versions in which they were turned into hymns, many of which survive to this day. William Kethe's 'All people that on earth do dwell' and the Scottish Psalter's 'The Lord's my shepherd' are but two famous examples, and H.F. Lyte's 'Praise, my soul, the King of heaven' is a later one. In recent years *Psalm Praise* and *Songs from the Psalms* have developed this process, and much of the music of charismatic renewal has taken the Book of Psalms as its inspiration. Classical Anglican chant has taken Coverdale's words and set them to music, whereas other churches use simple 'response' forms. The choices seem almost endless.

CONNECTIONS
▣ The Coverdale Psalter in *The Book of Common Prayer* – pp.248–9
▣ Psalm 23 – pp.250–51

The Psalter in the Church of England

For many people the Psalter is still that of Coverdale, the version printed in *The Book of Common Prayer*. Especially where psalms are said or sung on a daily basis, a full translation for worship has been essential. The popularity of Anglican chant in the last 150 years has also required a full, non-metrical translation of the Psalms, and a recent survey of churches revealed that over half of them were still using the version of the Psalms from *The Book of Common Prayer*. However, though Coverdale clearly retains his hold, the pattern of liturgical change in the Church of England has seen various new translations emerge in recent years.

Recent translations

The first attempt at a new translation was The Revised Psalter (1963). This aimed to revise Coverdale in a conservative fashion and did not survive the great change in liturgical prayer of the

1970s: the move from 'thou' to 'you'. One of the architects of Series 3, Professor David Frost, along with Dr Andrew Macintosh and Professor John Emerton, thus began to make a brand-new translation, and their psalms began to appear in new liturgical texts.

Eventually *The Liturgical Psalter* was published in 1976, and bound into the ASB in 1980. Twenty years of use convinced the Liturgical Commission that, though *The Liturgical Psalter* had many strengths, its very newness was a dislocation from the established praying tradition of the Church. Although it had been altered to use language inclusive of men and women, it was felt that a new translation, deriving more obviously from Coverdale, would be appropriate for *Common Worship*. The Psalter for *Common Worship* is a revision of a translation made for the Anglican Church in the United States (ECUSA), at a similar time to *The Liturgical Psalter*, and is familiar to many from its use in the Franciscan Office Book, *Celebrating Common Prayer*. Its overwhelming acceptance by General Synod is a sign that the Psalms are alive and well in today's Church of England.

Why use the Psalms?

Originally the Psalms were a hymn book of worship songs collected together and used in the restored Temple in Jerusalem. As with many hymns today, they were also used by individuals to express a range of emotions, from despair to ecstatic praise. There are many reasons to use the Psalms today for the same purposes: to gather God's people together in worship, and to provide texts for private prayer and praise.

● Jesus used them in worship, and quoted from them at other times (see Mark 12:36, for example).

Doxology

An ascription of praise to the Trinity is commonly added to the end of psalms when they are used in Christian liturgy:

Glory to the Father and to the Son
and to the Holy Spirit;
as it was in the beginning is now
and shall be for ever. Amen.

In this way a Christian framework of understanding and interpretation is provided; something which is seen even more explicitly in the provision in some psalters of Christian 'psalm prayers' to conclude each psalm.

- The early Church continued their use and found in them not just good worship, but songs which looked forward to Jesus, the centre of worship.
- At the Reformation, figures such as Luther found in the Psalms 'the Bible in miniature'. Much of what we believe about God, and what God feels about us, is written in the Psalms.
- The Psalms give us words to express ourselves. In the Psalter are expressions of love, lament, anger, despair, betrayal, hope and joy which have given generations of worshippers words for their deepest feelings.
- The worship of the Church of England has been soaked in the Psalms, and we would be denying our denominational as well as our Christian heritage if we were to discard them now.

An adaptable and wide-ranging resource

The Psalter is capable of nurturing Christian communities, of being recited morning and evening, day by day, by individuals and groups, of being sung by choirs and congregations, and of being prayed in retreat houses, living rooms and churches alike.

Using the Psalms in church

The early Church records the use of the Psalms in between the readings at Communion from the earliest days. The tradition developed such that the psalm follows the Old Testament reading, and in the *Common Worship* Lectionary the psalm reflects the theme of that reading. In the Church of England's daily Morning and Evening Prayer the Psalms have traditionally been read 'in course' – i.e. consecutively, from beginning to end, so that all are used in one month. This can make for some exciting clashes with the other set readings, so the *Common Worship* Weekday Lectionaries will allow the use of specially chosen psalms in the seasons, with a sequential pattern for the rest of the year. For Sunday use, especially where there is one service on a Sunday, it is best to use the psalm and readings set for the Principal Service.

A Psalter for *Common Worship* is not technically 'authorized' in the same way as other parts of *Common Worship*. Approval has been given to include this version in the publication of *Common Worship*, but, under the Versions of the Bible Measure, it is possible to use any version of the Psalter which is 'not prohibited'. Coverdale, The Liturgical Psalter, the New Revised Standard Version and others can, therefore, still be used.

CONNECTIONS
☒ **The Sunday Lectionary** – pp.236–7
☒ **The Weekday Lectionary** – pp.200–201

A Psalter for *Common Worship*

The version of the Psalter prepared by the Liturgical Commission and its consultants to complement the *Common Worship* services is a modern language Psalter which sets out to enable the worshipper to pray the Psalms afresh within the worshipping traditions of the Church. It builds on the traditions and scholarship encapsulated in the Psalter of Miles Coverdale, printed in *The Book of Common Prayer*, or *The Liturgical Psalter*, printed in *The Alternative Service Book 1980*, and other versions of the Psalter which are familiar to Anglican worshippers.

Why do we need a new Psalter for the Church of England?

The saying and singing of psalms in worship has helped to shape the spirituality of generations of Anglicans. These habits of saying and singing psalms continue to need nurturing and encouragement, and new ways of using psalms in worship continually need to be developed.

Language

Although any Psalter can be used in a Church of England service, worshippers have tended to use the Psalter which is printed in their service

books. The language of these Psalters has therefore been subject to many of the same criticisms that have been levelled at the services printed in *The Book of Common Prayer* and *The Alternative Service Book*. The Psalter for *Common Worship* aims to address a range of these criticisms. It differs from any Psalter previously printed in Church of England service books, and yet is clearly related to them. It is written in modern language, is discreetly inclusive of men and women, pays attention to the worshipping traditions which have shaped the Church, is rhythmic and singable, is reasonably accessible to a wide range of worshippers, and sits well within the parameters of contemporary Hebrew scholarship.

Key features of A Psalter for *Common Worship*
- Texts which have been prepared with close attention both to the received Hebrew text

and to scholarly discussions about its original form.
- Texts which reflect the use of the Psalms in the Christian tradition from its earliest days, and also within the traditions of the Church of England.
- Language which enables the Psalms to be said or sung with ease.
- Language which is memorable, resonating with the tradition of Coverdale.
- Language which is generally inclusive of men and women.
- Language which is accessible to a wide range of worshippers.

The example of Psalm 23 from the Psalter in *Common Worship* shows how the well-known phraseology of Coverdale remains in this translation. Only one verse is completely rewritten, and for the most part only Coverdale's mistranslations (he himself was translating the Latin version) and archaisms have been changed. Words which have taken root in people's praying and singing take on deep resonances, and tradition is best described as the best of the old reshaped and enlivened by the new. The Church today needs to find new ways of mining the treasures hidden in the Psalms, and this reworking of the old may just speak into the technological, fast-moving twenty-first century in a way which enables these gems to be handed on.

Psalm 23 in *Common Worship*
Exact Coverdale phrases are shown in red.
Close matches (e.g. 'you' for 'thou') are blue.

1. The Lord is my shepherd:
therefore can I lack nothing.

2. He makes me lie down in green pastures:
and leads me beside still waters.

3. He shall **refresh** my soul:
and guide me in the paths of righteousness for his name's sake.

4. Though I walk through the valley of the shadow of death,
I will fear no evil:
for **you are** with me
your rod and **your** staff, **they** comfort me.

5. **You spread** a table before me
in the presence of those who trouble me:
you have anointed my head with oil
and my cup shall be full.

6. Surely goodness and loving mercy shall follow me all the days of my life:
and I will dwell in the house of the Lord for ever.

CONNECTIONS
Psalm 23 –
pp.246–7

Using the Psalms

Any modern hymn book contains hymns and songs for different occasions, ranging from Harvest Festival to national events, from times of day to exclamations of praise. The Book of Psalms does just this, and is very clearly a collection of songs put together for worship. Many begin with a heading which talks about their author and use. Seventy-three claim to have been written by David, and some of them probably were, but like many hymns the psalms were changed and 'improved' over time.

What are they about?

As they date from David's time onwards, many psalms are about the rule and power of the King (e.g. Psalm 2), or national events like a coronation (Psalm 110) or a royal wedding (Psalm 45). Others refer to the Temple, and to the journey made by faithful pilgrims up the hill to Jerusalem (e.g. Psalm 122). Other psalms celebrate creation (Psalm 19), harvest (Psalm 65), God's work in history (Psalm 78), and the glory of God's Word in the law (Psalm 119). Many psalms are more personal: there are cries of anguish and fear (Psalm 22) and joy and gladness, sometimes in the same Psalm (e.g. Psalm 43). If there is a human emotion, it is expressed somewhere in the Psalms.

Poetry and song

The Psalms are poetry and song. Many contain what are assumed to be musical instructions (e.g. 'Selah', Psalm 48:8), or have an explanation at the beginning which gives the author and its type (e.g. 'To the leader. Of the Korahites. A Maskil', Psalm 44), though not all Bibles

> **DID YOU KNOW?** Even worship books get things wrong: Psalms 14 and 53 are nearly identical, and Psalms 42 and 43 are presumably one psalm which has been split up.

print these. Others conform to a strict scheme, like Psalm 119 where, in the Hebrew, the first word of every line in each section begins with the same letter. The first section begins with the first letter of the Jewish alphabet, the second with the second, and so on.

Imaginative use of the Psalms

Considering what the Psalms are about, where and how they were used, and their original form, gives some clues about using them creatively in today's Church. Some were clearly stately and majestic, and require that treatment. Others were sung on the move by those on pilgrimage. Some were cries of the heart, requiring subtle music for their expression. It seems clear that some psalms were designed to be sung by the whole assembly,

'The land has produced its harvest' (Psalm 67:6)

while others were sung by the professional musicians. It is assumed that the musical instructions in some psalms indicate places where instrumentalists could play in between the singing.

With music...

This means that the Psalms will be best used in a variety of ways. Anglican chant may indeed be appropriate for some: some think that plainsong may be close to some of the music used in the Temple in Jerusalem, and simple, chant-like forms are easy to pick up. Responsorial psalms enable the congregation to sing a chorus, and a small group or soloist to sing the verses. Versions are printed out like this in many Sunday lectionaries. It is worth checking, though, that the musical form is appropriate to the psalm in question, and it may be that a simple song form or metrical version would best suit the theme and shape. A cry for help has a very different character from the national anthem, and the same musical form is not necessarily going to work for both.

...and without

There is a long tradition of saying the Psalms, especially at daily prayer. Here again the poetic form can help. Much Hebrew poetry worked on parallelism, so that the same idea was reworked in the second half of a verse, or in a new verse. So psalms can be said by different groups (antiphonally) by half verses or full verses (just as church choirs swap verses). Others contain a 'chorus' which could be said by all.

Praise and prayer

Anglican liturgy has also made much of using texts from the Psalms as acts of praise or prayer within the service. The words of the shorter Litany at Matins and Evensong ('O Lord, show thy mercy upon us…') are entirely drawn from the Psalms, and it may be that the best use of a psalm which is a cry to God is within the intercessions. Other versicles and responses drawn from the Psalms make good acclamations for all to join in as a welcome to worship. Above all, they should be used, studied, preached and prayed.

CONNECTIONS
Using the Psalms at funerals – pp.220–21

Index of Themes and Common Threads

Subject Index

Index of Bible References